Pasta &
Italian

p

This is a Parragon Book
This edition published in 2002

Parragon
Queen Street House
4 Queen Street
Bath BA1 1HE, UK

Copyright © Parragon 2000

ISBN: 0-75257-554-6

A copy of the CIP data for this book is available from the British
Library, upon request

Printed in China

Note

Cup measurements used in this book are for American cups.
Tablespoons are assumed to be 15 ml. Unless otherwise stated,
milk is assumed to be full fat, eggs are medium and pepper is
freshly ground black pepper.

Contents

Introduction

Pasta has existed since the days of the Roman Empire and remains one of the most versatile cooking ingredients: no store cupboard should be without it. It can be combined with meat fish, vegetables, fruit or even a simple herb sauce, to create a mouth-watering and nutritious meal within minutes.

Most pasta is made from durum wheat flour and contains protein and carbohydrates. It is a good source of slow-release energy and has the additional advantage of being value for money. There are many different types of pasta, some of which are listed on the opposite page. Many are available both dried and fresh. Unless you have access to a good Italian delicatessen, it is probably not worth buying fresh unfilled pasta, but even supermarkets sell high-quality tortellini, capelletti, ravioli and agnolotti.

Best of all make fresh pasta at home. It takes a little time, but it is quite easy and well worth the effort. You can mix the dough by hand or prepare it in a food processor.

Pasta may be coloured and flavoured with extra ingredients that are usually added with the beaten egg:

Black: add 1 tsp squid or cuttlefish ink.
Green: add 115 g/4 oz well-drained, cooked spinach when kneading.
Purple: work 1 large, cooked beetroot (beet) in a food processor and add with an extra 60 g/2 oz/ ½ cup flour.
Red: add 2 tbsp tomato purée (paste).

To cook pasta, bring a large pan of lightly salted water to the boil, add the pasta and 1 tbsp olive oil, but do not cover or the water will boil over. Quickly bring the water back to a rolling boil. When the pasta is tender, but still firm to the bite, drain and toss with butter, olive oil or your prepared sauce. The cooking times given here are guidelines only:

Fresh unfilled pasta: *2–3 minutes*
Fresh filled pasta: *8–10 minutes*
Dried unfilled pasta: *10–12 minutes*
Dried filled pasta: *15–20 minutes*

BASIC PASTA DOUGH

If you wish to make your own pasta for the dishes in this book, follow this simple recipe.

Serves 4

INGREDIENTS
450 g/1 lb/4 cups durum wheat flour
4 eggs, lightly beaten
1 tbsp olive oil
salt

1 Lightly flour a work surface (counter). Sift the flour with a pinch of salt into a mound. Make a well in the centre and add the eggs and olive oil.

2 Using a fork or your fingertips, gradually work the mixture until the ingredients are combined. Knead vigorously for 10–15 minutes.

3 Set the dough aside to rest for 25 minutes, before rolling it out as thinly and evenly as possible.

TYPES OF PASTA

There are as many as 200 different pasta shapes and about three times as many names for them. New shapes are being designed – and named – all the time and the same shape may be called a different name in different regions of Italy.

Cannelloni

Conchigliette

Fusilli

Conchiglie

Orecchiette tricolori

Rigatoni

Lumaconi

Fettuccine

Spaghetti

anelli, anellini: *small rings for soup*

bucatini: *long, medium-thick tubes*

cannelloni: *large, thick, round pasta tubes*

capelli d'angelo: *thin strands of 'angel hair'*

conchiglie: *ridged shells*

conchigliette: *little shells*

cresti di gallo: *curved-shaped*

ditali, ditalini: *short tubes*

eliche: *loose spirals*

farfalle: *bows*

fettuccine: *medium ribbons*

fusilli: *spirals*

gemelli: *two pieces wrapped together as 'twins'*

lasagne: *flat, rectangular sheets*

linguini: *long, flat ribbons*

lumache: *snail-shaped shells*

lumaconi: *big shells*

macaroni: *long- or short-cut tubes*

orecchiette: *ear-shaped*

penne: *quill-shaped*

rigatoni: *thick, ridged tubes*

spaghetti: *fine or medium rods*

tagliarini: *thin ribbons*

tagliatelle: *broad ribbons*

vermicelli: *fine pasta, usually folded into skeins*

Each region in Italy has its distinctive culinary style, although in general the north favours the use of milk and butter and the south of olive oil in their cooking.

Piedmont

The food here is substantial, peasant-type fare, although the expensive fragrant white truffle is found in this region. Truffles can be finely flaked or grated and added to many of the more sophisticated dishes. There is an abundance of wild mushrooms throughout the region. Garlic features strongly in the recipes and polenta, gnocchi, and rice are eaten in larger quantities than pasta, the former being offered as a first course when soup is not served. A large variety of game is also widely available.

Lombardy

Milan is home to the wonderful risotto named after the city and also the Milanese soufflé flavoured strongly with lemon. Veal dishes, including *vitello tonnato* and *osso buco*, are specialties of the region and other excellent meat dishes, particularly pot roasts, feature widely. The lakes of the area produce a wealth of fresh fish. Rice and polenta are again popular but pasta also appears in many guises. The famous sweet yeasted cake *panettone* is a product of this region.

Trentino-Alto Adige

The foods are robust and basic here, where fish are plentiful. In the Trentino area particularly, pasta and simple meat dishes are popular, while in the Adige, soups and pot roasts are favoured, often with added dumplings and spiced sausages.

Veneto

Polenta is served with almost everything here and pasta is less in evidence, with gnocchi and rice more favoured. Fish, particularly shellfish, is in abundance and especially good seafood salads are widely available. There are also excellent robust soups and risottos.

Liguria

All along the Italian Riviera can be found excellent trattorias which produce amazing fish dishes flavoured with the local olive oil. Pesto sauce flavoured with basil, cheese, and pine nuts comes from this area, along with other excellent sauces.

Emilia-Romagna

Tortellini and lasagne feature widely here, along with many other pasta dishes, as do *saltimbocca* and other veal dishes. Parma is famous for its ham, *prosciutto di Parma*, thought to be the best in the world. Balsamic vinegar is also produced here.

Tuscany

Tuscany has everything: an excellent coastal area providing splendid fish, hills covered in vineyards, and fertile plains where every conceivable vegetable and fruit grow. There is plenty of game in the region, providing many interesting recipes; tripe cooked in a thick tomato sauce is popular along with many liver recipes; beans in many guises appear frequently, as well as pot roasts, steaks, and full-bodied soups. Florence has a wide variety of specialties, while Siena boasts the famous candied fruit cake called *Panforte di Siena*.

Umbria/Marches

Inland Umbria is famous for its pork, and the character of the cuisine is marked by the use of the local fresh ingredients, including lamb, game, and fish from the lakes. Spit-roasting and broiling is popular, and the excellent local olive oil is used both in cooking and to pour over dishes before serving. Black truffles, olives, fruit, and herbs are plentiful and feature in many recipes. First-class sausages and cured pork come from the Marches, particularly on the Umbrian border, and pasta features all over the region.

Lazio

Here, there are many pasta dishes with delicious sauces, gnocchi in various forms, and plenty of dishes featuring lamb and veal (*saltimbocca* being just one), and a variety of meats, all with plenty of herbs and seasonings giving really robust flavours and delicious sauces. Vegetables feature along with fantastic fruits; and beans appear both in soups and many other dishes.

Abruzzi and Molise

The cuisine here is deeply traditional, with local hams and cheeses from the mountain areas, interesting sausages with plenty of garlic and other seasonings, cured meats, and wonderful fish and seafood. Lamb features widely: tender, juicy, and well-flavoured with herbs.

Campania

Naples is the home of pasta dishes, served with a splendid tomato sauce (with many variations). Pizza is said to have been created in Naples. Fish abounds, with *fritto misto* and *fritto pesce* being great favourites. Fish stews are robust and varied and shellfish in particular is often served with pasta. Cutlets and steaks are excellent, served with strong sauces flavoured with garlic, tomatoes, and herbs: pizzaiola steak is one of the favourites. Mozzarella cheese is produced locally and used to create the crispy Mozzarella in Carozza, again served with a garlicky tomato sauce. Sweet dishes are popular too, often with flaky pastry and Ricotta cheese, and the seasonal fruit salads are laced with wine or liqueur.

Puglia (Apulia)

The ground in this region is stony but it produces good fruit, olive groves, vegetables, and herbs, and, of course, there is a large amount of seafood from the sea. Many of the excellent pasta dishes are exclusive to the region both in shape and ingredients. Mushrooms abound and are always added to the local pizzas. Oysters and mussels are plentiful, and so is octopus. Brindisi is famous for its shellfish – both the seafood salads and risottos are truly memorable.

Basilicata

Here potent wines are produced to accompany a robust cuisine largely based on pasta, lamb, pork, game, and dairy produce. The salamis and cured meats are excellent, as are the mountain hams. Lamb is flavoured with the herbs and grasses on which it feeds. Wonderful thick soups – true minestrone – are produced in the mountains, and eels and fish are plentiful in the lakes. Chilli peppers are grown in this region and appear in many of the recipes.

Calabria

This is the toe of Italy, where orange and lemon groves flourish along with olive trees and a profusion of vegetables, especially aubergines (eggplants) which are cooked in a variety of ways. Chicken, rabbit, and guinea fowl are often on the menu. Pizzas feature largely, often with a fishy topping. Mushrooms grow well in the Calabrian climate and feature in many dishes from sauces and stews to salads. Pasta comes with a variety of sauces including baby artichokes, eggs, meat, cheese, mixed vegetables, the large sweet (bell) peppers of the region, and of course garlic. Fish is excellent too and fresh tuna and swordfish are available, along with many other varieties. Many desserts and cakes are flavoured with aniseed, honey, and almonds and feature the plentiful figs of the region.

Sicily

This is the largest island in the Mediterranean and the cuisine is based mainly on fish and vegetables. Fish soups, stews, and salads appear in unlimited forms, including tuna, swordfish, mussels, and many more; citrus fruits are widely grown along with almonds and pistachio nuts, and the local wines, including the dessert wine Marsala, are excellent. Meat is often given a long, slow cooking, or else is ground and shaped before cooking. Game is plentiful and is often cooked in sweet-sour sauces containing the local black olives. Pasta abounds with more unusual sauces as well as the old favourites. Sicilians love desserts, cakes, and especially ice-cream. *Cassata* and other icecreams from Sicily are famous all over the world.

Sardinia

The national dish of Sardinia is suckling pig or newborn lamb cooked on an open fire or spit, and rabbit, game, and a variety of meat dishes are also very popular. Fish is top quality, with excellent sea bass, lobsters, tuna, mullet, eels, and mussels in good supply. Myrtle *(mirto)*, a local herb, is added to everything from chicken dishes to the local liqueur and will remain a fond memory of the island when you have returned home.

Starters & Light Meals

Pasta is so versatile: it can be used to make
soups more substantial, as a delicious and
unusual starter or as a quick and easy lunch
or light supper. The recipes in this chapter range
from traditional Italian dishes to new methods of
combining pasta with different ingredients.

Soup recipes include filling winter dishes
that, if served with some crusty bread, make a
meal in themselves. Others, are subtle and delicate.
Recipes for snacks and light meals offer something
for every taste – vegetable, cheese, meat and fish
sauces combined with every pasta shape from
linguine to lumache. You can also try delicious light
casseroles and roasts, pancakes and vegetable dishes.

Minestrone

Serves 8–10

INGREDIENTS

3 garlic cloves
3 large onions
2 celery sticks (stalks)
2 large carrots
2 large potatoes
100 g/3¹/₂ oz French (green) beans
100 g/3¹/₂ oz courgettes
   (zucchini)

60 g/2 oz/4 tbsp butter
50 ml/2 fl oz/¹/₄ cup olive oil
60 g/2 oz rindless fatty bacon,
   finely diced
1.5 litres/2³/₄ pints/6²/₃ cups
   vegetable or chicken stock
100 g/3¹/₂ oz chopped tomatoes
2 tbsp tomato purée (paste)

1 bunch fresh basil, finely
   chopped
100 g/3¹/₂ oz Parmesan cheese rind
85 g/3 oz dried spaghetti,
   broken up
salt and pepper
freshly grated Parmesan cheese,
   to serve

1 Finely chop the garlic, onions, celery, carrots, potatoes, beans and courgettes (zucchini).

2 Heat the butter and oil together in a large saucepan, add the bacon and cook for 2 minutes. Add the garlic and onion and fry for 2 minutes, then stir in the celery, carrots and potatoes and fry for a further 2 minutes.

3 Add the beans to the pan and fry for 2 minutes. Stir in the courgettes (zucchini) and fry for a further 2 minutes. Cover the pan and cook all the vegetables, stirring frequently, for 15 minutes.

4 Add the stock, tomatoes, tomato purée (paste), basil, and cheese rind and season to taste. Bring to the boil, lower the heat and simmer for 1 hour. Remove and discard the cheese rind.

5 Add the spaghetti pieces to the pan and cook for 20 minutes. Serve in large, warm soup bowls sprinkled with freshly grated Parmesan cheese.

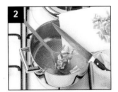

Italian Cream of Tomato Soup

Serves 4

INGREDIENTS

60 g/2 oz/4 tbsp unsalted butter
1 large onion, chopped
900 g/2 lb Italian plum tomatoes,
    skinned and roughly chopped
600 ml/1 pint/2¹/₂ cups
    vegetable stock

pinch of bicarbonate of soda
    (baking soda)
225 g/8 oz/2 cups dried fusilli
1 tbsp caster (superfine) sugar
150 ml/¹/₄ pint/⁵/₈ cup double
    (heavy) cream

salt and pepper
fresh basil leaves, to garnish
deep-fried croûtons, to serve

1 Melt the butter in a pan and fry the onion until softened. Add the chopped tomatoes, with 300 ml/ ¹/₂ pint/1¹/₄ cups of vegetable stock and the bicarbonate of soda (baking soda). Bring the soup to the boil and simmer for 20 minutes.

2 Remove the pan from the heat and set aside to cool. Purée the soup in a blender or food processor and pour through a fine strainer back into the saucepan.

3 Add the remaining vegetable stock and the fusilli to the pan, and season to taste.

4 Add the sugar to the pan, bring to the boil, then simmer for about 15 minutes.

5 Pour the soup into warm soup bowls, swirl the double (heavy) cream around the surface of the soup and garnish with fresh basil leaves. Serve immediately with deep-fried croûtons.

VARIATION

To make orange and tomato soup, simply use half the quantity of vegetable stock, topped up with the same amount of fresh orange juice and garnish the soup with orange rind. Or to make tomato and carrot soup, add half the quantity again of vegetable stock with the same amount of carrot juice and 175 g/6 oz/1¹/₄ cups grated carrot to the recipe, cooking the carrot with the onion.

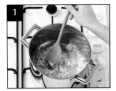

Potato & Parsley Soup with Pesto

Serves 4

INGREDIENTS

3 slices rindless, smoked, fatty
    bacon
450 g/1 lb floury potatoes
450 g/1 lb onions
25 g/1 oz/2 tbsp butter
600 ml/1 pint/2^1/$_2$ cups chicken
    stock
600 ml/1 pint/2^1/$_2$ cups milk
100 g/3^1/$_2$ oz/^{1}/$_4$ cup
    dried conchigliette

150 ml/^{1}/$_4$ pint/^{5}/$_8$ cup double
    (heavy) cream
chopped fresh parsley
freshly grated Parmesan cheese
    and garlic bread, to serve

PESTO SAUCE:
60 g/2 oz/1 cup finely chopped
    fresh parsley
2 garlic cloves, crushed

60 g/2 oz/^{1}/$_2$ cup pine nuts
    (kernels), crushed
2 tbsp chopped fresh basil leaves
60 g/2 oz/^{2}/$_3$ cup freshly grated
    Parmesan cheese
white pepper
150 ml/^{1}/$_4$ pint/^{5}/$_8$ cup
    olive oil

1 To make the pesto sauce, process all of the ingredients in a blender or food processor for 2 minutes, or blend together by hand (see Cook's Tip).

2 Finely chop the bacon, potatoes and onions. Fry the bacon in a pan for 4 minutes. Stir in the butter, potatoes and onions and cook for 12 minutes.

3 Add the stock and milk to the pan, bring to the boil and simmer for 10 minutes. Add the pasta and simmer for a further 12-14 minutes.

4 Blend in the cream and simmer for 5 minutes. Add the parsley and 2 tbsp pesto sauce. Transfer the soup to serving bowls and serve with the Parmesan cheese and garlic bread

COOK'S TIP

If you are making pesto by hand, it is best to use a mortar and pestle. Thoroughly grind together the parsley, garlic, pine nuts (kernels) and basil to make a smooth paste, then mix in the cheese and pepper. Finally, gradually beat in the oil.

Ravioli alla Parmigiana

Serves 4

INGREDIENTS

285 g/10 oz Basic Pasta Dough
1.2 litres/2 pints/5 cups veal
  stock
freshly grated Parmesan cheese,
  to serve

FILLING:
100 g/3¹/₂ oz/1 cup freshly grated
  Parmesan cheese
100 g/3¹/₂ oz/1¹/₃ cups fine
  white breadcrumbs
2 eggs

125 ml/4 fl oz/¹/₂ cup Espagnole
  Sauce (see Cook's Tip, below)
1 small onion, finely chopped
1 tsp freshly grated nutmeg

1 Make the basic pasta dough Carefully roll out 2 sheets of the pasta dough and cover with a damp tea towel (dish cloth) while you make the filling for the ravioli.

2 To make the filling, mix together the grated Parmesan cheese, white breadcrumbs, eggs, espagnole sauce (see Cook's Tip, right), chopped onion and the freshly grated nutmeg in a large mixing bowl.

3 Place spoonfuls of the filling at regular intervals on 1 sheet of pasta dough. Cover with the second sheet of pasta dough, then cut into squares and seal the edges.

4 Bring the veal stock to the boil in a large pan. Add the ravioli and cook for about 15 minutes.

5 Transfer the soup and ravioli to warm serving bowls and serve at once, generously sprinkled with Parmesan cheese.

COOK'S TIP

For espagnole sauce, melt 2 tbsp butter and stir in 25g/1 oz/¹/₄ cup plain flour until smooth. Stir in 1 tsp tomato purée, 250 ml/ 9 fl oz/1¹/₈ cups hot veal stock, 1 tbsp Madeira and 1¹/₂ tsp white wine vinegar. Dice 25 g/1 oz each bacon, carrot and onion and 15 g/ ¹/₂ oz each celery, leek and fennel. Fry with a thyme sprig and a bay leaf in oil. Drain, add to the sauce and simmer for 4 hours. Strain.

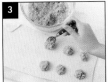

Pea & Egg Noodle Soup with Parmesan Cheese Croûtons

Serves 4

INGREDIENTS

3 slices smoked, rindless, fatty
   bacon, diced
1 large onion, chopped
15 g/¹/₂ oz/1 tbsp butter
450 g/1 lb/2¹/₂ cups dried peas,
   soaked in cold water for 2
   hours and drained

2.3 litres/4 pints/10 cups
   chicken stock
225 g/ 8 oz dried egg noodles
150 ml/. pint/⁵/₈ cup double
   (heavy) cream
salt and pepper
chopped fresh parsley, to garnish

Parmesan cheese croûtons
   (see Cook's Tip, below),
   to serve

1 Put the bacon, onion and butter in a large pan and cook over a low heat for about 6 minutes.

2 Add the peas and the chicken stock to the pan and bring to the boil. Season lightly with salt and pepper, cover and simmer for 1¹/₂ hours.

3 Add the egg noodles to the pan and simmer for a further 15 minutes.

4 Pour in the cream and blend thoroughly. Transfer to soup bowls, garnish with parsley and top with Parmesan cheese croûtons (see Cook's Tip, right). Serve immediately.

VARIATION

Use other pulses, such as dried haricot (navy) beans, borlotti or pinto beans, instead of the peas.

COOK'S TIP

To make Parmesan cheese croûtons, cut a French stick into slices. Coat each slice lightly with olive oil and sprinkle with Parmesan cheese. Grill (broil) for about 30 seconds.

Haricot (Navy) Bean & Pasta Soup

Serves 4

INGREDIENTS

250 g/9 oz/1¹⁄₃ cups haricot
    (navy) beans, soaked for 3
    hours in cold water and
    drained
4 tbsp olive oil
2 large onions, sliced
3 garlic cloves, chopped
425 g/14 oz can chopped
    tomatoes

1 tsp dried oregano
1 tsp tomato purée (paste)
850 ml/1¹⁄₂ pints/3¹⁄₂ cups water
90 g/3¹⁄₂ oz/³⁄₄ cup dried fusilli or
    conchigliette
115 g/4 oz sun-dried tomatoes,
    drained and thinly sliced
1 tbsp chopped fresh coriander
    (cilantro) or flat leaf parsley

salt and pepper
2 tbsp Parmesan cheese
    shavings, to serve

1 Put the haricot (navy) beans in a large pan. Cover with cold water and bring to the boil. Boil vigorously for 15 minutes. Drain and keep warm.

2 Heat the oil in a pan over a medium heat and fry the onions for 2–3 minutes or until soft. Stir in the garlic and cook for 1 minute. Stir in the tomatoes, oregano and tomato purée (paste).

3 Add the water and the reserved beans to the pan. Bring to the boil, cover, then simmer for about 45 minutes, or until the beans are almost tender.

4 Add the pasta to the pan and season to taste. Stir in the sun-dried tomatoes, bring back to the boil, partly cover and simmer for 10 minutes, or until the pasta is tender, but still firm to the bite.

5 Stir the herbs into the soup. Ladle the soup into warm serving bowls, sprinkle with Parmesan and serve.

COOK'S TIP

Place the beans in a pan of cold water and bring to the boil. Remove from the heat and leave the beans to cool in the water. Drain and rinse before using.

Chick Pea (Garbanzo Bean) & Chicken Soup

Serves 4

INGREDIENTS

25 g/1 oz/2 tbsp butter
3 spring onions (scallions), chopped
2 garlic cloves, crushed
1 fresh marjoram sprig, finely chopped

350 g/12 oz boned chicken breasts, diced
1.2 litres/2 pints/5 cups chicken stock
350 g/12 oz can chick peas (garbanzo beans), drained
1 bouquet garni

1 red (bell) pepper, diced
1 green (bell) pepper, diced
115 g/4 oz/1 cup small dried pasta shapes, such as elbow macaroni
salt and white pepper
croûtons, to serve

1 Melt the butter in a large saucepan. Add the spring onions (scallions), garlic, sprig of fresh marjoram and the diced chicken and cook, stirring frequently, over a medium heat for 5 minutes.

2 Add the chicken stock, chick peas (garbanzo beans) and bouquet garni to the pan and season with salt and white pepper.

3 Bring the soup to the boil, lower the heat and then simmer gently for about 2 hours.

4 Add the diced (bell) peppers and pasta to the pan, then simmer for a further 20 minutes.

5 Transfer the soup to a warm tureen. To serve, ladle the soup into individual serving bowls and serve immediately, garnished with the croûtons.

COOK'S TIP

If preferred, use dried chick peas (garbanzo beans). Cover with cold water and set aside to soak for 5–8 hours. Drain and add the peas to the soup, according to the recipe, and allow an additional 30 minutes–1 hour cooking time.

Cream of Lemon & Chicken Soup with Spaghetti

Serves 4

INGREDIENTS

60 g/2 oz/4 tbsp butter
8 shallots, thinly sliced
2 carrots, thinly sliced
2 celery sticks (stalks), thinly sliced
225 g/8 oz boned chicken
   breasts, finely chopped
3 lemons

1.2 litres/2 pints/5 cups chicken
   stock
225 g/8 oz dried spaghetti,
   broken into small pieces
150 ml/¼ pint/⅝ cup double
   (heavy) cream
salt and white pepper

TO GARNISH:
fresh parsley sprig
3 lemon slices, halved

1 Melt the butter in a large saucepan. Add the shallots, carrots, celery and chicken and cook over a low heat, stirring occasionally, for 8 minutes.

2 Thinly pare the lemons and blanch the lemon rind in boiling water for 3 minutes. Squeeze the juice from the lemons.

3 Add the lemon rind and juice to the pan,

together with the chicken stock. Bring slowly to the boil over a low heat and simmer for 40 minutes.

4 Add the spaghetti to the pan and cook for 15 minutes. Season with salt and white pepper and add the cream. Heat through, but do not allow the soup to boil.

5 Pour the soup into a tureen or individual

bowls, garnish with the parsley and half slices of lemon and serve immediately.

COOK'S TIP

You can prepare this soup up to the end of step 3 in advance, so that all you need do before serving is heat it through before adding the pasta and the finishing touches.

Chicken & Sweetcorn Soup

Serves 4

INGREDIENTS

450 g/1 lb boned chicken breasts, cut into strips

1.2 litres/2 pints/5 cups chicken stock

150 ml/¼ pint/⅝ cup double (heavy) cream

100 g/3½ oz/¾ cup dried vermicelli

1 tbsp cornflour (cornstarch)

3 tbsp milk

175 g/6 oz sweetcorn (corn) kernels

salt and pepper

1 Put the chicken, stock and cream into a large saucepan and bring to the boil over a low heat. Reduce the heat slightly and simmer for about 20 minutes. Season with salt and pepper to taste.

2 Meanwhile, cook the vermicelli in lightly salted boiling water for 10-12 minutes, until just tender. Drain the pasta and keep warm.

3 Mix together the cornflour (cornstarch) and milk to make a smooth paste, then stir into the soup until thickened.

4 Add the sweetcorn (corn) and pasta to the pan and heat through.

5 Transfer the soup to a warm tureen or individual soup bowls and serve immediately.

COOK'S TIP

If you are short of time, buy ready-cooked chicken, remove any skin and cut it into slices.

VARIATION

For crab and sweetcorn soup, substitute 450 g/1 lb cooked crabmeat for the chicken breasts. Flake the crabmeat well before adding it to the saucepan and reduce the cooking time by 10 minutes. For a Chinese-style soup, substitute egg noodles for the vermicelli and use canned, creamed sweetcorn (corn).

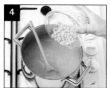

Veal & Ham Soup with Sherry

Serves 4

INGREDIENTS

60 g/2 oz/4 tbsp butter
1 onion, diced
1 carrot, diced
1 celery stick (stalk), diced
450 g/1 lb very thinly sliced veal
450 g/1 lb thinly sliced ham

60 g/2 oz/^{1}/$_2$ cup plain
   (all purpose) flour
1 litre/1^3/$_4$ pints/4^1/$_8$ cups beef stock
1 bay leaf
8 black peppercorns
pinch of salt

3 tbsp redcurrant jelly
150 ml/^{1}/$_4$ pint/^{5}/$_8$ cup cream
   sherry
100 g/3^1/$_2$ oz/^{3}/$_4$ cup dried
   vermicelli
garlic croûtons, to serve

1 Melt the butter in a large saucepan. Cook the onions, carrot, celery, veal and ham over a low heat for 6 minutes.

2 Sprinkle over the flour and cook, stirring, for a further 2 minutes. Gradually stir in the stock, then add the bay leaf, peppercorns and salt. Bring to the boil and simmer for 1 hour.

3 Remove from the heat and add the redcurrant jelly and cream sherry. Set aside for about 4 hours.

4 Discard the bay leaf from the pan and reheat the soup over a low heat until warmed through.

5 Meanwhile, cook the vermicelli in a pan of lightly salted boiling water for 10-12 minutes. Stir the vermicelli into the soup and transfer to warm soup bowls. Serve with garlic croûtons (see Cook's Tip, right).

COOK'S TIP

To make garlic croûtons, remove the crusts from 3 slices of day-old white bread. Cut the bread into 5 mm/^{1}/$_4$ inch cubes. Heat 3 tbsp olive oil over a low heat and stir-fry 1–2 finely chopped garlic cloves for 1–2 minutes. Remove the garlic and add the bread. Cook, stirring frequently, until golden brown. Remove from the pan and drain on kitchen paper (towels).

Tuscan Veal Broth

Serves 4

INGREDIENTS

60 g/2 oz/¹/₃ cup dried peas,
    soaked for 2 hours and
    drained
900 g/2 lb boned neck of
    veal, diced
1.2 litres/2 pints/5 cups beef or
    brown stock (see Cook's Tip)

600 ml/1 pint/2¹/₂ cups water
60 g/2 oz/¹/₃ cup barley, washed
1 large carrot, diced
1 small turnip (about
    175 g/6 oz), diced
1 large leek, thinly sliced
1 red onion, finely chopped

100 g/3¹/₂ oz chopped tomatoes
1 fresh basil sprig
100 g/3¹/₂ oz/³/₄ cup dried
    vermicelli
salt and white pepper

1 Put the peas, veal, stock and water into a large saucepan and gently bring to the boil. Using a slotted spoon, skim off any scum that rises to the surface of the liquid.

2 When all of the scum has been removed, add the barley and a pinch of salt to the mixture. Simmer gently over a low heat for 25 minutes.

3 Add the carrot, turnip, leek, onion, tomatoes and basil to the pan, and season to taste. Simmer for about 2 hours, skimming the surface from time to time. Remove the pan from the heat and set aside for 2 hours.

4 Set the pan over a medium heat and bring to the boil. Add the vermicelli and cook for 12 minutes. Season with salt and pepper to taste and remove and discard the basil. Ladle into soup bowls and serve immediately.

COOK'S TIP

Brown stock is made with veal bones and shin of beef roasted with dripping (drippings) in the oven for 40 minutes. Transfer the bones to a pan, add sliced leeks, onion, celery and carrots, a bouquet garni, white wine vinegar and a thyme sprig and cover with water. Simmer over a very low heat for 3 hours. Strain and blot the fat from the surface with kitchen paper.

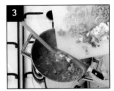

Veal & Wild Mushroom Soup with Vermicelli

Serves 4

INGREDIENTS

450 g/1 lb veal, thinly sliced
450 g/1 lb veal bones
1.2 litres/2 pints/5 cups water
1 small onion
6 peppercorns
1 tsp cloves

pinch of mace
140 g/5 oz oyster and shiitake
  mushrooms, roughly
  chopped
150 ml/¼ pint/⅝ cup double
  (heavy) cream

100 g/3½ oz/¾ cup dried
  vermicelli
1 tbsp cornflour (cornstarch)
3 tbsp milk
salt and pepper

1 Put the veal, bones and water into a large saucepan. Bring to the boil and lower the heat. Add the onion, peppercorns, cloves and mace and simmer for about 3 hours, until the veal stock is reduced by one-third.

2 Strain the stock, skim off any fat on the surface with a slotted spoon, and pour the stock into a clean saucepan. Add the veal meat to the pan.

3 Add the mushrooms and cream, bring to the boil over a low heat and simmer for 12 minutes. Meanwhile, cook the vermicelli in lightly salted boiling water until tender, but still firm to the bite. Drain and keep warm.

4 Mix together the cornflour (cornstarch) and milk to form a smooth paste. Stir into the soup to thicken. Season to taste with salt and pepper and

just before serving, add the vermicelli. Transfer the soup to a warm tureen and serve immediately.

COOK'S TIP

You can make this soup with the more inexpensive cuts of veal, such as breast or neck slices. These are lean and the long cooking time ensures that the meat is really tender.

Mussel & Potato Soup

Serves 4

INGREDIENTS

750 g/1 lb 10 oz mussels

2 tbsp olive oil

100 g/3¹/₂ oz/7 tbsp unsalted butter

2 slices rindless, fatty bacon, chopped

1 onion, chopped

2 garlic cloves, crushed

60 g/2 oz/¹/₂ cup plain (all purpose) flour

450 g/1 lb potatoes, thinly sliced

100 g/3¹/₂ oz/³/₄ cup dried conchigliette

300 ml/¹/₂ pint/1¹/₄ cups double (heavy) cream

1 tbsp lemon juice

2 egg yolks

salt and pepper

TO GARNISH:

2 tbsp finely chopped fresh parsley

lemon wedges

1 Debeard the mussels and scrub them under cold water for 5 minutes. Discard any mussels that do not close immediately when sharply tapped.

2 Bring a large pan of water to the boil, add the mussels, oil and a little pepper and cook until the mussels open.

3 Drain the mussels, reserving the cooking liquid. Discard any mussels that are closed. Remove the mussels from their shells.

4 Melt the butter in a large saucepan and cook the bacon, onion and garlic for 4 minutes. Stir in the flour, then 1.2 litres/ 2 pints/5 cups of the reserved cooking liquid.

5 Add the potatoes to the pan and simmer for 5 minutes. Add the conchigliette and simmer for a further 10 minutes.

6 Add the cream and lemon juice, season to taste, then add the mussels to the pan.

7 Blend the egg yolks with 1-2 tbsp of the remaining cooking liquid, stir into the pan and cook for 4 minutes.

8 Ladle the soup into 4 warm individual soup bowls, garnish with the chopped fresh parsley and lemon wedges and serve.

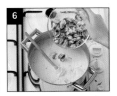

Italian Fish Soup

Serves 4

INGREDIENTS

60 g/2 oz/4 tbsp butter
450 g/1 lb assorted fish fillets,
　such as red mullet and
　snapper
450 g/1 lb prepared seafood,
　such as squid and prawns
　(shrimp)
225 g/8 oz fresh crabmeat

1 large onion, sliced
25 g/1 oz/¼ cup plain
　(all purpose) flour
1.2 litres/2 pints/5 cups fish
　stock
100 g/3½ oz/¾ cup dried pasta
　shapes, such as ditalini or
　elbow macaroni

1 tbsp anchovy essence
grated rind and juice of
　1 orange
50 ml/2 fl oz/¼ cup dry sherry
300 ml/½ pint/1¼ cups double
　(heavy) cream
salt and black pepper
crusty brown bread, to serve

1 Melt the butter in a
large saucepan and
cook the fish fillets,
seafood, crabmeat and
onion over a low heat for
6 minutes.

2 Stir the flour into the
mixture.

3 Gradually add the fish
stock and bring to the
boil, stirring constantly.
Reduce the heat and
simmer for 30 minutes.

4 Add the pasta and cook
for 10 minutes.

5 Stir in the anchovy
essence, orange rind,
orange juice, sherry and
double (heavy) cream.
Season to taste.

6 Heat the soup until
completely warmed
through. Transfer the soup
to a tureen or to warm soup
bowls and serve with crusty
brown bread.

COOK'S TIP

*The heads, tails, trimmings
and bones of most non-oily
fish can be used to make fish
stock. Simmer 900 g/2 lb
fish pieces in a pan with
150 ml/5 fl oz white wine,
1 chopped onion, 1 sliced
carrot, 1 sliced celery stick
(stalk), 4 black peppercorns,
1 bouquet garni and 1.75
litres/3 pints/7½ cups water
for 30 minutes, then strain.*

Chicken & Pasta Broth

Serves 6

INGREDIENTS

350 g/12 oz boneless chicken breasts

2 tbsp sunflower oil

1 medium onion, diced

250 g/9 oz/1¹/₂ cups carrots, diced

250 g/9 oz cauliflower florets

850 ml/1¹/₂ pints/3³/₄ cups chicken stock

2 tsp dried mixed herbs

125 g/4¹/₂ oz/1 cup small pasta shapes

salt and pepper

Parmesan cheese (optional) and crusty bread, to serve

1 Using a sharp knife, finely dice the chicken, discarding any skin.

2 Heat the oil in a large saucepan and quickly sauté the chicken and vegetables until they are lightly coloured.

3 Stir in the stock and herbs. Bring to the boil and add the pasta shapes. Return to the boil, cover and simmer for 10 minutes, stirring occasionally to prevent the pasta shapes sticking together.

4 Season with salt and pepper to taste and sprinkle with Parmesan cheese, if using. Serve with fresh crusty bread.

COOK'S TIP

You can use any small pasta shapes for this soup – try conchigliette or ditalini or even spaghetti broken up into small pieces. To make a fun soup for children you could add animal-shaped or alphabet pasta.

VARIATION

Broccoli florets can be used to replace the cauliflower florets. Substitute 2 tablespoons chopped fresh mixed herbs for the dried mixed herbs.

Chicken, Guinea Fowl & Spaghetti Soup

Serves 6

INGREDIENTS

500 g/1 lb 2 oz skinless chicken,
    chopped
500 g/1 lb 2 oz skinless guinea fowl
    meat
600 ml/1 pint/2¹/₂ cups chicken stock
1 small onion

6 peppercorns
1 tsp cloves
pinch of mace
150 ml/¹/₄ pint/²/₃ cup double (heavy)
    cream
2 tsp butter

2 tsp plain (all-purpose) flour
125 g/4¹/₂ oz/1 cup quick-cook
    spaghetti, broken into short
    lengths and cooked
2 tbsp chopped fresh parsley, to
    garnish

1 Put the chicken and guinea fowl meat into a large saucepan with the chicken stock.

2 Bring to the boil and add the onion, peppercorns, cloves and mace. Simmer gently for about 2 hours until the stock is reduced by one-third.

3 Strain the soup, skim off any fat and remove any bones from the chicken and guinea fowl.

4 Return the soup and meat to a clean saucepan. Add the double (heavy) cream and bring to the boil slowly.

5 To make a roux, melt the butter and stir in the flour until it has a paste-like consistency. Add to the soup, stirring until slightly thickened.

6 Just before serving, add the cooked quick-cook spaghetti.

7 Transfer the soup to individual serving bowls, garnish with parsley and serve.

VARIATION

Instead of spaghetti, use small pasta shapes such as ziti or macaroni.

Tuscan Bean Soup

Serves 4

INGREDIENTS

225 g/8 oz dried butter beans
soaked overnight or 2 x
420 g/14¹⁄₂ oz can butter beans
1 tbsp olive oil

2 garlic cloves, crushed
1 vegetable or chicken stock cube,
crumbled
150 ml/5 fl oz/²⁄₃ cup milk

2 tbsp chopped fresh oregano
salt and pepper

1 If you are using dried beans that have been soaked overnight, drain them thoroughly. Bring a large pan of water to the boil, add the beans and boil for 10 minutes. Cover the pan and simmer for a further 30 minutes or until tender. Drain the beans, reserving the cooking liquid. If you are using canned beans, drain them thoroughly and reserve the liquid.

2 Heat the oil in a large frying pan (skillet) and fry the garlic for 2–3 minutes or until just beginning to brown.

3 Add the beans and 400 ml/14 fl oz/1⅔ cup of the reserved liquid to the pan (skillet), stirring. You may need to add a little water if there is insufficient liquid. Stir in the crumbled stock cube. Bring the mixture to the boil and then remove the pan from the heat.

4 Place the bean mixture in a food processor and blend to form a smooth purée. Alternatively, mash the bean mixture to a smooth consistency. Season to taste with salt and pepper and stir in the milk.

5 Pour the soup back into the pan and gently heat to just below boiling point. Stir in the chopped oregano just before serving.

VARIATION

If you prefer, use 3 teaspoons of dried oregano instead of fresh, but add with the beans in step 3. This soup can also be made with cannellini or borlotti beans following the same method.

Brown Lentil Soup with Pasta

Serves 4

INGREDIENTS

4 rashers streaky bacon, cut into
small squares
1 onion, chopped
2 garlic cloves, crushed
2 sticks celery, chopped

50 g/1³/₄oz/¹/₄ cup farfalline
or spaghetti broken into
small pieces
1 x 420 g/14¹/₂ oz can brown
lentils, drained

1.2 litres/2 pints/5 cups hot ham
or vegetable stock
2 tbsp chopped, fresh mint

1 Place the bacon in a
large frying pan
(skillet) together with the
onions, garlic and celery.
Dry fry for 4–5 minutes,
stirring, until the onion is
tender and the bacon is just
beginning to brown.

2 Add the farfalline or
spaghetti pieces to
the pan (skillet) and cook,
stirring, for about 1
minute to coat the pasta
in the oil.

3 Add the lentils and the
stock and bring to the
boil. Reduce the heat and
leave to simmer for 12–15

minutes or until the pasta
is tender.

4 Remove the pan
(skillet) from the heat
and stir in the chopped
fresh mint.

5 Transfer the soup to
warm soup bowls and
serve immediately.

VARIATION

*Any type of pasta can be used in
this recipe, try fusilli, conchiglie
or rigatoni, if you prefer.*

COOK'S TIP

*If you prefer to use dried
lentils, add the stock before
the pasta and cook for
1–1¹/₄ hours until the lentils
are tender. Add the pasta
and cook for a further
12–15 minutes.*

Vegetable Soup with Cannelini Beans

Serves 4

INGREDIENTS

1 small aubergine (eggplant)	850 ml/1½ pints/3¾ cups hot	50 g/1¾ oz/½ cup vermicelli
2 large tomatoes	vegetable or chicken stock	3 tbsp pesto
1 potato, peeled	2 tsp dried basil	freshly grated Parmesan cheese,
1 carrot, peeled	10 g/½ oz dried porcini mushrooms,	to serve (optional)
1 leek	soaked for 10 minutes in	
420 g/14½ oz can cannelini beans	enough warm water to cover	

1 Slice the aubergine (eggplant) into rings about 10 mm/½ inch thick, then cut each ring into 4.

2 Cut the tomatoes and potato into small dice. Cut the carrot into sticks, about 2.5 cm/1 inch long and cut the leek into rings.

3 Place the cannelini beans and their liquid in a large saucepan. Add the aubergine (eggplant), tomatoes, potatoes, carrot and leek, stirring to mix.

4 Add the stock to the pan and bring to the boil. Reduce the heat and leave to simmer for 15 minutes.

5 Add the basil, dried mushrooms, their soaking liquid and the vermicelli and simmer for 5 minutes or until all of the vegetables are tender.

6 Remove the pan from the heat and stir in the pesto.

7 Serve with freshly grated Parmesan cheese, if using.

COOK'S TIP

Porcini are a wild mushroom grown in southern Italy. When dried and rehydrated they have a very intense flavour, so although they are expensive to buy only a small amount are required to add flavour to soups or risottos.

Tuscan Onion Soup

Serves 4

INGREDIENTS

50 g/1¾ oz pancetta ham, diced
1 tbsp olive oil
4 large white onions, sliced
    thinly in rings

3 garlic cloves, chopped
850 ml/1½ pints/3¾ cups hot
    chicken or ham stock
4 slices ciabatta or other

Italian bread
50 g/1¾ oz/3 tbsp butter
75 g/2¾ oz Gruyère or Cheddar
salt and pepper

1 Dry fry the pancetta in a large saucepan for 3–4 minutes until it begins to brown. Remove the pancetta from the pan and set aside until required.

2 Add the oil to the pan and cook the onions and garlic over a high heat for 4 minutes. Reduce the heat, cover and cook for 15 minutes until lightly caramelized.

3 Add the stock to the saucepan and bring to the boil. Reduce the heat and leave the mixture to simmer, covered, for about 10 minutes.

4 Toast the slices of ciabatta on both sides, under a preheated grill (broiler), for 2–3 minutes or until golden. Spread the ciabatta with butter and top with the Gruyère or Cheddar cheese. Cut the bread into bite-size pieces.

5 Add the reserved pancetta to the soup and season to taste with salt and pepper. Pour into 4 soup bowls and top with the toasted bread.

COOK'S TIP

Pancetta is similar to bacon, but it is air- and salt-cured for about 6 months. Pancetta is available from most delicatessens and some large supermarkets. If you cannot obtain pancetta use unsmoked bacon instead.

Green Soup

Serves 4

INGREDIENTS

1 tbsp olive oil
1 onion, chopped
1 garlic clove, chopped
200 g/7 oz potato, peeled and
    cut into 2.5 cm/1 inch cubes

700 ml/1¼ pint/scant 3 cups
    vegetable or chicken stock
1 small cucumber or ½ large
    cucumber, cut into chunks
80 g/3 oz bunch watercress

125 g/4½ oz green (dwarf) beans,
    trimmed and halved
    in length
salt and pepper

1 Heat the oil in a large pan and fry the onion and garlic for 3–4 minutes or until softened. Add the cubed potato and fry for a further 2–3 minutes.

2 Stir in the stock, bring to the boil and leave to simmer for 5 minutes.

3 Add the cucumber to the pan and cook for a further 3 minutes or until the potatoes are tender. Test by inserting the tip of a knife into the potato cubes – it should pass through easily.

4 Add the watercress and allow to wilt. Then place the soup in a food processor and blend until smooth. Alternatively, before adding the watercress, mash the soup with a potato masher and push through a sieve, then chop the watercress finely and stir into the soup.

5 Bring a small pan of water to the boil and steam the beans for 3–4 minutes or until tender.

6 Add the beans to the soup, season and warm

through.

VARIATION

Try using 125 g/4½ oz mange tout (snow peas) instead of the beans, if you prefer.

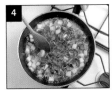

Artichoke Soup

Serves 4

INGREDIENTS

1 tbsp olive oil
1 onion, chopped
1 garlic clove, crushed
2 x 400 g/14 oz can artichoke
  hearts, drained

600 ml/1 pint/2¹⁄₂ cups hot
  vegetable stock
150 ml/5 fl oz/²⁄₃ cup
  single (light) cream
2 tbsp fresh thyme,

stalks removed
2 sun-dried tomatoes,
  cut into strips

1 Heat the oil in a large saucepan and fry the chopped onion and crushed garlic until just softened.

2 Using a sharp knife, roughly chop the artichoke hearts. Add the artichoke pieces to the onion and garlic mixture in the pan. Pour in the hot vegetable stock, stirring.

3 Bring the mixture to the boil, then reduce the heat and leave to simmer, covered, for about 3 minutes.

4 Place the mixture into a food processor and blend until smooth. Alternatively, push the mixture through a sieve to remove any lumps.

5 Return the soup to the saucepan. Stir the single (light) cream and fresh thyme into the soup.

6 Transfer the soup to a large bowl, cover, and leave to chill in the refrigerator for about 3–4 hours.

7 Transfer the chilled soup to individual soup bowls and garnish with strips of sun-dried tomato. Serve with lots of fresh, crusty bread.

VARIATION

Try adding 2 tablespoons of dry vermouth, such as Martini, to the soup in step 5 if you wish.

Orange, Thyme & Pumpkin Soup

Serves 4

INGREDIENTS

2 tbsp olive oil
2 medium onions, chopped
2 cloves garlic, chopped
900 g/2 lb pumpkin, peeled and
    cut into 2.5 cm/1 inch chunks

1.5 litres /2³/₄ pints/6¹/₄ cups
    boiling vegetable or
    chicken stock
finely grated rind and juice
    of 1 orange

3 tbsp fresh thyme, stalks
    removed
150 ml/5 fl oz/²/₃ cup milk
salt and pepper
crusty bread, to serve

1 Heat the olive oil in a large saucepan. Add the onions to the pan and cook for 3–4 minutes or until softened. Add the garlic and pumpkin and cook for a further 2 minutes, stirring well.

2 Add the boiling vegetable or chicken stock, orange rind and juice and 2 tablespoons of the thyme to the pan. Leave to simmer, covered, for 20 minutes or until the pumpkin is tender.

3 Place the mixture in a food processor and blend until smooth. Alternatively, mash the mixture with a potato masher until smooth. Season to taste with salt and pepper.

4 Return the soup to the saucepan and add the milk. Reheat the soup for 3–4 minutes or until it is piping hot but not boiling. Sprinkle with the remaining fresh thyme just before serving.

5 Divide the soup among 4 warm soup bowls and serve with lots of fresh crusty bread.

COOK'S TIP

Pumpkins are usually large vegetables. To make things a little easier, ask the greengrocer to cut a chunk off for you. Alternatively, make double the quantity and freeze the soup for up to 3 months.

Calabrian Mushroom Soup

Serves 4

INGREDIENTS

2 tbsp olive oil

1 onion, chopped

450g/1 lb mixed mushrooms, such as ceps, oyster and button

300 ml/^{1}/$_2$ pint/1^1/$_4$ cup milk

850 ml1^1/$_2$ pints/3^3/$_4$ cups hot vegetable stock

8 slices of rustic bread or French stick

50 g/1^3/$_4$ oz/3 tbsp butter, melted

2 garlic cloves, crushed

75 g/2^3/$_4$oz Gruyère cheese, finely grated

salt and pepper

1 Heat the oil in a large frying pan (skillet) and cook the onion for 3–4 minutes or until soft and golden.

2 Wipe each mushroom with a damp cloth and cut any large mushrooms into smaller, bite-size pieces.

3 Add the mushrooms to the pan, stirring quickly to coat them in the oil.

4 Add the milk to the pan, bring to the boil, cover and leave to simmer for about 5 minutes.

Gradually stir in the hot vegetable stock.

5 Under a preheated grill (broiler), toast the bread on both sides until golden.

6 Mix together the garlic and butter and spoon generously over the toast.

7 Place the toast in the bottom of a large tureen or divide it among 4 individual serving bowls and pour over the hot soup. Top with the grated Gruyère cheese and serve at once.

COOK'S TIP

Mushrooms absorb liquid, which can lessen the flavour and affect cooking properties. Wipe them with a damp cloth rather than rinsing them in water.

VARIATION

Supermarkets stock a wide variety of wild mushrooms. If you prefer, use a combination of cultivated and wild mushrooms.

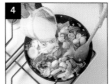

Tomatoes Stuffed with Tuna Mayonnaise

Serves 4

INGREDIENTS

4 plum tomatoes
2 tbsp sun-dried tomato paste
2 egg yolks
2 tsp lemon juice
finely grated rind of 1 lemon

4 tbsp olive oil
1 x 115g/4 oz can tuna, drained
2 tbsp capers, rinsed
salt and pepper

TO GARNISH:
2 sun-dried tomatoes, cut into
    strips
fresh basil leaves

1 Halve the tomatoes and scoop out the seeds. Divide the sun-dried tomato paste among the tomato halves and spread around the inside of the skin.

2 Place on a baking tray (cookie sheet) and roast in a preheated oven at 200°C/400°F/Gas Mark 6 for 12–15 minutes. Leave to cool slightly.

3 Meanwhile, make the mayonnaise. In a food processor, blend the egg yolks and lemon juice with the lemon rind until smooth. Once mixed and with the motor still running slowly, add the olive oil. Stop the processor as soon as the mayonnaise has thickened. Alternatively, use a hand whisk, beating the mixture continuously until it thickens.

4 Add the tuna and capers to the mayonnaise and season.

5 Spoon the tuna mayonnaise mixture into the tomato shells and garnish with sun-dried tomato strips and basil leaves. Return to the oven for a few minutes or serve chilled.

COOK'S TIP

For a picnic, do not roast the tomatoes, just scoop out the seeds, drain, cut-side down on absorbent kitchen paper for 1 hour, and fill with the mayonnaise mixture. They are firmer to handle and easier to eat with the fingers this way. If you prefer, shop-bought mayonnaise may be used instead – just stir in the lemon rind.

Deep-Fried Risotto Balls

Serves 4

INGREDIENTS

2 tbsp olive oil	150 g/5 oz/³/₄ cup arborio	100 ml/3¹/₂ fl oz/¹/₂ scant cup dry
1 medium onion, finely chopped	(risotto) rice, washed	white wine
1 garlic clove, chopped	1 tsp dried oregano	75 g/2³/₄oz Mozzarella cheese
¹/₂ red (bell) pepper, diced	400 ml/14 fl oz/1²/₃ cup hot	oil, for deep-frying
	vegetable or chicken stock	fresh basil sprig, to garnish

1 Heat the oil in a frying pan (skillet) and cook the onion and garlic for 3–4 minutes or until just softened.

2 Add the (bell) pepper, rice and oregano to the pan. Cook for 2–3 minutes, stirring to coat the rice in the oil.

3 Mix the stock together with the wine and add to the pan a ladleful at a time, waiting for the liquid to be absorbed by the rice before you add the next ladleful of liquid.

4 Once all of the liquid has been absorbed and the rice is tender (it should take about 15 minutes in total), remove the pan from the heat and leave until the mixture is cool enough to handle.

5 Cut the cheese into 12 pieces. Taking about a tablespoon of risotto, shape the mixture around the cheese pieces to make 12 balls.

6 Heat the oil until a piece of bread browns in 30 seconds. Cook the risotto balls in batches of 4 for 2 minutes until golden.

7 Remove the risotto balls with a perforated spoon and drain thoroughly on absorbent kitchen paper. Garnish with a sprig of basil and serve hot.

VARIATION

Although Mozzarella is the traditional cheese for this recipe and creates the stringy 'telephone wire' effect, other cheeses, such as Cheddar may be used if you prefer.

Black Olive Pâté

Serves 4

INGREDIENTS

175 g/6 oz black olives, pitted and chopped
finely grated rind and juice of 1 lemon

50 g/1 1/2 oz unsalted butter
4 canned anchovy fillets, drained and rinsed

2 tbsp extra virgin olive oil
15 g/1/2 oz ground almonds

1 If you are making the pâté by hand, chop the olives very finely and then mash them along with the lemon rind, juice and butter, using a fork or potato masher. Alternatively, place the roughly chopped olives, lemon rind, juice and butter in a food processor and blend until all of the ingredients are finely chopped.

2 Using a sharp knife, chop the drained anchovies and add them to the olive and lemon mixture. Mash the pâté by hand or blend it in a food processor for about 20 seconds.

3 Gradually whisk in the olive oil and stir in the ground almonds. Place the black olive pâté in a serving bowl.

4 Leave the pâté to chill in the refrigerator for about 30 minutes. Serve accompanied by thin pieces of toast.

COOK'S TIP

The pâté will keep for up to 5 days in a serving bowl in the refrigerator if you pour a thin layer of extra-virgin olive oil over the top of the pâté to seal it. Then use the oil to brush on the toast before spreading the pâté.

COOK'S TIP

Extra-virgin olive oil is the finest grade of olive oil. It is made from the first, cold pressing of hand gathered olives.

Fresh Figs with Parma Ham (Prosciutto)

Serves 4

INGREDIENTS

40 g/1½ oz rocket (arugula)	4 tbsp olive oil	1 small red chilli
4 fresh figs	1 tbsp fresh orange juice	
4 slices Parma ham (prosciutto)	1 tbsp clear honey	

1 Tear the rocket (arugula) into more manageable pieces and arrange on 4 serving plates.

2 Using a sharp knife, cut each of the figs into quarters and place them on top of the rocket (arugula) leaves.

3 Using a sharp knife, cut the Parma ham (prosciutto) into strips and scatter over the rocket (arugula) and figs.

4 Place the oil, orange juice and honey in a screw-top jar. Shake the jar until the mixture emulsifies and forms a thick dressing. Transfer to a bowl.

5 Using a sharp knife, dice the chilli, remembering not to touch your face before you have washed your hands (see Cook's Tip, right). Add the chopped chilli to the dressing and mix well.

6 Drizzle the dressing over the Parma ham (prosciutto), rocket (arugula) and figs, tossing to mix well. Serve at once.

COOK'S TIP

Chillies can burn the skin for several hours after chopping, so it is advisable to wear gloves when you are handling the very hot varieties.

COOK'S TIP

Parma, in the Emilia-Romagna region of Italy, is famous for its ham, prosciutto di Parma, *thought to be the best in the world.*

Roasted (Bell) Peppers

Serves 4

INGREDIENTS

2 each, red, yellow and orange
(bell) peppers

4 tomatoes, halved

1 tbsp olive oil

3 garlic cloves, chopped

1 onion, sliced in rings

2 tbsp fresh thyme

salt and pepper

1 Halve and deseed the (bell) peppers. Place them, cut-side down, on a baking tray (cookie sheet) and cook under a preheated grill (broiler) for 10 minutes.

2 Add the tomatoes to the baking tray (cookie sheet) and grill (broil) for 5 minutes, until the skins of the (bell) peppers and tomatoes are charred.

3 Put the (bell) peppers into a polythene bag for 10 minutes to sweat, which will make the skin easier to peel. Remove the tomato skins and roughly chop the flesh.

4 Peel the skins from the (bell) peppers and slice the flesh into strips.

5 Heat the oil in a large frying pan (skillet) and fry the garlic and onion for 3–4 minutes or until softened.

6 Add the (bell) peppers and tomatoes to the frying pan (skillet) and cook for 5 minutes. Stir in the fresh thyme and season to taste with salt and pepper.

7 Transfer to serving bowls and serve warm or chilled.

COOK'S TIP

You can preserve the (bell) peppers in the refrigerator by placing them in a sterilized jar and pouring olive oil over the top to seal. Alternatively, heat 300 ml/½ pint/¼ cup white wine vinegar with a bay leaf and 4 juniper berries and bring to the boiling point. Pour over the (bell) peppers and set aside until completely cold. Pack into sterilized jars – they will keep for up to 1 month.

Baked Aubergines (Eggplant) & Tomatoes

Serves 4

INGREDIENTS

3–4 tbsp olive oil	100 g/3½ oz Mozzarella cheese,	50 g/1¾ oz Parmesan cheese,
2 garlic cloves, crushed	sliced thinly	grated
2 large aubergines (eggplants)	200 g/7 oz passata (tomato purée)	

1 Heat 2 tablespoons of the olive oil in a large frying pan (skillet). Add the garlic to the frying pan (skillet) and sauté for 30 seconds.

2 Slice the aubergines (eggplants) lengthwise. Add the slices to the pan and cook in the oil for 3–4 minutes on each side or until tender. (You will probably have to cook them in batches, so add the remaining oil as necessary.)

3 Remove the aubergines (eggplants) with a perforated spoon and drain on absorbent kitchen paper.

4 Place a layer of aubergine (eggplant) slices in a shallow ovenproof dish. Cover the aubergines (eggplants) with a layer of Mozzarella and then pour over a third of the passata (tomato purée). Continue layering in the same order, finishing with a layer of passata (tomato purée) on top.

5 Generously sprinkle the grated Parmesan cheese over the top and bake in a preheated oven at 200°C/400°F/Gas Mark 6 for 25–30 minutes.

6 Transfer to serving plates and serve warm or chilled.

COOK'S TIP

Passata (tomato purée) is a simple tomato sauce, which can be bought from most supermarkets. Alternatively, you can purée and sieve a can of tomatoes and season with salt and pepper.

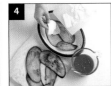

Courgette (Zucchini) & Thyme Fritters

Makes 16

INGREDIENTS

100 g/3½ oz self-raising flour
2 eggs, beaten
50 ml/2 fl oz milk

300 g/10½ oz courgettes
(zucchini)
2 tbsp fresh thyme

1 tbsp oil
salt and pepper

1 Sift the self-raising flour into a large bowl and make a well in the centre. Add the egg to the well, and using a wooden spoon, gradually draw in the flour.

2 Slowly add the milk to the mixture, stirring constantly to form a thick batter.

3 Meanwhile, wash the courgettes (zucchini). Grate the courgettes (zucchini) over a sheet of kitchen paper placed in a bowl to absorb some of the juices.

4 Add the courgettes (zucchini), thyme, salt and pepper to taste to the batter and mix thoroughly.

5 Heat the oil in a large, heavy-based frying pan (skillet). Taking a tablespoon of the batter for a medium-sized fritter or half a tablespoon of batter for a smaller-sized fritter, spoon the mixture into the hot oil and cook, in batches, for 3–4 minutes on each side.

6 Remove the fritters with a perforated spoon and drain thoroughly on absorbent kitchen paper.

Keep each batch of fritters warm in the oven while making the rest. Serve hot.

VARIATION

Try adding ½ teaspoon of dried, crushed chillies in step 4 for spicier tasting fritters.

Cured Meats with Olives & Tomatoes

Serves 4

INGREDIENTS

4 plum tomatoes

1 tbsp balsamic vinegar

6 canned anchovy fillets, drained
    and rinsed

2 tbsp capers, drained and rinsed

125 g/4$^1/_2$ oz green olives, pitted

175 g/6 oz mixed, cured meats,
    sliced

8 fresh basil leaves

1 tbsp extra virgin olive oil

salt and pepper

crusty bread, to serve

---

1 Using a sharp knife, cut the tomatoes into evenly-sized slices. Sprinkle the tomato slices with the balsamic vinegar and a little salt and pepper to taste and set aside.

2 Chop the anchovy fillets into pieces measuring about the same length as the olives.

3 Push a piece of anchovy and a caper into each olive.

4 Arrange the sliced . meat on 4 individual serving plates together with the tomatoes, filled olives and basil leaves.

5 Lightly drizzle the olive oil over the sliced meat, tomatoes and olives.

6 Serve the cured meats, olives and tomatoes with lots of fresh crusty bread.

COOK'S TIP

Fill a screw-top jar with the stuffed olives, cover with olive oil and use when required – they will keep for 1 month in the refrigerator.

COOK'S TIP

The cured meats for this recipe are up to your individual taste.
They can include a selection of Parma ham (prosciutto), pancetta, bresaola (dried salt beef) and salame di Milano (pork and beef sausage).

Spinach & Ricotta Patties

Serves 4

INGREDIENTS

450 g/1 lb fresh spinach
250 g/9 oz ricotta cheese
1 egg, beaten
2 tsp fennel seeds, lightly crushed

50 g/1¾ oz pecorino or Parmesan
cheese, finely grated
25 g/1 oz plain (all-purpose) flour,
mixed with 1 tsp dried thyme

75 g/2¾ oz/5 tbsp butter
2 garlic cloves, crushed
salt and pepper

1 Wash the spinach and trim off any long stalks. Place in a pan, cover and cook for 4–5 minutes until wilted. This will probably have to be done in batches as the volume of spinach is quite large. Place in a colander and leave to drain and cool.

2 Mash the ricotta and beat in the egg and the fennel seeds. Season with plenty of salt and pepper, then stir in the pecorino or Parmesan cheese.

3 Squeeze as much excess water as possible from the spinach

and finely chop the leaves. Stir into the cheese mixture.

4 Taking about 1 tablespoon of the spinach and cheese mixture, shape it into a ball and flatten it slightly to form a patty. Gently roll in the seasoned flour. Continue this process until all of the mixture has been used up.

5 Half fill a large frying pan (skillet) with water and bring to the boil. Carefully add the patties and cook for 3–4 minutes or until they rise to the surface. Remove with a perforated spoon.

6 Melt the butter in a pan. Add the garlic and cook for 2–3 minutes. Pour the garlic butter over the patties, season with freshly ground black pepper and serve at once.

COOK'S TIP

Once it is washed, spinach holds enough water on the leaves to cook without adding any extra liquid. If you use frozen spinach instead of fresh, simply defrost it and squeeze out the excess water.

Sweet & Sour Baby Onions

Serves 4

INGREDIENTS

350 g/12 oz baby or pickling onions

2 tbsp olive oil

2 fresh bay leaves, torn into strips

thinly pared rind of 1 lemon

1 tbsp soft brown sugar

1 tbsp clear honey

4 tbsp red wine vinegar

1 Soak the onions in a bowl of boiling water – this will make them easier to peel. Using a sharp knife, peel and halve the onions.

2 Heat the oil in a large frying pan (skillet). Add the bay leaves and onions to the pan and cook for 5–6 minutes over a medium-high heat or until browned all over.

3 Cut the lemon rind into thin matchsticks. Add to the frying pan (skillet) with the sugar and honey. Cook for 2–3 minutes, stirring occasionally, until the onions are lightly caramelized.

4 Add the red wine vinegar to the frying pan (skillet), being careful because it will spit. Cook for about 5 minutes, stirring, or until the onions are tender and the liquid has all but disappeared.

5 Transfer the onions to a serving dish and serve at once.

COOK'S TIP

Adjust the piquancy of this dish by adding more sugar for a sweeter, more caramelized taste or extra red wine vinegar for a sharper, tarter flavour.

COOK'S TIP

To make the onions easier to peel, place them in a large saucepan, pour over boiling water and leave for 10 minutes. Drain the onions thoroughly, and when they are cold enough to handle, peel them.

Stewed Artichokes

Serves 4

INGREDIENTS

4 small globe artichokes
4 garlic cloves, peeled

2 bay leaves
finely grated rind and juice
    of 1 lemon

olive oil
2 tbsp fresh marjoram
lemon wedges, to serve

1 Using a sharp knife, carefully peel away the tough outer leaves surrounding the artichokes. Trim the stems to about 2.5 cm/1 inch.

2 Using a knife, cut each artichoke in half and scoop out the choke (heart).

3 Place the artichokes in a large heavy based pan. Pour over enough olive oil to half cover the artichokes in the pan.

4 Add the garlic cloves, bay leaves and half of the grated lemon rind.

5 Start to heat the artichokes gently, cover the pan and continue to cook over a low heat for about 40 minutes. The artichokes should be stewed in the oil, not fried.

6 Once the artichokes are tender, remove them with a perforated spoon and drain thoroughly. Remove the bay leaves.

7 Transfer the artichokes to warm serving plates. Serve the artichokes sprinkled with the remaining grated lemon rind, fresh marjoram and a little lemon juice.

COOK'S TIP

To prevent the artichokes from oxidizing and turning brown before cooking, brush them with a little lemon juice. In addition, use the oil used for cooking the artichokes for salad dressings – it will impart a lovely lemon and herb flavour.

Chick Peas with Parma Ham (Prosciutto)

Serves 4

INGREDIENTS

1 tbsp olive oil
1 medium onion, thinly sliced
1 garlic clove, chopped

1 small red (bell) pepper, deseeded
and cut into thin strips
200 g/7 oz Parma ham
(prosciutto), cut into chunks

1 x 400g/14 oz can chick peas,
drained and rinsed
1 tbsp chopped parsley, to garnish
crusty bread, to serve

1 Heat the oil in a large frying pan (skillet). Add the sliced onion, chopped garlic and sliced (bell) pepper and cook for 3–4 minutes or until the vegetables have softened.

2 Add the Parma ham (prosciutto) to the frying pan (skillet) and fry for 5 minutes or until the ham (prosciutto) is just beginning to brown.

3 Add the chick peas to the frying pan (skillet) and cook, stirring, for 2–3 minutes until warmed through.

4 Sprinkle with chopped parsley and transfer to warm serving plates. Serve with lots of fresh crusty bread.

COOK'S TIP

Whenever possible, use fresh herbs when cooking. They are becoming more readily available, especially since the introduction of 'growing' herbs, small pots of herbs which you can buy from the supermarket or greengrocer. This ensures the herbs are fresh and also provides a continuous supply.

VARIATION

Try adding a small finely diced chilli in step 1 for a spicier taste, if you prefer.

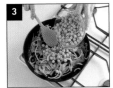

Deep-Fried Seafood

Serves 4

INGREDIENTS

200 g/7 oz prepared squid	deep-frying	TO SERVE:
200 g/7 oz blue (raw) tiger	50 g/1½ oz plain (all-purpose) flour	garlic mayonnaise (see Cook's Tip)
prawns (shrimp), peeled	1 tsp dried basil	lemon wedges
150 g/5½ oz whitebaitoil, for	salt and pepper	

1 Carefully rinse the squid, prawns (shrimp) and whitebait under cold running water, completely removing any dirt or grit.

2 Using a sharp knife, slice the squid into rings, leaving the tentacles whole.

3 Heat the oil in a large saucepan to 180°–190°C/350°–375°F or until a cube of bread browns in 30 seconds.

4 Place the flour in a bowl and season with the salt, pepper and basil.

5 Roll the squid, prawns (shrimp) and whitebait in the seasoned flour until coated all over. Carefully shake off any excess flour.

6 Cook the seafood in the heated oil in batches for 2–3 minutes or until crispy and golden all over. Remove all of the seafood with a perforated spoon and leave to drain thoroughly on kitchen paper.

7 Transfer the deep-fried seafood to serving plates and serve with garlic mayonnaise (see Cook's Tip) and lemon wedges.

COOK'S TIP

To make garlic mayonnaise for serving with the deep-fried seafood, crush 2 garlic cloves, stir into 8 tablespoons of mayonnaise and season with salt and pepper and a little chopped parsley.

Tuscan Bean Salad with Tuna

Serves 4

INGREDIENTS

1 small white onion or 2 spring
  onions (scallions),
  finely chopped
2 x 400g/14 oz cans butter
  beans, drained

2 medium tomatoes
1 x 185 g/6¹/₂ oz can tuna, drained
2 tbsp flat leaf parsley, chopped
2 tbsp olive oil

1 tbsp lemon juice
2 tsp clear honey
1 garlic clove, crushed

1 Place the chopped onions or spring onions (scallions) and butter beans in a bowl and mix well to combine.

2 Using a sharp knife, cut the tomatoes into wedges. Add the tomatoes to the onion and bean mixture.

3 Flake the tuna with a fork and add it to the onion and bean mixture together with the parsley.

4 In a screw-top jar, mix together the olive oil, lemon juice, honey and garlic. Shake the jar until the dressing emulsifies and thickens.

5 Pour the dressing over the bean salad. Toss the ingredients together using 2 spoons and serve.

COOK'S TIP

This salad will keep for several days in a covered container in the refrigerator. Make up the dressing just before serving and toss the ingredients together to mix well.

VARIATION

Substitute fresh salmon for the tuna if you wish to create a luxurious version of this recipe for a special occasion.

Italian Potato Salad

Serves 4

INGREDIENTS

450g/1 lb baby potatoes, unpeeled,
or larger potatoes, halved
4 tbsp natural yogurt

4 tbsp mayonnaise
8 sun-dried tomatoes

2 tbsp flat leaf parsley, chopped
salt and pepper

1 Rinse and clean the potatoes and place them in a large pan of water. Bring to the boil and cook for 8–12 minutes or until just tender. (The cooking time will vary according to the size of your potatoes.)

2 Using a sharp knife, cut the sun-dried tomatoes into thin slices.

3 To make the dressing, mix together the yogurt and mayonnaise in a bowl and season to taste with a little salt and pepper. Stir in the sun-dried tomato slices and the chopped flat leaf parsley.

4 Remove the potatoes with a perforated spoon, drain them thoroughly and then set them aside to cool. If you are using larger potatoes, cut them into 5 cm/2 inch chunks.

5 Pour the dressing over the potatoes and toss to mix.

6 Leave the potato salad to chill in the refrigerator for about 20 minutes, then serve as a starter or as an accompaniment.

COOK'S TIP

It is easier to cut the larger potatoes once they are cooked. Although smaller pieces of potato will cook more quickly, they tend to disintegrate and become mushy.

Green Salad

Serves 4

INGREDIENTS
---

25 g/1 oz pistachio nuts	rustic bread	(arugula)
5 tbsp extra virgin olive oil	1 tbsp red wine vinegar	25 g/1 oz red chard
1 tbsp rosemary, chopped	1 tsp wholegrain mustard	50 g/1¾ oz green olives, pitted
2 garlic cloves, chopped4 slices	1 tsp sugar25 g/1 oz rocket	2 tbsp fresh basil, shredded

1 Shell the pistachios and roughly chop them, using a sharp knife.

2 Place 2 tablespoons of the extra virgin olive oil in a frying pan (skillet). Add the rosemary and garlic and cook for 2 minutes.

3 Add the slices of bread to the pan and fry for 2–3 minutes on both sides until golden. Remove the bread from the pan and leave to drain on absorbent kitchen paper.

4 To make the dressing, mix together the remaining olive oil with the red wine vinegar, mustard and sugar.

5 Place a slice of bread on to a serving plate and top with the rocket (arugula) and red chard. Sprinkle with the olives.

6 Drizzle the dressing over the top of the salad leaves. Sprinkle with the chopped pistachios and shredded basil leaves and serve the salad immediately.

COOK'S TIP

If you cannot find red chard, try slicing a tomato into very thin wedges to add a splash of vibrant red colour to the salad.

VARIATION

Watercress may be used instead of the rocket (arugula), if preferred.

Minted Fennel Salad

Serves 4

INGREDIENTS

1 bulb fennel	1 small or $\frac{1}{2}$ a large cucumber	1 tbsp virgin olive oil
2 small oranges	1 tbsp chopped mint	2 eggs, hard boiled (cooked)

1 Using a sharp knife, trim the outer leaves from the fennel. Slice the fennel bulb thinly into a bowl of water and sprinkle with lemon juice (see Cook's Tip).

2 Grate the rind of the oranges over a bowl. Using a sharp knife, pare away the orange peel, then segment the orange by carefully slicing between each line of pith. Do this over the bowl in order to retain the juice.

3 Using a sharp knife, cut the cucumber into 12 mm/$\frac{1}{2}$ inch rounds and then cut each round into quarters.

Add the cucumber to the fennel and orange mixture together with the mint.

4 Pour the olive oil over the fennel and cucumber salad and toss well.

5 Peel and quarter the eggs and use these to decorate the top of the salad. Serve at once.

COOK'S TIP

Virgin olive oil, which has a fine aroma and flavour, is made by the cold pressing of olives. However, it may have a slightly higher acidity level than extra virgin oil.

COOK'S TIP

Fennel will discolour if it is left for any length of time without a dressing. To prevent any discoloration, place it in a bowl of water and sprinkle with lemon juice.

Capri Salad

Serves 4

INGREDIENTS

2 beef tomatoes	8 basil leaves	salt and pepper
125 g/4¹/₂ oz Mozzarella cheese	1 tbsp balsamic vinegar	basil leaves, to garnish
12 black olives	1 tbsp olive oil	

1 Using a sharp knife, cut the tomatoes into thin slices.

2 Using a sharp knife, cut the Mozzarella into slices.

3 Pit the olives and slice them into rings.

4 Layer the tomato, Mozzarella cheese and olives in a stack, finishing with a layer of cheese on top.

5 Place each stack under a preheated hot grill (broiler) for 2–3 minutes or just long enough to melt the Mozzarella.

6 Drizzle over the vinegar and olive oil, and season to taste with salt and pepper.

7 Transfer to serving plates and garnish with basil leaves. Serve immediately.

COOK'S TIP

Balsamic vinegar, which has grown in popularity over the past decade, is produced in the Emilia-Romagna region of Italy. It is made from wine which is distilled until it is dark brown and extremely strongly flavoured.

COOK'S TIP

Buffalo mozzarella cheese, although it is usually more expensive because of the comparative rarity of buffalo, does have a better flavour than the cow's milk variety. It is popular in salads, but also provides a tangy layer in baked dishes.

Mushroom Salad

Serves 4

INGREDIENTS

150 g/5½ oz firm white
mushrooms
4 tbsp virgin olive oil

1 tbsp lemon juice
5 anchovy fillets, drained and
chopped

1 tbsp fresh marjoram
salt and pepper

1 Gently wipe each mushroom with a damp cloth to remove any excess dirt. Slice the mushrooms thinly, using a sharp knife.

2 Mix together the olive oil and lemon juice and pour the mixture over the mushrooms. Toss together so that the mushrooms are completely coated with the lemon juice and oil.

3 Stir the chopped anchovy fillets into the mushrooms. Season the mushroom mixture with black pepper and garnish with the fresh marjoram.

4 Leave the mushroom salad to stand for 5 minutes before serving in order for all the flavours to be absorbed. Season with a little salt (see Cook's Tip, below) and then serve.

COOK'S TIP

Do not season the mushroom salad with salt until the very last minute as it will cause the mushrooms to blacken and the juices to leak. The result will not be as tasty as it should be as the full flavours won't be absorbed and it will also look very unattractive.

COOK'S TIP

If you use dried herbs rather than fresh, remember that you need only about one third of dried to fresh.

Yellow (Bell) Pepper Salad

Serves 4

| INGREDIENTS |

4 rashers streaky bacon, chopped

2 yellow (bell) peppers

8 radishes, washed and trimmed

1 stick celery, finely chopped

3 plum tomatoes, cut into
wedges

3 tbsp olive oil

1 tbsp fresh thyme

1 Dry fry the chopped bacon in a frying pan (skillet) for 4–5 minutes or until crispy. Remove the bacon from the frying pan (skillet), set aside and leave to cool until required.

2 Using a sharp knife, halve and deseed the (bell) peppers. Slice the (bell) peppers into long strips.

3 Using a sharp knife, halve the radishes and cut them into wedges.

4 Mix together the (bell) peppers, radishes, celery and tomatoes and toss the mixture in the olive oil and fresh thyme. Season to taste with a little salt and pepper.

5 Transfer the salad to serving plates and garnish with the reserved crispy bacon.

COOK'S TIP

Tomatoes are actually berries and are related to potatoes. There are many different shapes and sizes of this versatile fruit. The one most used in Italian cooking is the plum tomato which is very flavoursome.

COOK'S TIP

Pre-packaged diced bacon can be purchased from most supermarkets, which helps to save on preparation time.

Spinach Salad

Serves 4

INGREDIENTS

100 g/3¹/₂ oz baby spinach, washed
75 g/2³/₄ oz radicchio leaves, shredded
50 g/1³/₄ oz mushrooms

100 g/3¹/₂ oz cooked chicken, preferably breast
50 g/1³/₄ oz Parma ham (prosciutto)

2 tbsp olive oil
finely grated rind of ¹/₂ orange and juice of 1 orange
1 tbsp natural yogurt

1 Wipe the mushrooms with a damp cloth to remove any excess dirt.

2 Gently mix together the spinach and radicchio in a large salad bowl.

3 Thinly slice the wiped mushrooms and add them to the bowl containing the spinach and radicchio.

4 Tear the cooked chicken breast and Parma ham (prosciutto) into strips and mix them into the salad.

5 To make the dressing, place the olive oil,

orange rind, juice and yogurt into a screw-top jar. Shake the jar until the mixture is well combined. Season to taste with salt and pepper.

6 Drizzle the dressing over the spinach salad and toss to mix well. Serve immediately.

COOK'S TIP

Radiccio is a variety of chicory (endive) originating in Italy. It has a slightly bitter flavour.

VARIATION

Spinach is delicious when served raw. Try raw spinach in a salad garnished with bacon or garlicky croutons. The young leaves have a wonderfully sharp flavour.

Sweet & Sour Aubergine (Eggplant) Salad

Serves 4

INGREDIENTS

6 tbsp olive oil
1 onion, chopped
2 garlic cloves, chopped
2 sticks celery, chopped
450 g/1 lb aubergines (eggplant)

1 x 400 g/14 oz can tomatoes, chopped
50 g/1³/₄ oz green olives, stoned and chopped
25 g/1 oz granulated sugar

100 ml/3¹/₂ fl oz/2¹/₃ cup red wine vinegar
25 g/1 oz capers, drained
salt and pepper
1 tbsp flat leaf parsley, roughly chopped, to garnish

1 Heat 2 tablespoons of the oil in a large frying pan (skillet). Add the prepared onions, garlic and celery to the frying pan (skillet) and cook, stirring, for 3–4 minutes.

2 Using a sharp knife, slice the aubergines (eggplants) into thick rounds, then cut each round into 4 pieces.

3 Add the aubergine (eggplant) pieces to the frying pan (skillet) with the remaining olive oil and fry for 5 minutes or until golden.

4 Add the tomatoes, olives and sugar to the pan, stirring until the sugar has dissolved.

5 Add the red wine vinegar, reduce the heat and leave to simmer for 10–15 minutes or until the sauce is thick and the aubergines (eggplants) are tender.

6 While the pan is still on the heat, stir in the capers. Season to taste with salt and pepper.

7 Transfer to serving plates and garnish with the chopped fresh parsley.

COOK'S TIP

This salad is best served cold the day after it is made, which allows the flavours to mingle and be fully absorbed.

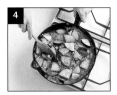

Lentil & Tuna Salad

Serves 4

INGREDIENTS

3 tbsp virgin olive oil
1 tbsp lemon juice
1 tsp wholegrain mustard
1 garlic clove, crushed

$\frac{1}{2}$ tsp cumin powder
$\frac{1}{2}$ tsp ground coriander
1 small red onion
2 ripe tomatoes
1 x 400 g/14 oz can lentils, drained

1 x 185 g/6$\frac{1}{2}$ cans tuna, drained
2 tbsp fresh coriander (cilantro), chopped
pepper

1 Using a sharp knife, deseed the tomatoes and chop them into fine dice.

2 Using a sharp knife, finely chop the red onion.

3 To make the dressing, whisk together the virgin olive oil, lemon juice, mustard, garlic, cumin powder and ground coriander in a small bowl. Set aside until required.

4 Mix together the chopped onion, diced tomatoes and drained lentils in a large bowl.

5 Flake the tuna and stir it into the onion, tomato and lentil mixture.

6 Stir in the chopped fresh coriander (cilantro).

7 Pour the dressing over the lentil and tuna salad and season with freshly ground black pepper. Serve at once.

VARIATION

Nuts would add extra flavour and texture to this salad.

COOK'S TIP

Lentils are a good source of protein and contain important vitamins and minerals. Buy them dried for soaking and cooking yourself, or buy canned varieties for speed and convenience.

Bruschetta with Tomatoes

Serves 4

INGREDIENTS

300 g/10½ oz cherry tomatoes
4 sun-dried tomatoes
4 tbsp extra virgin olive oil

16 fresh basil leaves, shredded
8 slices ciabatta
2 garlic cloves, peeled

salt and pepper

1 Using a sharp knife, cut the cherry tomatoes in half.

2 Using a sharp knife, slice the sun-dried tomatoes into strips.

3 Place the cherry tomatoes and sun-dried tomatoes in a bowl. Add the olive oil and the shredded basil leaves and toss to mix well. Season to taste with a little salt and pepper.

4 Using a sharp knife, cut the garlic cloves in half. Lightly toast the ciabatta bread.

5 Rub the garlic, cut-side down, over both sides of the toasted ciabatta bread.

6 Top the ciabatta bread with the tomato mixture and serve immediately.

COOK'S TIP

Ciabatta is an Italian rustic bread which is slightly holey and quite chewy. It is very good in this recipe as it absorbs the full flavour of the garlic and extra virgin olive oil.

VARIATION

Plum tomatoes are also good in this recipe. Halve them, then cut them into wedges. Mix them with the sun-dried tomatoes in step 3.

Italian Omelette

Serves 4

| INGREDIENTS |

900 g/2 lb potatoes	cut into strips	2 tbsp milk
1 tbsp oil	1 x 400g/14 oz can artichoke	50 g/1³/₄ oz Parmesan cheese,
1 large onions, sliced	hearts, drained and halved	grated
2 garlic cloves, chopped	250 g/9 oz ricotta cheese	3 tbsp chopped thyme
6 sun-dried tomatoes,	4 large eggs, beaten	

1 Peel the potatoes and place them in a bowl of cold water (see Cook's Tip). Cut the potatoes into thin slices.

2 Bring a large pan of water to the boil and add the potato slices. Leave the potatoes to simmer for 5–6 minutes or until just tender.

3 Heat the oil in a large frying pan (skillet). Add the onions and garlic to the pan and cook, stirring occasionally, for about 3–4 minutes.

4 Add the sun-dried tomatoes and continue cooking for a further 2 minutes.

5 Place a layer of potatoes at the bottom of a deep, ovenproof dish. Top with a layer of the onion mixture, artichokes and ricotta cheese. Repeat the layers in the same order, finishing with a layer of potatoes on top.

6 Beat the eggs, milk, half of the Parmesan, thyme and salt and pepper to taste together and pour over the potatoes.

7 Top with the remaining Parmesan cheese and bake in a preheated oven, at 190°C/375°F/Gas Mark 5, for 20–25 minutes or until golden brown. Cut into slices and serve.

COOK'S TIP

Placing the potatoes in a bowl of cold water will prevent them from turning brown while you cut the rest into slices.

Casserole of Beans in Tomato Sauce

Serves 4

INGREDIENTS

1 x 400g/14 oz can cannellini beans	1 stick celery	450 g/1 lb tomatoes
1 x 400g/14 oz can borlotti beans	2 garlic cloves, chopped	75 g/2¹⁄₄ oz rocket (arugula)
2 tbsp olive oil	175 g/6 oz baby onions, halved	

1 Drain both cans of beans and reserve 6 tbsp of the liquid.

2 Heat the oil in a large pan. Add the celery, garlic and onions and sauté for 5 minutes or until the onions are golden.

3 Cut a cross in the base of each tomato and plunge them into a bowl of boiling water for 30 seconds until the skins split. Remove them with a perforated spoon and leave until cool enough to handle. Peel off the skin and chop the flesh. Add the tomato flesh and the reserved bean liquid to the pan and cook for 5 minutes.

4 Add the beans to the pan and cook for a further 3–4 minutes or until the beans are hot.

5 Stir in the rocket (arugula) and allow to wilt slightly before serving.

VARIATION

For a spicier tasting dish, add 1–2 teaspoons of hot pepper sauce with the beans in step 4.

COOK'S TIP

Another way to peel tomatoes is once you have cut a cross in the base, push it on to a fork and hold it over a gas flame, turning it slowly so that the skin heats evenly all over. The skin will start to bubble and split, and should then slide off easily.

Small Pancakes with Smoked Fish

Makes 12 Pancakes

INGREDIENTS

PANCAKES:
100 g/3½ oz flour
½ tsp salt
1 egg, beaten
300 ml/½ pint/1¼ cups milk
1 tbsp oil, for frying

SAUCE:
450 g/1lb smoked haddock, skinned
300 ml/½ pint/1¼ cups milk
40 g/1½ oz/3 tbsp butter or
  margarine
40 g/1½ oz flour
300 ml/½ pint/1¼ cups fish stock

75 g/2¾ oz Parmesan cheese, grated
100 g/3½ oz peas, frozen and
  defrosted
100 g/3½ oz prawns (shrimp),
  cooked and peeled
50 g/1¾ oz Gruyère cheese, grated
salt and pepper

1 To make the pancake batter, sift the flour and salt into a large bowl and make a well in the centre. Add the egg and, using a wooden spoon, begin to draw in the flour. Slowly add the milk and beat to form a smooth batter. Set aside until required.

2 Place the fish in a large frying pan (skillet), add the milk and bring to the boil. Simmer for 10 minutes or until the fish begins to flake. Drain, reserving the milk.

3 Melt the butter in a saucepan. Add the flour, mix to a paste and cook for 2–3 minutes. Remove the pan from the heat and add the reserved milk a little at a time, stirring to make a smooth sauce. Repeat with the fish stock. Return to the heat and bring to the boil, stirring. Stir in the Parmesan and season with salt and pepper.

4 Grease a frying pan (skillet) with oil. Add 2 tablespoons of the pancake batter, swirling it round and

cook for 2–3 minutes. Loosen the sides with a palette knife (spatula) and flip over the pancake. Cook for 2–3 minutes until golden; repeat. Stack the pancakes with sheets of baking parchment between them and keep warm in the oven.

5 Stir the flaked fish, peas and prawns (shrimp) into half of the sauce and use to fill each pancake. Pour over the remaining sauce, top with the Gruyère and bake for 20 minutes until golden.

Roasted Seafood

Serves 4

INGREDIENTS

600 g/1lb 5 oz new potatoes
3 red onions, cut into wedges
2 courgettes (zucchini), sliced
  into chunks

8 garlic cloves, peeled
2 lemons, cut into wedges
4 sprigs rosemary
4 tbsp olive oil

350 g/12 oz shell-on prawns
  (shrimp), preferably uncooked
2 small squid, chopped into rings
4 tomatoes, quartered

1 Scrub the potatoes to remove any excess dirt. Cut any large potatoes in half. Place the potatoes in a large roasting tin (pan), together with the onions, courgettes (zucchini), garlic, lemon and rosemary.

2 Pour over the oil and toss to coat all of the vegetables in the oil.

3 Cook in a preheated oven, at 200°C/400°F/Gas Mark 6, for about 40 minutes, turning occasionally, until the potatoes are tender.

4 Once the potatoes are tender, add the prawns (shrimp), squid and tomatoes, tossing to coat them in the oil, and roast for 10 minutes. All of the vegetables should be cooked through and slightly charred for full flavour.

5 Transfer to serving plates and serve hot.

COOK'S TIP

Squid and octopus are great favourites in Italy and all around the Mediterranean.

VARIATION

Most vegetables are suitable for roasting in the oven. Try adding 450 g/1 lb pumpkin, squash or aubergine (eggplant), if you prefer.

Omelette Strips in Tomato Sauce

Serves 4

INGREDIENTS

25 g/1 oz/2 tbsp butter
1 onion, finely chopped
2 garlic cloves, chopped
4 eggs, beaten
150 ml/5 fl oz/²/₃ cup milk

75 g/2³/₄ oz Gruyère cheese, diced
1 x 400g/14 oz can tomatoes, chopped
1 tbsp rosemary, stalks removed
150 ml/5 fl oz/²/₃ cup vegetable stock

freshly grated Parmesan cheese, for sprinkling
crusty bread, to serve

1 Melt the butter in a large frying pan (skillet). Add the onion and garlic and cook for 4–5 minutes, until softened.

2 Beat together the eggs and milk and add the mixture to the frying pan (skillet).

3 Using a spatula, gently raise the cooked edges of the omelette and tip any uncooked egg around the edge of the pan.

4 Scatter over the cheese. Cook for 5 minutes, turning once,

until golden on both sides. Remove from the pan and roll up.

5 Add the tomatoes, rosemary and vegetable stock to the frying pan (skillet), stirring, and bring to the boil.

6 Leave the tomato sauce to simmer for about 10 minutes until reduced and thickened.

7 Slice the omelette into strips and add to the tomato sauce in the frying pan (skillet). Cook for 3–4 minutes until piping hot.

8 Sprinkle the freshly grated Parmesan cheese over the omelette strips in tomato sauce and serve with fresh crusty bread.

VARIATION

Try adding 100 g/3¹/₂ oz diced pancetta or unsmoked bacon in step 1 and cooking the meat with the onions.

Mozzarella in Carriages

Serves 4

INGREDIENTS

8 slices bread, preferably slightly stale, crusts removed	8 canned anchovy fillets, drained and chopped	4 eggs, beaten
100 g/3¹/₂ oz Mozzarella cheese, sliced thickly	16 fresh basil leaves	150 ml/5 floz/²/₃ cup milk
	50 g/1³/₄ oz black olives, chopped	oil, for deep-frying
		salt and pepper

1 Cut each slice of bread into 2 triangles. Top 8 of the bread triangles with the Mozzarella slices and chopped anchovies.

2 Place the basil leaves and olives on top and season with salt and pepper to taste.

3 Lay the other 8 triangles of bread over the top and press down round the edges to seal.

4 Mix together the eggs and milk and pour over the sandwiches. Leave to soak for 5 minutes.

5 Heat the oil in a large saucepan to 180°–190°C/ 350°–375°F or until a cube of bread browns in 30 seconds.

6 Before cooking the sandwiches, squeeze the edges together again.

7 Carefully place the sandwiches in the oil and deep-fry for 2 minutes or until golden, turning once. Remove the sandwiches with a perforated spoon and drain on absorbent kitchen paper. Serve immediately while still hot.

COOK'S TIP

If you prefer, try adding a peeled prawn (shrimp) to each triangle. For smaller sandwiches, cut the bread into 4 triangles.

Baked Fennel

Serves 4

INGREDIENTS

2 fennel bulbs	6 sun-dried tomatoes, halved	2 tsp dried oregano
2 celery sticks cut into 7.5 cm/	200 g/7 oz passata (tomato	50 g/1¾ oz Parmesan cheese,
3 inch sticks	paste)	grated

1 Using a sharp knife, trim the fennel, discarding any tough outer leaves, and cut the bulb into quarters.

2 Bring a large pan of water to the boil, add the fennel and celery and cook for 8–10 minutes or until just tender. Remove with a perforated spoon and drain.

3 Place the fennel pieces, celery and sun-dried tomatoes in an ovenproof dish.

4 Mix the passata (tomato paste) and oregano and pour the mixture over the fennel.

5 Sprinkle with the Parmesan cheese and bake in a preheated oven at 190°C/375°F/ Gas Mark 5 for 20 minutes or until hot.

6 Serve as a starter with bread or as a vegetable side dish.

VARIATION

If you cannot find any fennel in the shops, leeks make a delicious alternative. Use about 750 g/1 lb 10 oz, chopped, making sure that they are washed thoroughly to remove all traces of soil.

VARIATION

Add 1 x 400 g/14 oz can butter beans, drained, in step 3 for a substantial vegetarian supper dish.

Garlic & Pine Nut Tarts

Serves 4

INGREDIENTS

4 slices wholemeal or granary bread
50 g/1¾ oz pine nuts
150 g/5½ oz/10 tbsp butter

5 garlic cloves, peeled and halved
2 tbsp fresh oregano, chopped,
plus extra for garnish

4 black olives, halved
oregano leaves, to garnish

---

1 Using a rolling pin, flatten the bread slightly. Using a pastry cutter, cut out 4 circles to fit your individual tart tins – they should measure about 10 cm/4 inches across. Reserve the offcuts of bread and leave them in the refrigerator for 10 minutes or until required.

2 Meanwhile, place the pine nuts on a baking tray (cookie sheet). Toast the pine nuts under a preheated grill (broiler) for 2–3 minutes or until golden.

3 Put the bread offcuts, pine nuts, butter, garlic and oregano into a food processor and blend for about 20 seconds. Alternatively, pound the ingredients by hand in a mortar and pestle. The mixture should have a rough texture.

4 Spoon the pine nut butter mixture into the lined tin and top with the olives. Bake in a preheated oven at 200°C/400°F/Gas Mark 6 for 10–15 minutes or until golden.

5 Transfer the tarts to serving plates and serve warm garnished with the fresh oregano leaves.

VARIATION

Puff pastry can be used instead of the bread for the tart cases. Use 200 g/7oz puff pastry to line 4 tart tins. Leave the puff pastry to chill in the refrigerator for 20 minutes. Line the tart tins with the pastry and foil and bake blind for 10 minutes. Remove the foil and bake for 3–4 minutes or until the pastry is just set. Leave to cool, then continue from step 2, adding 2 tablespoons of breadcrumbs to the mixture.

Potatoes with Olives & Anchovies

Serves 4

INGREDIENTS

450 g/1lb baby new potatoes, scrubbed	2 fennel bulbs, trimmed and sliced	8 canned anchovy fillets, drained and chopped
2 tbsp olive oil	2 sprigs rosemary, stalks removed	
	75 g/2³/₄ oz mixed olives	

1 Bring a large saucepan of water to the boil and cook the potatoes for 8–10 minutes or until tender. Remove the potatoes from the saucepan using a perforated spoon and set aside to cool slightly.

2 Once the potatoes are just cool enough to handle, cut them into wedges, using a sharp knife.

3 Pit the mixed olives and cut them in half, using a sharp knife.

4 Using a sharp knife, chop the anchovy fillets into smaller strips.

5 Heat the oil in a large frying pan (skillet). Add the potato wedges, sliced fennel and rosemary. Cook for 7–8 minutes or until the potatoes are golden.

6 Stir in the olives and anchovies and cook for 1 minute or until warmed through.

7 Transfer to serving plates and serve immediately.

COOK'S TIP

Fresh rosemary is a particular favourite with Italians, but you can experiment with your favourite herbs in this recipe, if you prefer.

Tuscan Chicken Livers on Toast

Serves 4

INGREDIENTS

2 tbsp olive oil
1 garlic clove, finely chopped
225 g/8 oz fresh or frozen
    chicken livers

4 fresh sage leaves, finely chopped
    or 1 tsp dried, crumbled sage
2 tbsp white wine
2 tbsp lemon juice

salt and pepper
4 slices ciabatta or other Italian
    bread
wedges of lemon, to garnish

1 Heat the olive oil in a frying pan (skillet) and cook the garlic for 1 minute.

2 Rinse and roughly chop the chicken livers, using a sharp knife.

3 Add the chicken liver to the frying pan (skillet) together with the white wine and lemon juice. Cook for 3–4 minutes or until the juices from the chicken liver run clear.

4 Stir in the sage and season to taste with salt and pepper.

5 Under a preheated grill (broiler), toast the bread for 2 minutes on both sides or until golden-brown.

6 Spoon the hot chicken livers on top of the toasted bread and serve garnished with a wedge of lemon.

COOK'S TIP

Overcooked liver is dry and tasteless. Cook the chopped liver for only 3–4 minutes – it should be soft and tender.

VARIATION

Another way to make crostini is to slice a crusty loaf or a French loaf into small rounds or squares. Heat the olive oil in a frying pan (skillet) and fry the slices of bread until golden brown and crisp on both sides. Remove the crostini from the pan with a perforated spoon and leave to drain on paper towels. Top with the chicken livers.

Onion & Mozzarella Tarts

Serves 4

INGREDIENTS

1 x 250 g/9 oz packet puff pastry, defrosted if frozen
2 medium red onions, cut into thin wedges

1 red (bell) pepper, halved and deseeded
8 cherry tomatoes, halved

100g/3³/₄ oz Mozzarella cheese, cut into chunks
8 sprigs thyme

1 Roll out the pastry to make 4 x 7.5 cm/3 inch squares. Using a sharp knife, trim the edges of the pastry, reserving the trimmings. Leave the pastry to chill in the refrigerator for 30 minutes.

2 Place the pastry squares on a baking tray (cookie sheet). Brush a little water along each edge of the pastry squares and use the reserved pastry trimmings to make a rim around each tart.

3 Cut the red onions into wedges and halve and deseed the (bell) peppers.

4 Place the onions and (bell) pepper in a roasting tin (pan). Cook under a preheated grill (broiler) for 15 minutes or until charred.

5 Place the roasted (bell) pepper halves in a polythene bag and leave to sweat for 10 minutes. Peel off the skin from the (bell) peppers and cut the flesh into strips.

6 Line the pastry squares with squares of foil. Bake in a preheated oven at 200°C/400°F/Gas Mark 10 minutes. Remove the foil squares and bake for a further 5 minutes.

7 Place the onions, (bell) pepper strips, tomatoes and cheese in each tart and sprinkle with the fresh thyme.

8 Bake in the oven for 15 minutes or until the pastry is golden. Serve hot.

Spaghetti alla Carbonara

Serves 4

INGREDIENTS

425 g/15 oz dried spaghetti
2 tbsp olive oil
1 large onion, thinly sliced
2 garlic cloves, chopped
175 g/6 oz rindless bacon, cut
   into thin strips

25 g/1 oz/2 tbsp butter
175 g/6 oz mushrooms,
   thinly sliced
300 ml/^{1}/$_2$ pint/1^1/$_4$ cups double
   (heavy) cream
3 eggs, beaten

100 g /3^1/$_2$ oz/1 cup freshly
   grated Parmesan cheese, plus
   extra to serve (optional)
salt and pepper
fresh sage sprigs, to garnish

1 Warm a large serving dish or bowl. Bring a large pan of lightly salted water to the boil. Add the spaghetti and 1 tbsp of the oil and cook until tender, but still firm to the bite. Drain, return to the pan and keep warm.

2 Heat the remaining oil in a frying pan (skillet) over a medium heat. Add the onion and fry until it is transparent. Add the garlic and bacon and fry until the bacon is crisp. Transfer to the warm dish.

3 Melt the butter in the frying pan (skillet). Add the mushrooms and fry, stirring occasionally, for 3-4 minutes. Return the bacon mixture to the pan. Cover and keep warm.

4 Mix together the cream, eggs and cheese in a large bowl and then season to taste with salt and pepper.

5 Working very quickly, tip the spaghetti into the bacon and mushroom mixture and pour over the eggs. Toss the spaghetti quickly into the egg and cream mixture, using 2 forks. garnish and serve with extra grated Parmesan cheese, if using.

COOK'S TIP

The key to success with this recipe is not to overcook the egg. That is why it is important to keep all the ingredients hot enough just to cook the egg and to work rapidly to avoid scrambling it.

Smoked Ham Linguini

Serves 4

INGREDIENTS

450 g/1 lb dried linguini
450 g/1 lb broccoli florets

150 ml/¼ pint/⅝ cup Italian
Cheese Sauce (see Cook's Tip,
below right)

225 g/8 oz Italian smoked ham
salt and pepper
Italian bread, to serve

1 Bring a large pan of lightly salted water to the boil. Add the linguini and broccoli florets and cook for 10 minutes, until the linguini is tender, but still firm to the bite.

2 Drain the linguini and broccoli thoroughly, set aside and keep warm.

3 Meanwhile, make the Italian Cheese Sauce (see Cook's Tip, right).

4 Using a sharp knife, cut the Italian smoked ham into thin strips. Toss the linguini, broccoli and ham into the Italian Cheese Sauce and gently warm through over a very low heat.

5 Transfer the pasta mixture to a warm serving dish. Sprinkle with black pepper and serve with Italian bread.

COOK'S TIP

There are many types of Italian bread which would be suitable to serve with this dish. Ciabatta is made with olive oil and is available plain and with different ingredients, such as olives or sun-dried tomatoes.

COOK'S TIP

For Italian Cheese Sauce, melt 2 tbsp butter in a pan. Stir in 25 g/1 oz/¼ cup plain (all purpose) flour and cook gently until the roux is crumbly in texture. Stir in 300 ml/½ pint/1¼ cups hot milk and cook for 15 minutes. Add a pinch of nutmeg, a pinch of dried thyme, 2 tbsp white wine vinegar. Season. Stir in 3 tbsp double (heavy) cream, 60 g/2 oz/½ cup grated Mozzarella, 60 g/2 oz/ ⅔ cup grated Parmesan, 1 tsp English mustard and 2 tbsp soured cream.

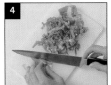

Chorizo & Wild Mushrooms with a Spicy Vermicelli

Serves 6

INGREDIENTS

680 g/1½ lb dried vermicelli	225 g/8 oz wild mushrooms	salt and pepper
125 ml/4 fl oz/½ cup olive oil	3 fresh red chillies, chopped	10 anchovy fillets, to garnish
2 garlic cloves	2 tbsp freshly grated	
125 g/4½ oz chorizo, sliced	Parmesan cheese	

1 Bring a large pan of lightly salted water to the boil. Add the vermicelli and 1 tbsp of the oil and cook until just tender, but still firm to the bite. Drain, place on a warm serving plate and keep warm.

2 Meanwhile heat the remaining oil in a large frying pan (skillet). Add the garlic and fry for 1 minute. Add the chorizo and wild mushrooms and cook for 4 minutes, then add the chopped chillies and cook for 1 further minute.

3 Pour the chorizo and wild mushroom mixture over the vermicelli and season. Sprinkle over the freshly grated Parmesan cheese, garnish with a lattice of anchovy fillets and serve immediately.

VARIATION

Fresh sardines may be used instead of the anchovies. However, ensure that you gut and clean the sardines, removing the backbone, before using them.

COOK'S TIP

Always obtain wild mushrooms from a reliable source: never pick them yourself unless you are sure of their identity. Many varieties of mushrooms are now cultivated and most are indistinguishable from the wild varieties. Mixed colour oyster mushrooms are used here, but you could also use chanterelles. However, chanterelles shrink during cooking, so you may need more.

Pancetta & Pecorino Cakes
on a Bed of Farfalle

Serves 4

INGREDIENTS

25 g/1 oz/2 tbsp butter, plus
extra for greasing
100 g/3¹/₂ oz pancetta, rind
removed
225 g/8 oz/2 cups self-raising
(self-rising) flour

75 g/4 oz/⁷/₈ cup grated
pecorino cheese
150 ml/¹/₄ pint/⁵/₈ cup milk, plus
extra for glazing
1 tbsp tomato ketchup
1 tsp Worcestershire sauce

400 g/14 oz/3¹/₂ cups dried
farfalle
1 tbsp olive oil
salt and black pepper
3 tbsp Pesto or anchovy sauce
(optional)
green salad, to serve

1 Grease a baking (cookie) sheet. Grill (broil) the pancetta until it is cooked, then allow it to cool and chop finely

2 Sift the flour and a pinch of salt into a bowl. Rub in the butter with your fingertips, then add the pancetta and one-third of the grated cheese.

3 Mix together the milk, tomato ketchup and Worcestershire sauce and add to the dry ingredients, mixing to make a soft dough.

4 Roll out the dough on a lightly floured board to make an 18 cm/7 inch round. Brush with milk to glaze and cut into 8 wedges.

5 Arrange the dough wedges on the prepared baking (cookie) sheet and sprinkle over the remaining cheese. Bake in a preheated oven at 200°C/400°F/Gas 6 for 20 minutes.

6 Bring a pan of lightly salted water to the boil. Add the farfalle and the oil and cook until just tender, but still firm to the bite. Drain and transfer to a serving dish. Top with the pancetta and pecorino cakes. Serve with the sauce of your choice and a salad.

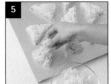

Orecchiette with Bacon & Tomatoes

Serves 4

INGREDIENTS

900 g/2 lb small, sweet tomatoes
6 slices rindless, smoked bacon
60 g/2 oz/4 tbsp butter
1 onion, chopped
1 garlic clove, crushed

4 fresh oregano sprigs,
   finely chopped
450 g/1 lb/4 cups dried
   orecchiette
1 tbsp olive oil

salt and pepper
freshly grated Pecorino cheese,
   to serve
fresh basil sprigs, to garnish

1 Blanch the tomatoes in boiling water. Drain, skin and seed the tomatoes, then roughly chop the flesh. Chop the bacon into small dice.

2 Melt the butter in a saucepan and fry the bacon until it is golden. Add the onion and garlic and fry for 5-7 minutes, until softened.

3 Add the tomatoes and oregano to the pan and season to taste. Lower the heat and simmer for 10-12 minutes.

4 Bring a pan of lightly salted water to the boil. Add the orecchiette and oil and cook for 12 minutes, until just tender, but still firm to the bite. Drain and transfer to a serving dish. Spoon over the bacon and tomato sauce and toss to coat. Garnish and serve.

VARIATION

You could also use 450 g/ 1 lb spicy Italian sausages. Squeeze the meat out of the skins and add to the pan in step 2 instead of the bacon.

COOK'S TIP

For an authentic Italian flavour use pancetta, rather than ordinary bacon. This kind of bacon is streaked with fat and adds rich undertones of flavour to many traditional dishes. It is available both smoked and unsmoked and can be bought in a single, large piece or cut into slices. You can buy it in some supermarkets and all Italian delicatessens.

Creamed Veal Kidneys with Penne & Pesto Sauce

Serves 4

INGREDIENTS

75 g/2³/₄ oz/5 tbsp butter
12 veal kidneys, trimmed and thinly sliced
175 g/6 oz button mushrooms, sliced
1 tsp English mustard

pinch of freshly grated root ginger
2 tbsp dry sherry
150 ml/¹/₄ pint/⁵/₈ cup double (heavy) cream
2 tbsp Pesto Sauce

400 g/14 oz dried penne
1 tbsp olive oil
salt and pepper
4 slices of hot toast cut into triangles
fresh parsley sprigs, to garnish

1 Melt the butter in a frying pan (skillet) and fry the kidneys for 4 minutes. Transfer the kidneys to an ovenproof dish and keep warm.

2 Add the mushrooms to the frying pan (skillet), and cook for 2 minutes.

3 Add the mustard and ginger to the pan and season to taste. Cook for 2 minutes, then add the sherry, cream and pesto sauce. Cook for a further 3 minutes, then pour the sauce over the kidneys. Bake in a preheated oven at 190°C/375°F/ Gas 5 for 10 minutes.

4 Bring a pan of lightly salted water to the boil. Add the penne and the oil and cook until just tender, but still firm to the bite. Drain and transfer to a warm serving dish.

5 Top the pasta with the kidneys in the pesto sauce. Place triangles of warm toast around the kidneys, garnish with fresh parsley and serve.

COOK'S TIP

Store the pesto sauce in an airtight container for up to a week in the refrigerator, or freeze (before adding the Parmesan) for 3 months.

Marinated Aubergine (Eggplant) on a Bed of Linguine

Serves 4

INGREDIENTS

150 ml/¼ pint/⅔ cup
    vegetable stock
150 ml/¼ pint/⅔ cup white
    wine vinegar
2 tsp balsamic vinegar
3 tbsp olive oil
fresh oregano sprig

450 g/1 lb aubergine (eggplant),
    peeled and thinly sliced
400 g/14 oz dried linguine

MARINADE:
2 tbsp extra virgin oil
2 garlic cloves, crushed
2 tbsp chopped fresh oregano

2 tbsp finely chopped
    roasted almonds
2 tbsp diced red (bell) pepper
2 tbsp lime juice
grated rind and juice of
    1 orange
salt and pepper

1 Put the vegetable stock, wine vinegar and balsamic vinegar into a saucepan and bring to the boil over a low heat. Add 2 tsp of the olive oil and the sprig of oregano and simmer gently for about 1 minute.

2 Add the aubergine slices to the pan, remove from the heat and set aside for 10 minutes.

3 Meanwhile, make the marinade. Combine the oil, garlic, fresh oregano, almonds, (bell) pepper, lime juice, orange rind and juice and seasoning in a large bowl.

4 Remove the aubergine (eggplant) from the saucepan with a slotted spoon, and drain well. Mix the aubergine (eggplant) slices into the marinade,

and set aside in the refrigerator for 12 hours.

5 Bring a pan of salted water to the boil. Add half the remaining oil and the linguine and cook until just tender. Drain the pasta and toss with the remaining oil. Arrange the pasta on a serving plate with the aubergine (eggplant) slices and the marinade and serve.

Spinach & Ricotta Shells

Serves 4

INGREDIENTS

400 g/14 oz dried lumache
   rigate grande
5 tbsp olive oil
60g/2 oz/1 cup fresh
   white breadcrumbs
125 ml/4 fl oz/^{1}/$_2$ cup milk

300 g/10^1/$_2$ oz frozen spinach,
   thawed and drained
225 g/8 oz/1 cup ricotta cheese
pinch of freshly grated nutmeg
400 g/14 oz can chopped
   tomatoes, drained

1 garlic clove, crushed
salt and pepper

1 Bring a large saucepan of lightly salted water to the boil. Add the lumache and 1 tbsp of the olive oil and cook until just tender, but still firm to the bite. Drain the pasta, refresh under cold water and set aside.

2 Put the breadcrumbs, milk and 3 tbsp of the remaining olive oil in a food processor and work to combine.

3 Add the spinach and ricotta cheese to the food processor and work to a smooth mixture. Transfer to a bowl, stir in the nutmeg, and season with salt and pepper to taste.

4 Mix together the tomatoes, garlic and remaining oil and spoon the mixture into the base of an ovenproof dish.

5 Using a teaspoon, fill the lumache with the spinach and ricotta mixture and arrange on top of the tomato mixture in the dish. Cover and bake in a preheated oven at 180°C/350°F/Gas 4 for 20 minutes. Serve hot.

COOK'S TIP

Ricotta is a creamy Italian cheese traditionally made from ewes' milk whey. It is soft and white, with a smooth texture and a slightly sweet flavour. It should be used within 2–3 days of purchase.

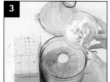

Rotelle with Spicy Italian Sauce

Serves 4

INGREDIENTS

200 ml/7 fl oz/$^7/_8$ cup Italian Red
   Wine Sauce (see Cook's Tip)

5 tbsp olive oil

3 garlic cloves, crushed

2 fresh red chillies, chopped

1 green chilli, chopped

400 g/14 oz/$3^1/_2$ cups dried
   rotelle

salt and pepper

warm Italian bread, to serve

---

1 Make the Italian Red
Wine Sauce (see
Cook's Tip, right).

2 Heat 4 tbsp of the oil
in a pan and fry the
garlic and chillies for
3 minutes.

3 Stir in the Italian Red
Wine Sauce, season to
taste and simmer gently for
20 minutes.

4 Bring a large saucepan
of lightly salted water
to the boil. Add the rotelle
and the remaining oil and
cook for 8 minutes, until
just tender. Drain the pasta.

5 Toss the rotelle in the
spicy sauce, transfer
to a warm serving dish
and serve immediately.

COOK'S TIP

*Take care when using fresh
chillies as they can burn
your skin. Handle them as
little as possible – wear
rubber gloves if necessary.
Always wash your hands
afterwards and don't touch
your face or eyes before you
have washed your hands.
Remove chilli seeds before
chopping the chillies, as they
are the hottest part.*

COOK'S TIP

*For Italian Red Wine
Sauce, first make a demi-
glace sauce: mix 150 ml/
$^1/_4$ pint/$^5/_8$ cup each Brown
Stock and Espagnole Sauce,
cook for 10 minutes and
strain. Mix 125 ml/4 fl
oz/$^1/_2$ cup red wine, 2 tbsp
red wine vinegar, 4 tbsp
chopped shallots, 1 bay leaf
and 1 thyme sprig in a pan.
Bring to the boil and reduce
by three-quarters. Add the
demi-glace sauce and
simmer for 20 minutes.
Season and strain.*

Tricolour Timballini

Serves 4

INGREDIENTS

15 g/¹⁄₂ oz/1 tbsp butter, softened
60 g/2 oz/1 cup dried white
    breadcrumbs
175 g/6 oz dried tricolour
    spaghetti, broken into
    5 cm/2 inch lengths
3 tbsp olive oil
1 egg yolk

125 g/4 oz/1 cup grated Gruyère
    (Swiss) cheese
300 ml/¹⁄₂ pint/1¹⁄₄ cups
    Béchamel Sauce
1 onion, finely chopped
1 bay leaf
150 ml/¹⁄₄ pint/⁶⁄₈ cup dry
    white wine

150 ml/¹⁄₄ pint/⁶⁄₈ cup passata
    (sieved tomatoes)
1 tbsp tomato purée (paste)
salt and pepper
fresh basil leaves, to garnish

1 Grease four 180 ml/
6 fl oz/³⁄₄cup ramekins
with the butter. Evenly coat
the insides with half the
breadcrumbs.

2 Bring a pan of lightly
salted water to the boil.
Add the spaghetti and
1 tbsp of the oil and cook
until just tender. Drain and
transfer to a mixing bowl.

3 Add the egg yolk and
cheese to the pasta and
season. Pour the Béchamel

sauce into the bowl and
mix. Spoon the mixture
into the ramekins and
sprinkle over the remaining
breadcrumbs.

4 Stand the ramekins on
a baking (cookie) sheet
and bake in a preheated
oven at 220°C/ 425°F/Gas 7
for 20 minutes. Set aside
for 10 minutes.

5 To make the sauce,
heat the remaining oil
in a pan and gently fry the

onion and bay leaf for
2-3 minutes.

6 Stir in the wine,
passata (sieved
tomatoes) and tomato
purée (paste). Season. and
simmer for 20 minutes,
until thickened. Discard
the bay leaf.

7 Turn the timballini
out on to individual
serving plates, garnish with
the basil leaves and serve
with the tomato sauce.

Tagliarini with Gorgonzola

Serves 4

INGREDIENTS

25 g/1 oz/2 tbsp butter

225 g/8 oz Gorgonzola cheese, roughly crumbled

150 ml/¼ pint/⅝ cup double (heavy) cream

30 ml/2 tbsp dry white wine

1 tsp cornflour (cornstarch)

4 fresh sage sprigs, finely chopped

400 g/14 oz dried tagliarini

2 tbsp olive oil

salt and white pepper

fresh herb sprigs, to garnish

1 Melt the butter in a heavy-based saucepan. Stir in 175 g/6 oz of the Gorgonzola and melt, over a low heat, for 2 minutes.

2 Add the cream, wine and cornflour (cornstarch) and beat with a whisk until fully incorporated.

3 Stir in the sage and season to taste. Bring to the boil over a low heat, whisking constantly, until the sauce thickens. Remove from the heat and set aside.

4 Bring a large saucepan of lightly salted water to the boil. Add the tagliarini and 1 tbsp of the olive oil. Cook the pasta for 12–14 minutes or until just tender, drain thoroughly and toss in the remaining olive oil. Transfer the pasta to a serving dish and keep warm.

5 Reheat the sauce over a low heat, whisking constantly. Spoon the Gorgonzola sauce over the tagliarini, sprinkle over the remaining cheese, garnish and serve.

COOK'S TIP

Gorgonzola is one of the world's oldest veined cheeses and, arguably, its finest. When buying, always check that it is creamy yellow with delicate green veining. Avoid hard or discoloured cheese. It should have a rich, piquant aroma, not a bitter smell. If you find Gorgonzola too strong or rich, you could substitute Danish blue.

Gnocchi Piemontese

Serves 4

INGREDIENTS

450 g/1 lb warm mashed potato
75 g/2³/₄ oz/⁵/₈ cup self-raising
     (self-rising) flour
1 egg

2 egg yolks
1 tbsp olive oil
150 ml/¹/₄ pint/⁵/₈ cup Espagnole
     sauce

SAUCE
60 g/2 oz/4 tbsp butter
175 g/6 oz/2 cups freshly grated
     Parmesan cheese
salt and pepper
fresh herbs, to garnish

1 Combine the mashed potato and flour in a bowl. Add the egg and egg yolks, season well and mix together to form a dough.

2 Break off pieces and roll between the palms of your hands to form small balls the size of a walnut. Flatten the balls with a fork into the shape of small cylinders.

3 Bring a pan of lightly salted water to the boil. Add the gnocchi and olive oil and poach for 10 minutes.

4 Mix the Espagnole sauce and the butter in a large saucepan over a gentle heat. Gradually blend in the grated Parmesan cheese.

5 Remove the gnocchi from the pan and toss in the sauce, transfer to individual serving plates, garnish and serve.

COOK'S TIP

This dish also makes an excellent main meal with a crisp salad.

VARIATION

These gnocchi would also taste delicious with a tomato sauce, in Trentino-style. Mix together 115 g/4 oz/ 1 cup finely chopped sun-dried tomatoes, 1 finely sliced celery stick (stalk), 1 crushed garlic clove and 6 tbsp red wine in a pan. Cook over a low heat for 15–20 minutes. Stir in 8 skinned, chopped, Italian plum tomatoes, season to taste with salt and pepper and simmer over a low heat for a further 10 minutes.

Pasta Omelette

Serves 2

INGREDIENTS

4 tbsp olive oil
1 small onion, chopped
1 fennel bulb, thinly sliced
125 g/4½ oz potato, diced
1 garlic clove, chopped

4 eggs
1 tbsp chopped fresh flat leaf
    parsley
pinch of chilli powder
100 g/3½ oz cooked short pasta

2 tbsp stuffed green olives,
    halved
salt and pepper
fresh marjoram sprigs, to garnish
tomato salad, to serve

1 Heat half the oil in a frying pan (skillet) and fry the onion, fennel and potato, stirring, for 8-10 minutes, until the potato is just tender.

2 Add the garlic and fry for 1 minute. Remove the pan from the heat and transfer the vegetables to a plate and set aside.

3 Beat the eggs until they are frothy. Stir in the parsley and season with salt, pepper and a pinch of chilli powder.

4 Heat 1 tbsp of the remaining oil in a clean frying pan (skillet). Add half of the egg mixture to the pan, then add the cooked vegetables, pasta and half of the olives. Pour in the remaining egg mixture and cook until the sides begin to set.

5 Lift up the edges of the omelette with a palette knife (spatula) to allow the uncooked egg to spread underneath. Cook until the underside is a light golden brown colour.

6 Slide the omelette out of the pan on to a plate. Wipe the pan with kitchen paper (kitchen towels) and heat the remaining oil. Invert the omelette into the pan and cook until the other side is golden brown.

7 Slide the omelette on to a warmed serving dish and garnish with the remaining olives and the fresh marjoram sprigs. Cut the omelette into wedges and serve with a tomato salad.

Spaghetti with Ricotta Cheese

Serves 4

INGREDIENTS

350 g/12 oz dried spaghetti
3 tbsp olive oil
40 g/1$^1/_2$ oz/3 tbsp butter
2 tbsp chopped fresh flat leaf
　parsley
125 g/4$^1/_2$ oz/1 cup freshly
　ground almonds

125 g/4$^1/_2$ oz/$^1/_2$ cup ricotta
　cheese
pinch of grated nutmeg
pinch of ground cinnamon
150 ml/$^1/_4$ pint/$^5/_8$ cup crème
　fraîche (unsweetened yogurt)
125 ml/4 fl oz hot chicken stock

1 tbsp pine nuts (kernels)
salt and pepper
fresh flat leaf parsley sprigs,
　to garnish

---

1 Bring a large pan of lightly salted water to the boil. Add the spaghetti and 1 tbsp of the oil and cook until tender, but still firm to the bite.

2 Drain the pasta, return to the pan and toss with the butter and chopped parsley. Set aside and keep warm.

3 To make the sauce, mix together the ground almonds, ricotta cheese, nutmeg, cinnamon and crème fraîche (unsweetened yogurt) over a low heat to form a thick paste. Stir in the remaining oil, then gradually stir in the hot chicken stock, until smooth. Season to taste.

4 Transfer the spaghetti to a warm serving dish, pour over the sauce and toss together well (see Cook's Tip, right). Sprinkle over the pine nuts (kernels), garnish with the flat leaf parsley sprigs and serve warm.

COOK'S TIP

Use two large forks to toss spaghetti or other long pasta, so that it is thoroughly coated with the sauce. Special spaghetti forks are available from some cookware departments and kitchen shops. Holding one fork in each hand, gently ease the prongs under the pasta on each side and lift them towards the centre. Continue until the pasta is completely coated.

Gnocchi Romana

Serves 4

INGREDIENTS

700 ml/1¼ pints/3⅛ cups milk	90 g/3 oz/6 tbsp butter, plus extra for greasing	2 eggs, beaten
pinch of freshly grated nutmeg	250 g/8 oz/1¼ cups semolina	60 g/2 oz/½ cup grated Gruyère (Swiss) cheese
	125 g/4½ oz/1½ cups grated Parmesan cheese	salt and pepper
		fresh basil sprigs, to garnish

1 Bring the milk to the boil in a saucepan. Remove from the heat and stir in the nutmeg, 25 g/ 1 oz/2 tbsp of the butter and salt and pepper to taste.

2 Stir the semolina into the milk, whisking to prevent lumps forming, and return the pan to a low heat. Simmer, stirring constantly, for about 10 minutes, until very thick.

3 Beat 60 g/2 oz/⅔ cup of Parmesan into the semolina mixture, then beat in the eggs. Continue beating until smooth. Set the mixture aside for a few minutes to cool slightly.

4 Spread out the semolina mixture in a smooth, even layer, about 1 cm/½ inch thick, on a sheet of baking parchment or in a large oiled baking tin (pan). Leave to cool completely, then chill in the refrigerator for 1 hour.

5 Once chilled, cut out rounds of gnocchi, measuring 4 cm/1½ inches in diameter, using a plain, greased pastry cutter.

6 Grease a shallow ovenproof dish and lay the gnocchi trimmings in the base of the dish. Cover with overlapping rounds of gnocchi.

7 Melt the remaining butter and drizzle over the gnocchi. Sprinkle over the remaining Parmesan, then sprinkle over the Gruyère (Swiss) cheese. Bake in a preheated oven at 200°C/400°F/Gas 6 for 25-30 minutes, until the top is crisp and golden brown. Garnish with the basil and serve.

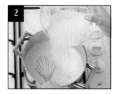
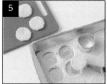

Three-Cheese Bake

Serves 4

INGREDIENTS

butter, for greasing	4 fresh basil sprigs	salt and black pepper
400 g/14 oz dried penne	100 g/3½ oz/1 cup grated	fresh basil leaves (optional), to
1 tbsp olive oil	mozzarella or halloumi	garnish
2 eggs, beaten	cheese	
350 g/12 oz/1½ cups ricotta	4 tbsp freshly grated	
cheese	Parmesan cheese	

1 Lightly grease an ovenproof dish.

2 Bring a large pan of lightly salted water to the boil. Add the penne and olive oil and cook until just tender, but still firm to the bite. Drain the pasta, set aside and keep warm.

3 Beat the eggs into the ricotta cheese and season to taste with salt and pepper.

4 Spoon half of the penne into the base of the dish and cover with half of the basil leaves.

5 Spoon over half of the ricotta cheese mixture. Sprinkle over the mozzarella or halloumi cheese and top with the remaining basil leaves. Cover with the remaining penne and then spoon over the remaining ricotta cheese mixture. Lightly sprinkle over the grated Parmesan cheese.

6 Bake in a preheated oven at 190°C/375°F/ Gas 5 for about 30–40 minutes, until golden brown and the cheese topping is hot and bubbling. Garnish with fresh basil leaves, if liked, and serve hot.

VARIATION

Try substituting smoked Bavarian cheese for the mozzarella or halloumi and grated Cheddar cheese for the Parmesan, for a slightly different but just as delicious flavour.

Baked Rigatoni Filled with Tuna & Ricotta Cheese

Serves 4

INGREDIENTS

butter, for greasing
450 g/1 lb dried rigatoni
1 tbsp olive oil
200 g /7 oz can flaked tuna,
    drained

225 g/ 8 oz ricotta cheese
125 ml/4 fl oz/¹/₂ cup double
    (heavy) cream
225 g/8 oz/2¹/₂ cups grated
    Parmesan cheese

125 g/4 oz sun-dried tomatoes,
    drained and sliced
salt and pepper

1 Lightly grease an ovenproof dish.

2 Bring a large saucepan of lightly salted water to the boil. Add the rigatoni and olive oil and cook until just tender, but still firm to the bite. Drain the pasta and set aside until cool enough to handle.

3 In a bowl, mix together the tuna and ricotta cheese to form a soft paste. Spoon the mixture into a piping bag and use to fill the rigatoni. Arrange the filled pasta tubes side by side in the prepared ovenproof dish.

4 To make the sauce, mix the cream and Parmesan cheese and season. Spoon the sauce over the rigatoni and top with the sun-dried tomatoes arranged in a criss-cross pattern. Bake in a preheated oven at 200°C/400°F/Gas 6 for 20 minutes. Serve hot straight from the dish.

VARIATION

For a vegetarian version of this recipe, simply substitute a mixture of stoned (pitted) and chopped black olives and chopped walnuts for the tuna. Follow exactly the same cooking method.

Spaghetti with Anchovy & Pesto Sauce

Serves 4

INGREDIENTS

90 ml/3 fl oz olive oil

2 garlic cloves, crushed

60 g/2 oz can anchovy fillets, drained

450 g/1 lb dried spaghetti

60 g/2 oz Pesto Sauce

2 tbsp finely chopped fresh oregano

90 g/3 oz/1 cup grated Parmesan cheese, plus extra for serving (optional)

salt and pepper

2 fresh oregano sprigs, to garnish

1 Heat 1 tbsp of the oil a in a small saucepan. Add the garlic and fry for 3 minutes.

2 Add the anchovies and cook, stirring, until the anchovies have disintegrated.

3 Bring a large saucepan of lightly salted water to the boil. Add the spaghetti and the remaining olive oil and cook until just tender, but still firm to the bite.

4 Add the Pesto Sauce and chopped fresh oregano to the anchovy mixture and then season with black pepper to taste.

5 Drain the spaghetti, using a slotted spoon, and transfer to a warm serving dish. Pour the Pesto Sauce over the spaghetti and then sprinkle over the grated Parmesan cheese. Garnish with oregano sprigs and serve with extra cheese, if using.

VARIATION

For a vegetarian version of this recipe, substitute drained sun-dried tomatoes for the anchovy fillets.

COOK'S TIP

If you find canned anchovies much too salty, soak them in a saucer of cold milk for 5 minutes, drain and pat dry with kitchen paper (kitchen towels) before using.

Fettuccine with Anchovy & Spinach Sauce

Serves 4

INGREDIENTS

900 g/2 lb fresh, young
spinach leaves
400 g/14 oz dried fettuccine

6 tbsp olive oil
3 tbsp pine nuts (kernels)
3 garlic cloves, crushed

8 canned anchovy fillets, drained
and chopped
salt

---

1 Trim off any tough spinach stalks. Rinse the spinach leaves and place them in a large saucepan with only the water that is clinging to them after washing. Cover and cook over a high heat, shaking the pan from time, until the spinach has wilted, but retains its colour. Drain well, set aside and keep warm.

2 Bring a large saucepan of lightly salted water to the boil. Add the fettuccine and 1 tbsp of the oil and cook for 2–3 minutes until it is just tender, but still firm to the bite.

3 Heat 4 tbsp of the remaining oil in a saucepan. Add the pine nuts (kernels) and fry until golden. Remove from the pan and set aside.

4 Add the garlic to the pan and fry until golden. Add the anchovies and stir in the spinach. Cook, stirring, for 2–3 minutes, until heated through. Return the pine nuts (kernels) to the pan.

5 Drain the fettuccine, toss in the remaining olive oil and transfer to a warm serving dish. Spoon the anchovy and spinach sauce over the fettuccine, toss lightly and serve immediately.

COOK'S TIP

If you are in a hurry, use frozen spinach. Thaw and drain it thoroughly, pressing out as much moisture as possible. Cut the leaves into strips and add to the dish with the anchovies in step 4.

Penne with Muscoli Fritti nell'Olio

Serves 4-6

INGREDIENTS

400/14 oz/3¹/₃ cups dried penne
125 ml/4 fl oz/¹/₂ cup olive oil
450 g/1 lb mussels, cooked
    and shelled
1 tsp sea salt

90 g/3 oz/³/₄ cup flour
100 g/3¹/₂ oz sun-dried
    tomatoes, sliced

2 tbsp chopped fresh basil leaves
salt and pepper
1 lemon, thinly sliced, to garnish

1 Bring a large pan of lightly salted water to the boil. Add the penne and 1 tbsp of the olive oil and cook until the pasta is just tender, but still firm to the bite.

2 Drain the pasta and place in a warm serving dish. Set aside and keep warm.

3 Sprinkle the mussels with the sea salt. Season the flour with salt and pepper, sprinkle into a bowl and toss the mussels in the flour until coated.

4 Heat the remaining oil in a frying pan (skillet) and fry the mussels until golden brown, stirring.

5 Toss the mussels with the penne and sprinkle with the sun-dried tomatoes and basil leaves. Garnish with lemon slices and serve immediately.

VARIATION

You could substitute clams for the mussels. If using fresh clams, try smaller varieties, such as Venus.

COOK'S TIP

Sun-dried tomatoes have been used in Mediterranean countries for a long time, but have become popular elsewhere only quite recently. They are dried and then preserved in oil. They have a concentrated, almost roasted flavour and a dense texture. They should be drained and chopped or sliced before using.

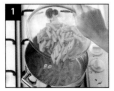

Chilli Polenta Chips

Serves 4

INGREDIENTS

350 g/12 oz instant polenta	1 tbsp olive oil	1 tbsp chopped parsley
2 tsp chilli powder	150 ml/5 fl oz/²/₃ cup soured cream	salt and pepper

1 Place 1.5 litres/2¾ pints/6¼ cups of water in a saucepan and bring to the boil. Add 2 teaspoons of salt and then add the polenta in a steady stream, stirring constantly.

2 Reduce the heat slightly and continue stirring for about 5 minutes. It is essential to stir the polenta, otherwise it will stick and burn. The polenta should have a thick consistency at this point and should be stiff enough to hold the spoon upright in the pan.

3 Add the chilli powder to the polenta mixture and stir well.

Season to taste with a little salt and pepper.

4 Spread the polenta out on to a board or baking tray (cookie sheet) to about 4 cm/1½ inch thick. Leave to cool and set.

5 Cut the cooled polenta mixture into thin wedges.

6 Heat 1 tablespoon of oil in a pan. Add the polenta wedges and fry for 3–4 minutes on each side until golden and crispy. Alternatively, brush with melted butter and grill for 6–7 minutes until golden. Drain the cooked polenta on paper towels.

7 Mix the soured cream with parsley and place in a bowl.

8 Serve the polenta with the soured cream and parsley dip.

COOK'S TIP

Easy-cook instant polenta is widely available in supermarkets and is quick to make. It will keep for up to 1 week in the refrigerator. The polenta can also be baked in a preheated oven, at 200°C/400°F/Gas Mark 6, for 20 minutes.

Polenta Kebabs (Kabobs)

Serves 4

INGREDIENTS

175 g/6 oz instant polenta
175 ml/1 pint/scant 3¹/₄ cups water
2 tbsp fresh thyme, stalks removed

8 slices Parma ham (prosciutto)
(about 75 g/2³/₄ oz)
1 tbsp olive oil

salt and pepper
fresh green salad, to serve

1 Cook the polenta, using 750 ml/1 pint 7 fl oz/3 ¹/₄ cups of water to 175 g/6 oz polenta, stirring occasionally. Alternatively, follow the instructions on the packet.

2 Add the fresh thyme to the polenta mixture and season to taste with salt and pepper.

3 Spread out the polenta, about 2.5 cm/1 inch thick, on to a board. Set aside to cool.

4 Using a sharp knife, cut the cooled polenta into 2.5 cm/1 inch cubes.

5 Cut the Parma ham (prosciutto) slices into 2 pieces lengthways. Wrap the Parma ham (prosciutto) around the polenta cubes.

6 Thread the Parma ham (prosciutto) wrapped polenta cubes on to skewers.

7 Brush the kebabs (kabobs) with a little oil and cook under a preheated grill (broiler), turning frequently, for 7–8 minutes. Alternatively, barbecue (grill) the kebabs (kabobs) until golden. Transfer to serving plates and serve with a green salad.

VARIATION

Try flavouring the polenta with chopped oregano, basil or marjoram instead of the thyme, if you prefer. You should use 3 tablespoons of chopped herbs to every 350 g/ 12 oz instant polenta.

Risotto-Stuffed (Bell) Peppers

Serves 4

INGREDIENTS

4 red or orange (bell) peppers
1 tbsp olive oil
1 large onion, finely chopped
350 g/12 oz arborio (risotto) rice,
 washed
about 15 strands saffron

150 ml/¼ pint white wine
850 ml/1½ pints hot vegetable or
 chicken stock
50 g/1¾ oz/3 tbsp butter
50 g/1¾ oz pecorino cheese,
 grated

50 g/1¾ oz Italian sausage,
 such as felino salame or
 other coarse Italian
 salame, chopped
200 g/7 oz Mozzarella cheese,
 sliced

1 Cut the (bell) peppers in half, retaining some of the stalk. Remove the seeds.

2 Place the (bell) peppers, cut side up, under a preheated grill (broiler) for 12–15 minutes until softened and charred.

3 Meanwhile, heat the oil in a large frying pan (skillet). Add the onion and cook for 3–4 minutes or until softened. Add the rice and saffron, stirring to coat in the oil, and cook for 1 minute.

4 Add the wine and stock slowly, a ladleful at a time, making sure that all of the liquid is absorbed before adding the next ladleful of liquid. When all of the liquid is absorbed, the rice should be cooked. Test by tasting a grain – if it is still crunchy add a little more water and continue cooking. It should take at least 15 minutes to cook.

5 Stir in the butter, pecorino cheese and the chopped Italian sausage.

6 Spoon the risotto into the (bell) peppers. Top

with a slice of Mozzarella and grill (broil) for 4–5 minutes or until the cheese is bubbling. Serve hot.

VARIATION

*Use tomatoes
instead of the (bell) peppers,
if you prefer. Halve 4 large
tomatoes and scoop out the
seeds. Follow steps 3–6 as
there is no need to
roast them.*

Potato Gnocchi with Tomato Sauce

Serves 4

INGREDIENTS

350 g/12 oz floury (mealy)
potatoes (those suitable for
baking or mashing), halved
75 g/2³/₄ oz self-raising flour, plus
extra for rolling out
2 tsp dried oregano

2 tbsp oil
1 large onion, chopped
2 garlic cloves, chopped
1 x 400g/14 oz can chopped
tomatoes
¹/₂ vegetable stock cube dissolved

in 100ml/3¹/₂ fl oz/¹/₂cup
boiling water
salt and pepper
2 tbsp basil, shredded, plus whole
leaves to garnish
Parmesan cheese, grated, to serve

1 Bring a large pan of water to the boil. Add the potatoes and cook for 12–15 minutes or until tender. Drain and leave to cool.

2 Peel and then mash the potatoes with the salt and pepper, sifted flour and oregano. Mix together with your hands to form a dough.

3 Heat the oil in a pan. Add the onions and garlic and cook for 3–4 minutes. Add the tomatoes and stock and cook,

uncovered, for 10 minutes. Season with salt and pepper to taste.

4 Roll the potato dough into a sausage about 2.5 cm/1 inch in diameter. Cut the sausage into 2.5 cm/1 inch lengths. Flour your hands, then press a fork into each piece to create a series of ridges on one side and the indent of your index finger on the other.

5 Bring a large pan of water to the boil and cook the gnocchi, in batches, for 2–3 minutes.

They should rise to the surface when cooked. Drain and keep warm.

6 Stir the basil into the tomato sauce and pour over the gnocchi. Garnish with basil leaves and freshly ground black pepper. Sprinkle with Parmesan and serve.

VARIATION

Try serving the gnocchi with Pesto Sauce for a change.

Baked Semolina Gnocchi

Serves 4

INGREDIENTS

425 ml/³/₄ pint/1³/₄ cups vegetable
stock
100 g/3¹/₂ oz semolina
1 tbsp thyme, stalks removed

1 egg, beaten
50 g/1³/₄ oz Parmesan cheese,
grated
50 g/1³/₄ oz/3 tbsp butter

2 garlic cloves, crushed
salt and pepper

1 Place the stock in a large saucepan and bring to the boil. Add the semolina in a steady trickle, stirring continuously. Keep stirring for 3–4 minutes until the mixture is thick enough to hold a spoon upright. Set aside and leave to cool slightly.

2 Add the thyme, egg and half of the cheese to the semolina mixture, and season to taste with salt and pepper.

3 Spread the semolina mixture on to a board to about 12 mm/¹/₂ inch thick. Set aside to cool and set.

4 When the semolina is cold, cut it into 2.5 cm/1 inch squares, reserving any offcuts.

5 Grease an ovenproof dish, placing the reserved offcuts in the bottom. Arrange the semolina squares on top and sprinkle with the remaining cheese.

6 Melt the butter in a pan, add the garlic and season with black pepper to taste. Pour the butter mixture over the gnocchi. Bake in a preheated oven at 220°C/425°F/Gas Mark 7 for 15–20 minutes until

puffed up and golden. Serve hot.

VARIATION

Try adding ¹/₂ tablespoon of sun-dried tomato paste or 50 g/1¹/₄ oz finely chopped mushrooms, fried in butter, to the semolina mixture in step 2. Follow the same cooking method.

Meat & Poultry

*Pasta with meat or poultry is a classic combination.
Dishes range from easy, economic mid-week suppers
to sophisticated and elegant meals for special occasions.*

*Most meat in Italy is sold ready boned and cut across the
grain. Veal is a great favourite and widely available. Pork
is also popular, cooked with lots of fragrant herbs, with
roast pig being the traditional dish of Umbria. Lamb is
often served for special occasions, cooked on a spit or
roasted in the oven with wine, garlic and herbs.*

*Poultry dishes provide some of Italy's finest food. Every
part of the chicken is used, the leftovers generally used for
making soups. Turkey, duck, goose and guinea fowl are
also popular, as is game. Wild rabbit, hare, wild boar
and deer being traditional fare, especially in Sardinia*

*The recipes in this chapter include many
family favourites and some exciting variations
on traditional themes. Finally, there is a superb
collection of mouth-watering original recipes
featuring pasta, beef, lamb, pork, chicken and game.
You will be astonished at how quickly and easily
you can prepare these gourmet dishes.*

Spaghetti Bolognese

Serves 4

INGREDIENTS

3 tbsp olive oil
2 garlic cloves, crushed
1 large onion, finely chopped
1 carrot, diced
225 g/8 oz/2 cups lean minced
   (ground) beef, veal or chicken

85 g/3 oz chicken livers,
   finely chopped
100 g/3¹/₂ oz lean, Parma ham
   (prosciutto), diced
150 ml/¹/₄ pint/⁵/₈ cup Marsala

285 g/10 oz can chopped
   plum tomatoes
1 tbsp chopped fresh basil leaves
2 tbsp tomato purée (paste)
salt and pepper
450 g/1 lb dried spaghetti

1 Heat 2 tbsp of the olive oil in a large saucepan. Add the garlic, onion and carrot and fry for 6 minutes.

2 Add the minced (ground) beef, veal or chicken, chicken livers and Parma ham (prosciutto) to the pan and cook over a medium heat for 12 minutes, until well browned.

3 Stir in the Marsala, tomatoes, basil and tomato purée (paste) and cook for 4 minutes. Season to taste with salt and pepper. Cover and simmer for about 30 minutes.

4 Remove the lid from the pan, stir and simmer for a further 15 minutes.

5 Meanwhile, bring a large pan of lightly salted water to the boil. Add the spaghetti and the remaining oil and cook for about 12 minutes, until tender, but still firm to the bite. Drain and transfer to a serving dish. Pour the sauce over the pasta, toss and serve hot.

VARIATION

Chicken livers are an essential ingredient in a classic Bolognese sauce to which they add richness. However, if you prefer not to use them, you can substitute the same quantity of minced (ground) beef.

Creamed Strips of Sirloin with Rigatoni

Serves 4

INGREDIENTS

75 g/3 oz/6 tbsp butter
450 g/1 lb sirloin steak, trimmed
    and cut into thin strips
175 g/6 oz button mushrooms,
    sliced
1 tsp mustard
pinch of freshly grated root ginger

2 tbsp dry sherry
150 ml/¼ pint/⅝ cup double
    (heavy) cream
salt and pepper
4 slices hot toast, cut into
    triangles, to serve

PASTA:
450 g/1 lb dried rigatoni
2 tbsp olive oil
2 fresh basil sprigs
115 g/4 oz/8 tbsp butter

1 Melt the butter in a frying pan (skillet) and fry the steak over a low heat for 6 minutes. Transfer to an ovenproof dish and keep warm.

2 Add the mushrooms to the remaining juices in the frying pan (skillet) and cook for 2–3 minutes. Add the mustard, ginger, salt and pepper. Cook for 2 minutes, then add the sherry and cream. Cook for 3 minutes, then pour the cream sauce over the steak.

3 Bake the steak and cream mixture in a preheated oven at 90°C/375°F/Gas 5 for 10 minutes.

4 Bring a pan of lightly salted water to the boil. Add the rigatoni, olive oil and 1 basil sprig and boil for 10 minutes. Drain and transfer to a warm serving plate. Toss the pasta with the butter and garnish with the remaining basil sprig.

5 Serve the steak with the pasta and triangles of warm toast.

Fresh Spaghetti with Italian Meatballs in Tomato Sauce

Serves 4

INGREDIENTS

150 g/5¹/₂ oz/2¹/₂ cups brown
  breadcrumbs
150 ml/¹/₄ pint/⁵/₈ cup milk
25 g/1 oz/2 tbsp butter
25 g/1 oz/¹/₄ cup wholemeal
  (wholewheat) flour
200 ml/7 fl oz/⁷/₈ cup beef stock

400 g/14 oz can chopped
  tomatoes
2 tbsp tomato purée (paste)
1 tsp sugar
1 tbsp finely chopped fresh
  tarragon
1 large onion, chopped

450 g/1 lb/4 cups minced steak
1 tsp paprika
4 tbsp olive oil
450 g/1 lb fresh spaghetti
salt and pepper
fresh tarragon sprigs, to garnish

1 Soak the breadcrumbs and the milk in a bowl for 30 minutes.

2 Melt half the butter in a pan. Stir in the flour for 2 minutes. Gradually stir in the beef stock and cook, stirring, for a further 5 minutes. Add the tomatoes, tomato purée (paste), sugar and tarragon. Season well and simmer for 25 minutes.

3 Mix the onion, steak and paprika into the breadcrumbs and season. Shape into 14 meatballs.

4 Fry the meatballs in the oil and remaining butter until brown all over. Place them in a casserole, pour over the tomato sauce, cover and bake in a preheated oven at 180°C/ 350°F/Gas 4 for 25 minutes.

5 Bring a pan of lightly salted water to the boil and cook the spaghetti for 2–3 minutes, until tender, but still firm to the bite.

6 Remove the meatballs from the oven and allow them to cool for 3 minutes. Serve the meatballs and their sauce with the spaghetti, garnished with fresh tarragon sprigs.

Layered Meat Loaf

Serves 6

INGREDIENTS

25 g/1 oz/2 tbsp butter, plus
    extra for greasing
1 small onion, finely chopped
1 small red (bell) pepper, cored,
    seeded and chopped
1 garlic clove, chopped
450 g/1 lb/4 cups minced
    (ground) beef

25 g/1 oz/1^1/$_2$ cup white
    breadcrumbs
^{1}/$_2$ tsp cayenne pepper
1 tbsp lemon juice
^{1}/$_2$ tsp grated lemon rind
2 tbsp chopped fresh parsley
90 g/3 oz/^{3}/$_4$ cup dried short
    pasta, such as fusilli
1 tbsp olive oil

250 ml/8 fl oz/1 cup Italian
    Cheese Sauce
4 bay leaves
175 g/6 oz fatty bacon,
    rinds removed
salt and pepper
salad leaves (greens), to garnish

1 Preheat the overn to
180°C/350°F/Gas 4.
Melt the butter in a pan
and fry the onion and (bell)
pepper for 3 minutes. Stir
in the garlic and cook for
1 minute.

2 Mash the meat with a
wooden spoon until
sticky. Mix in the onion
mixture, breadcrumbs,
cayenne pepper, lemon
juice, lemon rind, parsley
and seasoning.

3 Bring a pan of salted
water to the boil. Add
the pasta and oil and cook
for 8–10 minutes. Drain
and stir into the Italian
Cheese Sauce.

4 Grease a 1 kg/2 lb loaf
tin (pan) and arrange
the bay leaves in the base.
Stretch the bacon slices and
use to line the base and
sides of the tin (pan).
Spoon in half the meat
mixture and smooth the

surface. Cover with the
pasta mixed with Italian
Cheese Sauce, then spoon
in the remaining meat
mixture. Level the top and
cover with foil.

5 Bake the meat loaf for
1 hour or until the
juices run clear when a
skewer is inserted in the
centre. Pour off any excess
fat and turn out the loaf on
to a serving dish. Garnish
with salad leaves (greens).

Egg Noodles with Beef

Serves 4

INGREDIENTS

285 g/10 oz egg noodles

3 tbsp walnut oil

2.5 cm/1 inch piece fresh root
   ginger, cut into thin strips

5 spring onions (scallions),
   finely shredded

2 garlic cloves, finely chopped

1 red (bell) pepper, cored, seeded
   and thinly sliced

100 g/3 1/2 oz button mushrooms,
   thinly sliced

340 g/12 oz fillet steak, cut into
   thin strips

1 tbsp cornflour (cornstarch)

5 tbsp dry sherry

3 tbsp soy sauce

1 tsp soft brown sugar

225 g/8 oz/1 cup beansprouts

1 tbsp sesame oil

salt and pepper

spring onion (scallion) strips, to
   garnish

1 Bring a large saucepan
of water to the boil.
Add the noodles and cook
according to the
instructions on the packet.
Drain and set aside.

2 Heat the walnut oil in
a preheated wok. Add
the ginger, spring onions
(scallions) and garlic and
stir-fry for 45 seconds.
Add the (bell) pepper,
mushrooms and steak and
stir-fry for 4 minutes.
Season to taste.

3 Mix together the
cornflour (cornstarch),
sherry and soy sauce in a
small jug to form a paste,
and pour into the wok.
Sprinkle over the brown
sugar and stir-fry all of the
ingredients for 2 minutes.

4 Add the beansprouts,
drained noodles and
sesame oil to the wok, stir
and toss together for
1 minute. Garnish with
strips of spring onion
(scallion) and serve.

COOK'S TIP

*If you do not have a wok,
you could prepare this dish
in a frying pan (skillet).
However, a wok is
preferable, as the round base
ensures an even distribution
of heat and it is easier to
keep stirring and tossing the
contents when stir-frying.*

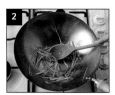

Tagliarini with Meatballs in Red Wine & Oyster Mushroom Sauce

Serves 4

INGREDIENTS

150 g/5 oz/2 cups white breadcrumbs
150 ml/¼ pint/⅔ cup milk
225 g/8 oz/3 cups sliced oyster mushrooms
25 g/1 oz/2 tbsp butter
9 tbsp olive oil

25 g/1 oz/¼ cup wholemeal (wholewheat) flour
200 ml/7 fl oz/⅞ cup beef stock
150 ml/¼ pint/⅔ cup red wine
4 tomatoes, skinned and chopped
1 tbsp tomato purée (paste)
1 tsp brown sugar

1 tbsp finely chopped fresh basil
12 shallots, chopped
450 g/1 lb/4 cups minced (ground) steak
1 tsp paprika
450 g/1 lb dried egg tagliarini
salt and pepper
fresh basil sprigs, to garnish

1 Soak the breadcrumbs in the milk for 30 minutes.

2 Fry the mushrooms in half the butter and 4 tbsp of the oil until soft. Stir in the flour. Add the stock and wine and simmer for 15 minutes. Add the tomatoes, tomato purée (paste), sugar and basil and simmer for 30 minutes.

3 Mix the shallots, steak and paprika with the breadcrumbs. Season then shape into 14 meatballs.

4 Heat 4 tbsp of the remaining oil and the butter in a frying pan (skillet). Fry the meatballs until brown all over. Transfer to a casserole, pour over the red wine and the mushroom sauce, cover and bake in a preheated oven at 180°C/350°F/Gas 4 for 30 minutes.

5 Bring a pan of salted water to the boil. Add the pasta and the remaining oil and cook until tender. Drain and transfer to a serving dish. Pour the meatballs and sauce on to the pasta. Garnish with fresh basil and serve.

Sicilian Spaghetti

Serves 4

INGREDIENTS

150 ml/$\frac{1}{4}$ pint/$\frac{2}{3}$ cup olive oil,
plus extra for brushing
2 aubergines (eggplants)
350 g/12 oz/3 cups minced
(ground) beef
1 onion, chopped
2 garlic cloves, crushed
2 tbsp tomato purée (paste)

400 g/14 oz can chopped
tomatoes
1 tsp Worcestershire sauce
1 tsp chopped fresh marjoram or
oregano or $\frac{1}{2}$ tsp dried
marjoram or oregano
60 g/2 oz/$\frac{1}{2}$ cup stoned (pitted)
black olives, sliced

1 green, red or yellow (bell)
pepper, cored, seeded and
chopped
175 g/6 oz dried spaghetti
115 g/4 oz/1 cup freshly grated
Parmesan cheese
salt and pepper

1 Brush a 20 cm/8 inch loose-based round cake tin (pan) with oil, line the base with baking parchment and brush with oil.

2 Slice the aubergines (eggplants). Fry the aubergines (eggplant) in a little oil until browned on both sides. Drain on kitchen paper (towels).

3 Cook the beef, onion and garlic in a pan, stirring, until browned. Add the tomato purée (paste), tomatoes, Worcestershire sauce, herbs and salt and pepper. Simmer for 10 minutes. Add the olives and (bell) pepper and cook for a further 10 minutes.

4 Bring a pan of salted water to the boil. Add the spaghetti and 1 tbsp olive oil and cook until tender. Drain and turn the spaghetti into a bowl. Add the meat mixture and cheese and toss to mix.

5 Arrange aubergine (eggplant) slices over the base and sides of the tin (pan). Add the pasta, then cover with the rest of the aubergine (eggplant). Bake in a preheated oven at 200°C/400°F/ Gas 6 for 40 minutes. Leave to stand for 5 minutes, then invert on to a serving dish. Discard the baking parchment and serve.

Beef & Pasta Bake

Serves 4

INGREDIENTS
---

900 g/2 lb steak, cut into cubes
150 ml/$^1/_4$ pint beef stock
450 g/1 lb dried macaroni
300 ml/$^1/_2$ pint/1$^1/_4$ cups double
    (heavy) cream
$^1/_2$ tsp garam masala
salt
fresh coriander and toasted
    almonds, to garnish

naan bread, to serve

KORMA PASTE:
60 g/2 oz/$^1/_2$ cup blanched
    almonds
6 garlic cloves
2.5 cm/1 inch piece fresh root
    ginger, coarsely chopped
6 tbsp beef stock

1 tsp ground cardamom
4 cloves, crushed
1 tsp cinnamon
2 large onions, chopped
1 tsp coriander seeds
2 tsp ground cumin seeds
pinch of cayenne pepper
6 tbsp of sunflower oil

1 Grind the almonds finely using a pestle and mortar. Blend the ground almonds and the rest of the korma paste ingredients in a food processor or blender to make a very smooth paste.

2 Put the steak in a shallow dish and spoon over the korma paste, turning to coat steak well. Marinate in the refrigerator for 6 hours.

3 Transfer the steak to a large saucepan, and simmer gently, for 35 minutes, adding a little beef stock if required.

4 Bring a large pan of lightly salted water to the boil. Add the macaroni and cook for 10 minutes, until tender. Drain the pasta and transfer to a deep casserole. Add the steak, double (heavy) cream and garam masala.

5 Bake in a preheated oven at 200°C/400°F/ Gas 6 for 30 minutes. Remove and let stand for 10 minutes. Garnish with fresh coriander and serve with naan bread.

VARIATION

You could also make this dish using diced chicken and chicken stock, instead of steak and beef stock.

Lasagne Verde

Serves 4–6

INGREDIENTS

butter, for greasing
14 sheets pre-cooked lasagne
850 ml/1½ pints/3¾ cups
   Béchamel Sauce
75 g/3 oz/¾ cup grated
   mozzarella cheese
fresh basil (optional), to garnish

MEAT SAUCE:
25 ml/1 fl oz/⅛ cup olive oil
450 g/1 lb/4 cups minced
   (ground) beef
1 large onion, chopped
1 celery stick (stalk), diced
4 cloves garlic, crushed
25g/1 oz/¼ cup plain
   (all purpose) flour

300 ml/½ pint/1¼ cups beef
   stock
150 ml/¼ pint/⅝ cup red wine
1 tbsp chopped fresh parsley
1 tsp chopped fresh marjoram
1 tsp chopped fresh basil
2 tbsp tomato purée (paste)

salt and pepper

1 To make the meat sauce, heat the olive oil in a large frying pan (skillet). Add the minced (ground) beef and fry, stirring frequently, until browned all over. Add the onion, celery and garlic and cook for 3 minutes.

2 Sprinkle over the flour and cook, stirring constantly, for 1 minute. Gradually stir in the stock and red wine. Season well

and add the parsley, marjoram and basil. Bring to the boil, lower the heat and simmer for 35 minutes. Add the tomato purée (paste) and simmer for a further 10 minutes.

3 Lightly grease an ovenproof dish with butter. Arrange sheets of lasagne over the base of the dish, spoon over a layer of meat sauce, then Béchamel Sauce. Place another layer

of lasagne on top and repeat the process twice, finishing with a layer of Béchamel Sauce. Sprinkle over the grated mozzarella cheese.

4 Bake the lasagne in a preheated oven at 190°C/375°F/Gas 5 for 35 minutes, until the top is golden brown and bubbling. Garnish with fresh basil, if liked, and serve immediately.

Pasticcio

Serves 6

INGREDIENTS

250 g/8 oz/2 cups dried fusilli
1 tbsp olive oil, plus extra
   for brushing
4 tbsp double (heavy) cream
mixed salad, to serve

SAUCE:
2 tbsp olive oil
1 onion, thinly sliced
1 red (bell) pepper, cored, seeded
   and chopped

2 garlic cloves, chopped
600 g/1 lb 5 oz/5¼ cups minced
   (ground) beef
400 g/14 oz can chopped
   tomatoes
125 ml/4 fl oz/½ cup dry white
   wine
2 tbsp chopped fresh parsley
60 g/2 oz can anchovies, drained
   and chopped
salt and pepper

TOPPING:
300 ml/½ pint/1¼ cups natural
   yogurt
3 eggs
pinch of freshly grated nutmeg
40 g/1½ oz/½ cup freshly grated
   Parmesan cheese

1 To make the sauce, heat the oil in a frying pan (skillet) and fry the onion and red (bell) pepper for 3 minutes. Add the garlic and cook for 1 minute. Add the beef and cook until browned.

2 Add the tomatoes and wine and bring to the boil. Simmer for 20 minutes, until thickened.

Stir in the parsley, anchovies and seasoning.

3 Bring a pan of salted water to the boil. Add the pasta and oil and cook for 10 minutes, until almost tender. Drain and transfer to a bowl. Stir in the cream.

4 For the topping, beat together the yogurt, eggs and nutmeg.

5 Brush an ovenproof dish with oil. Spoon in half the pasta and cover with half the meat sauce. Repeat, then spread over the topping and sprinkle with cheese.

6 Bake in a preheated oven at 190°C/375°F/ Gas 5 for 25 minutes until golden. Serve with a mixed salad.

Fettuccine with Fillet of Veal & Pink Grapefruit in a Rose-Petal Butter Sauce

Serves 4

INGREDIENTS

450 g/1 lb dried fettuccine
7 tbsp olive oil
1 tsp chopped fresh oregano
1 tsp chopped fresh marjoram
170 g/6 oz/³/₄ cup butter
450 g/1 lb veal fillet, thinly sliced

150 ml/¹/₄ pint/⁵/₈ cup rose petal
   vinegar (see Cook's Tip, below)
150 ml/¹/₄ pint/⁵/₈ cup fish stock
50 ml/2 fl oz/ ¹/₄ cup grapefruit juice
50 ml/2 fl oz/¹/₄ cup double
   (heavy) cream
salt

TO GARNISH:
12 pink grapefruit segments
12 pink peppercorns
rose petals
fresh herb leaves

1 Cook the fettuccine with 1 tbsp of the oil in a pan of salted boiling water for 12 minutes. Drain and transfer to a warm serving dish, sprinkle over 2 tbsp of the olive oil, the oregano and marjoram.

2 Heat 50 g/2 oz/4 tbsp of the butter with the remaining oil in a frying pan (skillet) and cook the veal for 6 minutes. Spoon the veal on top of the pasta.

3 Add the vinegar and fish stock to the pan and boil vigorously until reduced by two thirds. Add the grapefruit juice and cream and simmer for 4 minutes. Dice the remaining butter and add to the pan, whisking until fully incorporated.

4 Pour the sauce around the veal, garnish and serve.

COOK'S TIP

To make rose-petal vinegar, infuse the petals of 8 pesticide-free roses in 150 ml/¹/₄ pint/⁵/₈ cup white wine vinegar for 48 hours.

Neapolitan Veal Cutlets with Mascarpone Cheese & Marille

Serves 4

INGREDIENTS

200 g/7 oz/⅞ cup butter

4 x 250 g/9 oz veal cutlets, trimmed

1 large onion, sliced

2 apples, peeled, cored and sliced

175 g/6 oz button mushrooms

1 tbsp chopped fresh tarragon

8 black peppercorns

1 tbsp sesame seeds

400 g/14 oz dried marille

100 ml/3½ fl oz/scant ½ cup extra virgin olive oil

175 g/6 oz/¾ cup mascarpone cheese, broken into small pieces

salt and pepper

2 large beef tomatoes, cut in half

leaves of 1 fresh basil sprig

1 Melt 60 g/2 oz/4 tbsp of the butter in a frying pan (skillet). Gently fry the veal for 5 minutes on each side. Transfer to a dish and keep warm.

2 Fry the onion and apples until golden. Transfer to a dish, top with the veal and keep warm.

3 Fry the mushrooms, tarragon and peppercorns in the remaining butter for 3 minutes. Sprinkle over the sesame seeds.

4 Bring a pan of salted water to the boil. Add the pasta and 1 tbsp of the oil and cook until tender. Drain and transfer to a serving plate.

5 Top the pasta with the cheese and sprinkle over the remaining olive oil. Place the onions, apples and veal cutlets on top of the pasta. Spoon the mushrooms, peppercorns and pan juices on to the cutlets, place the tomatoes and basil leaves around the edge of the plate and place in a preheated oven at 150°C/300°F/Gas 2 for 5 minutes. Season to taste with salt and pepper and serve immediately.

Stir-Fried Pork with Pasta & Vegetables

Serves 4

INGREDIENTS

3 tbsp sesame oil
350 g/12 oz pork fillet
    (tenderloin), cut into thin
    strips
450 g/1 lb dried taglioni
1 tbsp olive oil
8 shallots, sliced
2 garlic cloves, finely chopped

2.5 cm/1 inch piece fresh root
    ginger, grated
1 fresh green chilli, finely
    chopped
1 red (bell) pepper, cored, seeded
    and thinly sliced
1 green (bell) pepper, cored,
    seeded and thinly sliced

3 courgettes (zucchini), thinly
    sliced
2 tbsp ground almonds
1 tsp ground cinnamon
1 tbsp oyster sauce
60 g/2 oz creamed coconut (see
    Cook's Tip, below), grated
salt and pepper

1 Heat the sesame oil in a preheated wok. Season the pork and stir-fry for 5 minutes.

2 Bring a pan of salted water to the boil. Add the taglioni and olive oil and cook for 12 minutes. Set aside and keep warm.

3 Add the shallots, garlic, ginger and chilli to the wok and stir-fry for 2 minutes. Add the (bell) peppers and courgettes and stir-fry for 1 minute.

4 Add the ground almonds, cinnamon, oyster sauce and coconut cream to the wok and stir-fry for 1 minute.

5 Drain the taglioni and transfer to a serving dish. Top with the stir-fry and serve immediately.

COOK'S TIP

Creamed coconut is available from Chinese and Asian food stores and some large supermarkets. It is sold in compressed blocks and adds a concentrated coconut flavour to the dish.

Orecchioni with Pork in Cream Sauce, Garnished with Quail Eggs

Serves 4

INGREDIENTS

450 g/1 lb pork fillet (tenderloin),
thinly sliced
4 tbsp olive oil
225 g/8 oz button mushrooms,
sliced

200 ml/7 fl oz/⁷/₈ cup Italian Red
Wine Sauce
1 tbsp lemon juice
pinch of saffron

350 g/12 oz/3 cups dried
orecchioni
4 tbsp double (heavy) cream
12 quail eggs (see Cook's Tip, below)
salt

1 Pound the slices of pork until wafer thin, then cut into strips.

2 Heat the olive oil in a frying pan (skillet) and stir-fry the pork for 5 minutes, then stir-fry the mushrooms for 2 minutes.

3 Pour over the Italian Red Wine Sauce and simmer for 20 minutes.

4 Meanwhile, bring a large saucepan of

lightly salted water to the boil. Add the lemon juice, saffron and orecchioni and cook for 12 minutes, until tender but still firm to the bite. Drain the pasta and keep warm.

5 Stir the cream into the pan with the pork and heat gently for 3 minutes.

6 Boil the quail eggs for 3 minutes, cool them in cold water and remove the shells.

7 Transfer the pasta to a warm serving plate, top with the pork and the sauce and garnish with the eggs. Serve immediately.

COOK'S TIP

In this recipe, the quail eggs are soft-boiled (soft-cooked). As they are very difficult to shell when warm, they should be thoroughly cooled first. Otherwise, they will break up unattractively.

206

Stuffed Cannelloni

Serves 4

INGREDIENTS

8 dried cannelloni tubes
1 tbsp olive oil
25 g/1 oz/^{1}/$_4$ cup freshly grated
    Parmesan cheese
fresh herb sprigs, to garnish

FILLING:
25 g/1 oz/2 tbsp butter
300 g/10^1/$_2$ oz frozen spinach,
    thawed and chopped

115 g/4 oz/1^1/$_2$ cup ricotta cheese
25 g/1 oz/^{1}/$_4$ cup freshly grated
    Parmesan cheese
60 g/2 oz/^{1}/$_4$ cup chopped ham
pinch of freshly grated nutmeg
2 tbsp double (heavy) cream
2 eggs, lightly beaten
salt and pepper

SAUCE:
25 g/1 oz/2 tbsp butter
25 g/1 oz/^{1}/$_4$ cup plain
    (all purpose) flour
300 ml/^{1}/$_2$ pint/1^1/$_4$ cups milk
2 bay leaves
pinch of freshly grated nutmeg

1 For the filling, melt the butter in a pan and stir-fry the spinach for 2–3 minutes. Remove from the heat and stir in the cheeses and the ham. Season with nutmeg, salt and pepper. Beat in the cream and eggs to make a thick paste.

2 Cook the pasta with the oil in a pan of salted boiling water until tender. Drain and set aside.

3 To make the sauce, melt the butter in a pan. Stir in the flour and cook for 1 minute. Gradually stir in the milk and the bay leaves and simmer for 5 minutes. Add the nutmeg and seasoning. Remove from the heat and discard the bay leaves.

4 Spoon the filling into a piping bag and fill the cannelloni.

5 Spoon a little sauce into the base of an ovenproof dish. Arrange the cannelloni in the dish in a single layer and pour over the remaining sauce. Sprinkle over the Parmesan cheese and bake in a preheated oven at 190°C/375°F/Gas 5 for about 40–45 minutes. Garnish with the fresh herb sprigs and serve immediately.

Wholemeal (Wholewheat) Spaghetti with Suprêmes of Chicken Nell Gwyn

Serves 4

INGREDIENTS

25 ml/1 fl oz/$^{1}/_{8}$ cup rapeseed oil
3 tbsp olive oil
4 x 225 g/8 oz chicken suprêmes
150 ml/$^{1}/_{4}$ pint/$^{2}/_{3}$ cup orange brandy
15 g/$^{1}/_{2}$ oz/2 tbsp plain (all purpose) flour
150 ml/$^{1}/_{4}$ pint/$^{2}/_{3}$ cup freshly squeezed orange juice

25 g/1 oz courgette (zucchini), cut into matchstick strips
25 g/1 oz red (bell) pepper, cut into matchstick strips
25 g/1 oz leek, finely shredded
400 g/14 oz dried wholemeal (whole wheat) spaghetti
3 large oranges, peeled and cut into segments

rind of 1 orange, cut into very fine strips
2 tbsp chopped fresh tarragon
150 ml/$^{1}/_{4}$ pint/$^{2}/_{3}$ cup fromage frais or ricotta cheese
salt and pepper

1 Heat the rapeseed oil and 1 tbsp of the olive oil in a frying pan (skillet). Add the chicken and cook quickly until golden brown. Add the orange brandy and cook for 3 minutes. Sprinkle over the flour and cook for 2 minutes.

2 Lower the heat and add the orange juice, courgette (zucchini), (bell) pepper and leek and season. Simmer for 5 minutes until the sauce has thickened.

3 Meanwhile, bring a pan of salted water to the boil. Add the spaghetti and 1 tbsp of the olive oil and cook for 10 minutes. Drain, transfer to a serving dish and drizzle over the remaining oil.

4 Add half the orange segments, half the orange rind, the tarragon and fromage frais or ricotta cheese to the sauce in the pan and cook for 3 minutes.

5 Place the chicken on top of the pasta, pour over a little sauce, garnish with orange segments and rind. Serve immediately.

Chicken & Wild Mushroom Lasagne

Serves 4

INGREDIENTS

butter, for greasing
14 sheets pre-cooked lasagne
850 ml/1¹/₂ pints/3³/₄ cups
    Béchamel Sauce
75 g/3 oz/1 cup grated
    Parmesan cheese

CHICKEN & WILD MUSHROOM
    SAUCE:
2 tbsp olive oil
2 garlic cloves, crushed
1 large onion, finely chopped
225 g/8 oz wild mushrooms,
    sliced
300 g/10¹/₂ oz/2¹/₂ cups minced
    (ground) chicken
80 g/3 oz chicken livers,
    finely chopped

115 g/4 oz Parma ham
    (prosciutto), diced
150 ml/¹/₄ pint/²/₃ cup Marsala
285g/10 oz can chopped
    tomatoes
1 tbsp chopped fresh basil leaves
2 tbsp tomato purée (paste)
salt and pepper

1 To make the sauce, heat the olive oil in a large saucepan. Add the garlic, onion and mushrooms and cook for 6 minutes.

2 Add the minced (ground) chicken, chicken livers and Parma ham (prosciutto) and cook for 12 minutes, until the meat has browned.

3 Stir the Marsala, tomatoes, basil and tomato purée (paste) into the pan and cook for 4 minutes. Season, cover and simmer for 30 minutes. Stir and simmer for a further 15 minutes.

4 Arrange the lasagne over the base of a greased ovenproof dish, spoon over a layer of chicken and wild mushroom sauce, then a layer of Béchamel Sauce. Place another layer of lasagne on top and repeat the process twice, finishing with a layer of Béchamel Sauce. Sprinkle over the grated cheese and bake in a preheated oven at 190°C/375°F/Gas 5 for 35 minutes until golden brown. Serve immediately.

Tagliatelle with Chicken Sauce

Serves 4

INGREDIENTS

250 g/9 oz fresh green tagliatelle
1 tbsp olive oil
fresh basil leaves, to garnish
salt

TOMATO SAUCE:
2 tbsp olive oil
1 small onion, chopped
1 garlic clove, chopped

400 g/14 oz can chopped
    tomatoes
2 tbsp chopped fresh parsley
1 tsp dried oregano
2 bay leaves
2 tbsp tomato purée (paste)
1 tsp sugar
salt and pepper

CHICKEN SAUCE:
60 g/2 oz/4 tbsp unsalted butter
400 g/14 oz boned chicken
    breasts, skinned and cut into
    thin strips
90 g/3 oz/³/₄ cup blanched
    almonds
300 ml/¹/₂ pint/1¹/₄ cups double
    (heavy) cream
salt and pepper

1 To make the tomato sauce, heat the oil and fry the onion until translucent. Add the garlic and fry for 1 minute. Stir in the tomatoes, herbs, tomato purée (paste), sugar and seasoning to taste. Bring to the boil and simmer for 15–20 minutes, until reduced by half. Remove from the heat and discard the bay leaves.

2 To make the chicken sauce, melt the butter in a frying pan (skillet) and stir-fry the chicken and almonds for 5–6 minutes, until the chicken is cooked.

3 Meanwhile, bring the cream to the boil over a low heat for about 10 minutes, until reduced by half. Pour the cream over the chicken and almonds,

stir and season to taste. Set aside and keep warm.

4 Bring a pan of salted water to the boil. Add the tagliatelle and olive oil and cook until tender. Drain and transfer to a warm serving dish. Spoon over the tomato sauce and arrange the chicken sauce on top. Garnish with the basil leaves and serve.

Mustard-Baked Chicken with Pasta Shells

Serves 4

INGREDIENTS

8 chicken pieces
(about 115 g/4 oz each)
60 g/2 oz/4 tbsp butter, melted
4 tbsp mild mustard (see Cook's Tip)

2 tbsp lemon juice
1 tbsp brown sugar
1 tsp paprika
3 tbsp poppy seeds
400 g/14 oz fresh pasta shells

1 tbsp olive oil
salt and pepper

1 Arrange the chicken, smooth side down, in an ovenproof dish.

2 Combine the butter, mustard, lemon juice, sugar, paprika and salt and pepper. Brush the mixture over the upper surfaces of the chicken pieces and bake in a preheated oven at 200°C/400°F/Gas 6 for 15 minutes.

3 Remove the dish from the oven and turn over the chicken pieces. Coat the upper surfaces of the chicken with the remaining mustard mixture, sprinkle with poppy seeds and return to the oven for a further 15 minutes.

4 Meanwhile, bring a large pan of lightly salted water to the boil. Add the pasta shells and olive oil and cook until tender, but still firm to the bite.

5 Drain the pasta and arrange on a warmed serving dish. Top with the chicken, pour over the sauce and serve immediately.

COOK'S TIP

Dijon is the type of mustard most often used in cooking, as it has a clean and only mildly spicy flavour. German mustard has a sweet-sour taste, with Bavarian mustard being slightly sweeter. American mustard is mild and sweet.

Tortellini

Serves 4

INGREDIENTS

115 g/4 oz boned chicken breast,
  skinned
60 g/2 oz Parma ham
  (prosciutto)
40 g/1¹⁄₂ oz cooked spinach,
  well drained
1 tbsp finely chopped onion
2 tbsp freshly grated

Parmesan cheese
pinch of ground allspice
1 egg, beaten
450 g/1 lb Basic Pasta Dough
salt and pepper
2 tbsp chopped fresh parsley,
  to garnish

SAUCE:
300 ml/¹⁄₂ pint/1¹⁄₄ cups single
  (light) cream
2 garlic cloves, crushed
115 g/4 oz button mushrooms,
  thinly sliced
4 tbsp freshly grated Parmesan
  cheese

1 Bring a pan of seasoned water to the boil. Add the chicken and poach for 10 minutes. Cool slightly, then process in a food processor, with the Parma ham (prosciutto), spinach and onion until finely chopped. Stir in the Parmesan cheese, allspice and egg and season to taste.

2 Thinly roll out the pasta dough and cut into 5 cm/2 inch rounds.

3 Place ¹⁄₂ tsp of the filling in the centre of each round. Fold the pieces in half and press the edges to seal. Then wrap each piece around your index finger, cross over the ends and curl the rest of the dough backwards to make a navel shape.

4 Bring a pan of salted water to the boil. Add the tortellini, bring back to the boil and cook for

5 minutes. Drain and transfer to a serving dish.

5 To make the sauce, bring the cream and garlic to the boil then simmer for 3 minutes. Add the mushrooms and half the cheese, season and simmer for 2–3 minutes. Pour the sauce over the tortellini. Sprinkle over the remaining Parmesan, garnish with the parsley and serve.

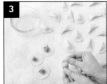

Chicken Suprêmes Filled with Tiger Prawns (Shrimp) on a Bed of Pasta

Serves 4

INGREDIENTS

4 x 200 g/7 oz chicken
   suprêmes, trimmed
115 g/4 oz large spinach leaves,
   trimmed and blanched in hot
   salted water
4 slices of Parma ham
   (prosciutto)

12–16 raw tiger prawns (shrimp),
   shelled and deveined
450 g/1 lb dried tagliatelle
1 tbsp olive oil
60 g/2 oz/4 tbsp butter, plus
   extra for greasing
3 leeks, shredded

1 large carrot, grated
150 ml/¹/₄ pint/⅝ cup
   thick mayonnaise
2 large cooked beetroot (beet)
salt

1 Place each suprême between 2 pieces of baking parchment and pound to flatten.

2 Divide half the spinach between the suprêmes, add a slice of ham to each and top with spinach. Place 3–4 prawns (shrimp) on top. Roll up each suprême to form a parcel. Wrap each parcel in greased foil, place on a baking (cookie) sheet and bake in a preheated oven at 200°C/400°F/Gas 6 for 20 minutes.

3 Cook the pasta with the oil in salted boiling water until tender. Drain and transfer to a warm dish.

4 Melt the butter and fry the leeks and carrot for 3 minutes. Transfer to the centre of the pasta.

5 Work the mayonnaise and 1 beetroot (beet) in a food processor until smooth. Rub through a strainer and pour around the pasta and vegetables.

6 Cut the remaining beetroot (beet) into diamond shapes and place them neatly around the mayonnaise. Remove the foil from the chicken and cut the suprêmes into thin slices. Arrange the slices on top of the vegetables and pasta, and serve.

Chicken & Lobster on a Bed of Penne

Serves 6

INGREDIENTS

butter, for greasing
6 chicken breasts
450 g/1 lb dried penne rigate
6 tbsp extra virgin olive oil
90 g/3 oz/1 cup freshly grated
    Parmesan cheese

salt
fresh herbs, to garnish

FILLING:
115 g/4 oz lobster meat, chopped
2 shallots, very finely chopped

2 figs, chopped
1 tbsp Marsala
2 tbsp breadcrumbs
1 large egg, beaten
salt and pepper

1 Grease 6 pieces of foil large enough to enclose each chicken breast and lightly grease a baking (cookie) sheet.

2 Place all of the filling ingredients into a mixing bowl and blend together thoroughly with a spoon.

3 Cut a pocket in each chicken breast with a sharp knife and fill with the lobster mixture. Wrap each chicken breast in foil, place the parcels on the

greased baking (cookie) sheet and bake in a preheated oven at 200°C/400°F/Gas 6 for 30 minutes.

4 Meanwhile, bring a large pan of lightly salted water to the boil. Add the pasta and 1 tbsp of the olive oil and cook for about 10 minutes, or until tender but still firm to the bite. Drain the pasta thoroughly and transfer to a large serving plate. Sprinkle over the remaining olive oil and the grated Parmesan

cheese, set aside and keep warm.

5 Carefully remove the foil from around the chicken breasts. Slice the breasts very thinly, arrange over the pasta. Garnish with fresh herbs and serve immediately.

COOK'S TIP

The cut of chicken known as suprême consists of the breast and wing. It is always skinned.

Chicken with Green Olives & Pasta

Serves 4

INGREDIENTS

4 chicken breasts, part boned
3 tbsp olive oil
25 g/1 oz/2 tbsp butter
1 large onion, finely chopped
2 garlic cloves, crushed
2 red, yellow or green (bell)
  peppers, cored, seeded and
  cut into large pieces

250 g/9 oz button mushrooms,
  sliced or quartered
175 g/6 oz tomatoes, skinned
  and halved
150 ml/¼ pint/⅝ cup dry
  white wine

175 g/6 oz/1½ cups stoned
  (pitted) green olives
4–6 tbsp double (heavy) cream
400 g/14 oz dried pasta
salt and pepper
chopped parsley, to garnish

1 Fry the chicken breasts in 2 tbsp of the oil and the butter until golden brown. Remove the chicken from the pan.

2 Add the onion and garlic to the pan and fry until beginning to soften. Add the (bell) peppers and mushrooms and cook for 2–3 minutes. Add the tomatoes and seasoning. Transfer the vegetables to a casserole with the chicken.

3 Add the wine to the pan and bring to the boil. Pour the wine over the chicken. Cover and cook in a preheated oven at 180°C/350°F/Gas 4 for 50 minutes.

4 Mix the olives into the casserole. Pour in the cream, cover and return to the oven for 10–20 minutes.

5 Meanwhile, bring a large pan of lightly

salted water to the boil. Add the pasta and the remaining oil and cook until tender, but still firm to the bite. Drain the pasta well and transfer to a serving dish.

6 Arrange the chicken on top of the pasta, spoon over the sauce, garnish with the parsley and serve immediately. Alternatively, place the pasta in a large serving bowl and serve separately.

Sliced Breast of Duckling with Linguine

Serves 4

INGREDIENTS

4 x 275 g/10½ oz boned breasts
    of duckling
25 g/1 oz/2 tbsp butter
50 g/2 oz/3⅜ cup finely
    chopped carrots
50 g/2 oz/4 tbsp finely
    chopped shallots
1 tbsp lemon juice

150 ml/¼ pint/⅝ cup meat stock
4 tbsp clear honey
115 g/4 oz/⅝ cup fresh or
    thawed frozen raspberries
25 g/1 oz/¼ cup plain (all
    purpose) flour
1 tbsp Worcestershire sauce
400 g/14 oz fresh linguine

1 tbsp olive oil
salt and pepper

TO GARNISH:
fresh raspberries
fresh sprig of flat-leaf parsley

1 Trim and score the duck breasts and season well. Melt the butter in a frying pan (skillet) and fry the duck breasts until lightly coloured.

2 Add the carrots, shallots, lemon juice and half the meat stock and simmer for 1 minute. Stir in half the honey and half the raspberries. Stir in half the flour and cook for 3 minutes. Add the pepper and Worcestershire sauce.

3 Stir in the remaining stock and cook for 1 minute. Stir in the remaining honey, raspberries and flour. Cook for a further 3 minutes.

4 Remove the duck from the pan, but continue simmering the sauce.

5 Bring a large pan of salted water to the boil. Add the linguine and olive oil and cook until tender. Drain and divide between 4 plates.

6 Slice the duck breast lengthways into 5 mm/¼ inch thick pieces. Pour a little sauce over the pasta and arrange the sliced duck in a fan shape on top. Garnish and serve.

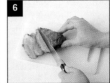

Rigatoni & Pesto-Baked Partridge

Serves 4

INGREDIENTS

8 partridge pieces (about 115 g/4 oz each)	1 tbsp brown sugar	115 g/4 oz/1⅓ cups freshly grated Parmesan cheese
60 g/2 oz/4 tbsp butter, melted	6 tbsp Pesto Sauce	salt and pepper
4 tbsp Dijon mustard	450 g/1 lb dried rigatoni	
2 tbsp lime juice	1 tbsp olive oil	

1 Arrange the partridge pieces, smooth side down, in a single layer in a large, ovenproof dish.

2 Mix together the butter, Dijon mustard, lime juice and brown sugar in a bowl. Season to taste. Brush the mixture over the upper surfaces of the partridge pieces and bake in a preheated oven at 200°C/400°F/Gas 6 for 15 minutes.

3 Remove the dish from the oven and coat the partridge pieces with 3 tbsp of the Pesto Sauce. Return to the oven and bake for a further 12 minutes.

4 Remove the dish from the oven and carefully turn over the partridge pieces. Coat the top of the partridges with the remaining mustard mixture and return to the oven for a further 10 minutes.

5 Meanwhile, bring a large saucepan of lightly salted water to the boil. Add the rigatoni and olive oil and cook for about 10 minutes until tender, but still firm to the bite. Drain and transfer to a serving dish. Toss the pasta with the remaining Pesto Sauce and the Parmesan.

6 Arrange the pieces of partridge on the serving dish with the rigatoni, pour over the cooking juices and serve immediately.

VARIATION

You could also prepare young pheasant in the same way.

Breast of Pheasant Lasagne with Baby Onions & Green Peas

Serves 4

INGREDIENTS

butter, for greasing
14 sheets pre-cooked lasagne
850 ml/1½ pints/3¾ cups
    Béchamel Sauce
75 g/3 oz/¾ cup grated
    mozzarella cheese

FILLING:
225 g/8 oz pork fat, diced
60 g/2 oz/2 tbsp butter
16 small onions
8 large pheasant breasts, thinly
    sliced

25 g/1 oz/¼ cup plain
    (all purpose) flour
600 ml/1 pint/2½ cups chicken
    stock
bouquet garni
450 g/1 lb fresh peas, shelled
salt and pepper

1 Put the pork fat into a pan of boiling, salted water and simmer for 3 minutes, drain and pat dry.

2 Fry the pork fat and onions in the butter until lightly browned. Remove from the pan.

3 Add the pheasant to the pan and cook over a low heat until browned all over. Transfer to an ovenproof dish.

4 Stir the flour into the pan and cook until brown, then blend in the stock. Pour over the pheasant, add the bouquet garni and cook in a preheated oven at 200°C/400°F/Gas 6 for 5 minutes.

5 Remove the bouquet garni. Add the onions, pork fat and peas and return to the oven for 10 minutes.

6 Mince the pheasant breasts and pork in a food processor.

7 Lower the oven to 190°C/375°F/Gas 5. Make layers of lasagne, pheasant sauce and Béchamel Sauce in an ovenproof dish, ending with Béchamel sauce. Sprinkle over the cheese and bake in the oven for 30 minutes. Serve surrounded by the peas and onions.

Chicken Lasagne

Serves 4

INGREDIENTS

350 g/12 oz fresh lasagne (about 9 sheets) or 150 g/5¹/₂ oz dried lasagne (about 9 sheets)
1 tbsp olive oil
1 red onion, finely chopped
1 garlic clove, crushed
100 g/3¹/₂ oz mushrooms, wiped and sliced

350 g/12 oz chicken or turkey breast, cut into chunks
150 ml/5 fl oz/²/₃ cup red wine, diluted with 100 ml/3¹/₂ fl oz/ scant ¹/₂ cup water
250 g/9 oz passata (tomato purée)
1 tsp sugar

BECHAMEL SAUCE:
75 g/2³/₄ oz/5 tbsp butter
50 g/1³/₄ oz plain (all-purpose) flour
600 ml/1 pint/2¹/₂ cups milk
1 egg, beaten
75 g/2³/₄ oz Parmesan cheese, grated
salt and pepper

1 Cook the lasagne in a pan of boiling water according to the instructions on the packet. Lightly grease a deep ovenproof dish.

2 Heat the oil in a pan. Add the onion and garlic and cook for 3–4 minutes. Add the mushrooms and chicken and stir-fry for 4 minutes or until the meat browns.

3 Add the wine, bring to the boil, then leave to simmer for 5 minutes. Stir in the passata (tomato purée) and sugar and cook for 3–5 minutes until the meat is tender and cooked through. The sauce should have thickened but still be quite runny.

4 To make the béchamel sauce, melt the butter in a pan, stir in the flour and cook for 2 minutes. Remove the pan from the heat and gradually add the milk, mixing to form a smooth sauce. Return the pan to the heat and bring to the boil, stirring until thickened. Leave to cool slightly, then beat in the egg and half of the cheese. Season to taste.

5 Place 3 sheets of lasagne in the base of the dish and spread with half of the chicken mixture. Repeat the layers. Top with the last 3 sheets of lasagne, pour over the Béchamel sauce and sprinkle with the Parmesan. Bake in a preheated oven at 190°C/375°F/Gas Mark 5 for 30 minutes until golden and the pasta is cooked.

Cannelloni

Serves 4

INGREDIENTS

20 tubes dried cannelloni
(about 200 g/7 oz) or 20
square sheets of fresh pasta
(about 350 g/12 oz)
250 g/9 oz ricotta cheese

150 g/5$^{1}/_{2}$ oz frozen spinach,
defrosted
$^{1}/_{2}$ small red (bell) pepper, diced
2 spring onions (scallions), chopped
150 ml/5 fl oz/$^{2}/_{3}$ cup hot vegetable
or chicken stock

1 portion of Basil and Tomato
Sauce
5 g/1 oz Parmesan or pecorino
cheese, grated
salt and pepper

1 If you are using dried
cannelloni, check the
packet instructions; many
varieties do not need
pre-cooking. If necessary,
pre-cook your pasta. Bring
a large saucepan of water to
the boil, add 1 tablespoon
of oil and cook the pasta
for 3–4 minutes – it is
easier to do this in batches.

2 In a bowl, mix
together the ricotta,
spinach, (bell) pepper, and
spring onions (scallions)
and season to taste with salt
and pepper.

3 Lightly butter an
ovenproof dish, large
enough to contain all of the
pasta tubes in a single layer.
Spoon the ricotta mixture
into the pasta tubes and
place them into the
prepared dish. If you are
using fresh sheets of pasta,
spread the ricotta mixture
along one side of each fresh
pasta square and roll up to
form a tube.

4 Mix together the stock
and Basil and Tomato
Sauce and pour over the
pasta tubes.

5 Sprinkle the cheese
over the cannelloni and
bake in a preheated oven,
190°C/375°F/Gas Mark 5,
for 20–25 minutes or until
the pasta is cooked through.

VARIATION

*If you would prefer a
creamier version, omit the
stock and the Basil and
Tomato sauce and replace
with Béchamel Sauce.*

Rich Beef Stew

Serves 4

INGREDIENTS

1 tbsp oil
15 g/$^1\!/_2$ oz/1 tbsp butter
225 g/8 oz baby onions, peeled
    and halved

600 g/1 lb 5 oz stewing steak, diced
    into 4 cm/1$^1\!/_2$ inch chunks
300 ml/$^1\!/_2$ pint/1$^1\!/_4$ cup beef stock
150 ml/5 fl oz/$^2\!/_3$ cup red wine
4 tbsp chopped oregano
1 tbsp sugar

1 orange
25 g/1 oz porcini or other dried
    mushrooms
225 g/8 oz fresh plum tomatoes
cooked rice or potatoes, to serve

1 Heat the oil and butter in a large frying pan (skillet). Add the onions and sauté for 5 minutes or until golden. Remove with a perforated spoon, set aside and keep warm.

2 Add the beef to the pan and cook, stirring, for 5 minutes or until browned all over.

3 Return the onions to the frying pan (skillet) and add the stock, wine, oregano and sugar, stirring to mix well. Transfer the mixture to an ovenproof casserole dish.

4 Pare the rind from the orange and cut it into strips. Slice the orange flesh into rings. Add the orange rings and the rind to the casserole. Cook in a preheated oven, at 180°C/350°F/Gas Mark 4, for 1$^1\!/_4$ hours.

5 Soak the porcini mushrooms for 30 minutes in a small bowl containing 4 tablespoons of warm water.

6 Peel and halve the tomatoes. Add the tomatoes, porcini mushrooms and their soaking liquid to the casserole. Cook for a further 20 minutes until the beef is tender and the juices thickened. Serve with cooked rice or potatoes.

VARIATION

Instead of fresh tomatoes, try using 8 sun-dried tomatoes, cut into wide strips, if you prefer.

Pork with Lemon & Garlic

Serves 4

INGREDIENTS

450 g/1 lb pork fillet
50 g/1¹/₄ oz chopped almonds
2 tbsp olive oil
100 g/3¹/₂ oz raw ham
  (prosciutto), finely chopped

2 garlic cloves, chopped
1 tbsp fresh oregano, chopped
finely grated rind of 2 lemons
4 shallots, finely chopped

200 ml/7 fl oz/¹/₄ cup ham or
  chicken stock
1 tsp sugar

1 Using a sharp knife, cut the pork fillet into 4 equal pieces. Place the pork between sheets of greaseproof paper and pound each piece with a meat mallet or the end of a rolling pin to flatten it.

2 Cut a horizontal slit in each piece of pork to make a pocket.

3 Place the almonds on a baking tray (cookie sheet). Lightly toast the almonds under a medium-hot grill (broiler) for 2–3 minutes or until golden.

4 Mix the almonds with 1 tablespoon of the olive oil, chopped ham (prosciutto), garlic, oregano and the finely grated rind from 1 lemon. Spoon the mixture into the pockets of the pork.

5 Heat the remaining oil in a large frying pan (skillet). Add the shallots and cook for 2 minutes.

6 Add the pork to the frying pan (skillet) and cook for 2 minutes on each side or until browned all over.

7 Add the stock to the pan, bring to the boil, cover and leave to simmer for 45 minutes or until the pork is tender. Remove the meat from the pan, set aside and keep warm.

8 Using a zester, pare the remaining lemon. Add the rind and sugar to the pan, boil for 3–4 minutes or until reduced and syrupy. Pour over the pork fillets and serve at once.

Pork Chops with Fennel & Juniper

Serves 4

INGREDIENTS

¹⁄₂ fennel bulb	finely grated rind and juice of	4 pork chops, each about
1 tbsp juniper berries, lightly crushed	1 orange	150 g/5¹⁄₂ oz
about 2 tbsp olive oil		fresh bread and a crisp salad, to serve

1 Using a sharp knife, finely chop the fennel bulb, discarding the green parts.

2 Grind the juniper berries in a mortar and pestle. Mix the crushed juniper berries with the fennel flesh, olive oil and orange rind.

3 Using a sharp knife, score a few cuts all over each chop.

4 Place the pork chops in a roasting tin (pan) or an ovenproof dish. Spoon the fennel and juniper mixture over the pork chops.

5 Carefully pour the orange juice over the top of each pork chop, cover and leave to marinate in the refrigerator for about 2 hours.

6 Cook the pork chops, under a preheated grill (broiler), for 10–15 minutes, depending on the thickness of the meat, until the meat is tender and cooked through, turning occasionally.

7 Transfer the pork chops to serving plates and serve with a crisp, fresh salad and plenty of fresh bread to mop up the cooking juices.

COOK'S TIP

Juniper berries are most commonly associated with gin, but they are often added to meat dishes in Italy for a delicate citrus flavour. They can be bought dried from most health food shops and some larger supermarkets.

Pork Cooked in Milk

Serves 4

INGREDIENTS

800 g/1 lb 12 oz leg of pork, boned	2 garlic cloves, chopped	2 fresh bay leaves
1 tbsp oil	75 g/2¾ oz pancetta, diced	2 tbsp marjoram
25 g/1 oz/2 tbsp butter	1.2 litres/2 pints/5 cups milk	2 tbsp thyme
1 onion, chopped	1 tbsp green peppercorns, crushed	

1 Using a sharp knife, remove the fat from the pork. Shape the meat into a neat form, tying it in place with a length of string.

2 Heat the oil and butter in a large saucepan. Add the onion, garlic and pancetta to the pan and cook for 2–3 minutes.

3 Add the pork to the pan and cook, turning occasionally, until it is browned all over.

4 Pour over the milk, add the peppercorns, bay leaves, marjoram and thyme and cook over a low heat for 1¼–1½ hours or until tender. Watch the liquid carefully for the last 15 minutes of the cooking time because it tends to reduce very quickly and will then burn. If the liquid reduces and the pork is still not tender, add another 100 ml/3½ fl oz milk and continue cooking. Reserve the cooking liquid.

5 Remove the pork from the saucepan. Using a sharp knife, cut the meat into slices. Transfer the pork slices to serving plates and serve immediately with the sauce (see Cook's Tip, right).

COOK'S TIP

As the milk reduces naturally in this dish, it forms a thick and creamy sauce, which curdles slightly but tastes delicious.

Neapolitan Pork Steaks

Serves 4

INGREDIENTS

2 tbsp olive oil
1 garlic clove, chopped
1 large onion, sliced
1 x 400 g/14 oz can tomatoes

2 tsp yeast extract
4 pork loin steaks, each about
125 g/4½ oz
75 g/2¾ oz black olives, pitted

2 tbsp fresh basil, shredded
freshly grated Parmesan cheese,
to serve

1 Heat the oil in a large frying pan (skillet). Add the onions and garlic and cook, stirring, for 3–4 minutes or until they just begin to soften.

2 Add the tomatoes and yeast extract to the frying pan (skillet) and leave to simmer for about 5 minutes or until the sauce starts to thicken.

3 Cook the pork steaks, under a preheated grill (broiler), for 5 minutes on both sides, until the the meat is golden and cooked through. Set the pork steaks aside and keep warm.

4 Add the olives and fresh shredded basil to the sauce in the frying pan (skillet) and stir quickly to combine.

5 Transfer the steaks to warm serving plates. Top the steaks with the sauce, sprinkle with freshly grated Parmesan cheese and serve immediately.

COOK'S TIP

Parmesan is a mature and exceptionally hard cheese produced in Italy. You only need to add a little as it has a very strong flavour.

COOK'S TIP

There are many types of canned tomato available – for example plum tomatoes, or tomatoes chopped in water, or chopped sieved tomatoes (passata). The chopped variety are often canned with added flavours such as garlic, basil, onion, chilli and mixed herbs, and are a good storecupboard standby.

Roman Pan-Fried Lamb

Serves 4

INGREDIENTS

1 tbsp oil
15 g/$^1/_2$ oz/1 tbsp butter
600 g/1 lb 5 oz lamb (shoulder or
   leg), cut in 2.5 cm/1 inch chunks
4 garlic cloves, peeled

3 sprigs thyme, stalks removed
6 canned anchovy fillets
150 ml/5 fl oz/$^2/_3$ cup red wine
150 ml/5 fl oz/$^2/_3$ cup lamb or
   vegetable stock

1 tsp sugar
50 g/1$^3/_4$ oz black olives, pitted and
   halved
2 tbsp chopped parsley, to garnish
mashed potato, to serve

1 Heat the oil and butter in a large frying pan (skillet). Add the lamb and cook for 4–5 minutes, stirring, until the meat is browned all over.

2 Using a pestle and mortar, grind together the garlic, thyme and anchovies to make a smooth paste.

3 Add the wine and lamb or vegetable stock to the frying pan (skillet). Stir in the garlic and anchovy paste together with the sugar.

4 Bring the mixture to the boil, reduce the heat, cover and leave to simmer for 30–40 minutes or until the lamb is tender. For the last 10 minutes of the cooking time, remove the lid in order to allow the sauce to reduce slightly.

5 Stir the olives into the sauce and mix to combine.

6 Transfer the lamb and the sauce to a serving bowl and garnish with freshly chopped parsley. Serve with creamy mashed potatoes.

COOK'S TIP

Rome is the capital of both the region of Lazio and Italy and thus has become a focal point for specialities from all over Italy. Food from this region tends to be fairly simple and quick to prepare, all with plenty of herbs and seasonings giving really robust flavours.

Lamb Noisettes with Bay & Lemon

Serves 4

INGREDIENTS

4 lamb chops	150 ml/5 fl oz/²/₃ cup white wine	2 bay leaves
1 tbsp oil	150 ml/5 fl oz/²/₃ cup lamb or	pared rind of 1 lemon
15 g/¹/₂ oz/1 tbsp butter	vegetable stock	salt and pepper

1 Using a sharp knife, carefully remove the bone from each lamb chop, keeping the meat intact. Alternatively, ask the butcher to prepare the lamb noisettes for you.

2 Shape the meat into rounds and secure with a length of string.

3 In a large frying pan (skillet), heat together the oil and butter until the mixture starts to froth. Add the lamb noisettes to the frying pan (skillet) and cook for 2–3 minutes on each side or until browned all over.

4 Remove the frying pan (skillet) fom the heat, drain off all of the fat and discard.

5 Return the frying pan (skillet) to the heat. Add the wine, stock, bay leaves and lemon rind to the frying pan (skillet) and cook for 20–25 minutes or until the lamb is tender.

6 Season the lamb noisettes and sauce to taste with a little salt and pepper.

7 Transfer to serving plates. Remove the string from each noisette and serve with the sauce.

COOK'S TIP

Your local butcher will offer you good advice on how to prepare the lamb noisettes, if you are wary of preparing them yourself.

Chicken Marengo

Serves 4

INGREDIENTS

1 tbsp olive oil	8 slices white bread	40 g/1³/₄ oz black olives, chopped
8 chicken pieces	40 g/1¹/₂ oz butter, melted	1 tsp sugar
300 g/10¹/₂ oz passata (tomato paste)	2 garlic cloves, crushed	fresh basil, to garnish
200 ml/7 fl oz/⁷/₈ cup white wine	100 g/3¹/₂ oz mixed mushrooms	
2 tsp dried mixed herbs	(such as button, oyster and ceps)	

1 Using a sharp knife, remove the bone from each of the chicken pieces.

2 Heat the oil in a large frying pan (skillet). Add the chicken pieces and cook for 4–5 minutes, turning occassionally, or until browned all over.

3 Add the passata (tomato paste), wine and mixed herbs to the frying pan (skillet). Bring to the boil and then leave to simmer for 30 minutes or until the chicken is tender and the juices run clear when a skewer is inserted into the thickest part of the meat.

4 Mix the melted butter and crushed garlic together. Lightly toast the slices of bread and brush with the garlic butter.

5 Add the remaining oil to a separate frying pan (skillet) and cook the mushrooms for 2–3 minutes or until just brown.

6 Add the olives and sugar to the chicken mixture and warm through.

7 Transfer the chicken and sauce to serving plates. Serve with the bruschetta (fried bread) and fried mushrooms.

COOK'S TIP

If you have time, marinate the chicken pieces in the wine and herbs and leave in the refrigerator for 2 hours. This will make the chicken more tender and accentuate the wine flavour of the sauce.

Parma-Wrapped Chicken

Serves 4

INGREDIENTS

4 chicken breasts, skin removed	8 slices Parma ham (prosciutto)	150 ml/5 fl oz/²/₃ cup chicken stock
100 g/3¹/₂ oz full fat soft cheese, flavoured with herbs and garlic	150 ml/5 fl oz/²/₃ cup red wine	1 tbsp brown sugar

1 Using a sharp knife, make a horizontal slit along the length of each chicken breast to form a pocket.

2 Beat the cheese with a wooden spoon to soften it. Spoon the cheese into the pocket of the chicken breasts.

3 Wrap 2 slices of Parma ham (prosciutto) around each chicken breast and secure in place with a length of string.

4 Pour the wine and chicken stock into a large frying pan (skillet) and bring to the boil.

When the mixture is just starting to boil, add the sugar and stir to dissolve.

5 Add the chicken breasts to the mixture in the frying pan (skillet). Leave to simmer for 12–15 minutes or the chicken is tender and the juices run clear when a skewer is inserted into the thickest part of the meat.

6 Remove the chicken from the pan, set aside and keep warm.

7 Reheat the sauce and boil until reduced and thickened. Remove the string from the chicken

and cut into slices. Pour the sauce over the chicken to serve.

VARIATION

Try adding 2 finely chopped sun-dried tomatoes to the soft cheese in step 2, if you prefer.

Chicken with Balsamic Vinegar

Serves 4

INGREDIENTS

4 chicken thighs, boned	1 tbsp oil	2 tbsp fresh thyme
2 garlic cloves, crushed	15 g/¹/₂ oz/1 tbsp butter	salt and pepper
200 ml/7 fl oz/³/₄ cup red wine	4 shallots	cooked polenta or rice, to serve
3 tbsp white wine vinegar	3 tbsp balsamic vinegar	

1 Using a sharp knife, make a few slashes in the skin of the chicken. Brush the chicken with the crushed garlic and place in a non-metallic dish.

2 Pour the wine and white wine vinegar over the chicken and season to taste with salt and pepper. Cover and leave to marinate in the refrigerator overnight.

3 Remove the chicken pieces with a perforated spoon, draining well, and reserve the marinade.

4 Heat the oil and butter in a frying pan (skillet).

Add the shallots and cook for 2–3 minutes or until they begin to soften.

5 Add the chicken pieces to the pan and cook for 3-4 minutes, turning, until browned all over. Reduce the heat and add half of the reserved marinade. Cover and cook for 15–20 minutes, adding more marinade when necessary.

6 Once the chicken is tender, add the balsamic vinegar and thyme and cook for a further 4 minutes.

7 Transfer the chicken and marinade to

serving plates and serve with polenta or rice.

COOK'S TIP

To make the chicken pieces look a little neater, use wooden skewers to hold them together or secure them with a length of string.

Saltimbocca

Serves 4

INGREDIENTS

4 turkey fillets or 4 veal escalopes, about 450 g/1 lb in total	8 sage leaves	200 ml/7 fl oz/^{3}/$_4$ cup white wine
100 g/3^1/$_4$ oz Parma ham (prosciutto)	1 tbsp olive oil	200 ml/7 fl oz/^{3}/$_4$ cup chicken stock
	1 onion, finely chopped	

1 Place the turkey or veal between sheets of greaseproof paper. Pound the meat with a meat mallet or the end of a rolling pin to flatten it slightly. Cut each escalope in half.

2 Trim the Parma ham (prosciutto) to fit each piece of turkey or veal and place over the meat. Lay a sage leaf on top. Roll up the escalopes and secure with a cocktail stick (toothpick).

3 Heat the oil in a frying pan (skillet) and cook the onion for 3–4 minutes. Add the turkey or veal rolls to the pan and cook for 5 minutes until brown all over.

4 Pour the wine and stock into the pan and leave to simmer for 15 minutes if using turkey, and 20 minutes for veal, or until tender. Serve immediately.

COOK'S TIP

If using turkey rather than veal, watch it carefully as turkey tends to turn dry very quickly if overcooked.

VARIATION

Try a similar recipe called Bocconcini, meaning 'little mouthfuls'. Follow the same method as here, but replace the sage leaf with a piece of Gruyère cheese.

Escalopes with Italian Sausage & Capers

Serves 4

INGREDIENTS

1 tbsp olive oil	finely grated rind and juice	4 turkey or veal escalopes, each
6 canned anchovy fillets, drained	of 1 orange	about 125 g/4^{1}/$_{2}$ oz
1 tbsp capers, drained	75 g/2^{3}/$_{4}$ oz Italian sausage, diced	salt and pepper
1 tbsp fresh rosemary, stalks	3 tomatoes, skinned and chopped	crusty bread or cooked polenta,
removed		to serve

1 Heat the oil in a large frying pan (skillet). Add the anchovies, capers, fresh rosemary, orange rind and juice, Italian sausage and tomatoes to the pan and cook for 5–6 minutes, stirring occasionally.

2 Meanwhile, place the turkey or veal escalopes between sheets of greaseproof paper. Pound the meat with a meat mallet or the end of a rolling pin to flatten it.

3 Add the meat to the mixture in the frying pan (skillet). Season to taste with salt and pepper, cover and cook for 3–5 minutes on each side, slightly longer if the meat is thicker.

4 Transfer to serving plates and serve with fresh crusty bread or cooked polenta.

VARIATION

Try using 4-minute steaks, slightly flattened, instead of the turkey or veal. Cook them for 4–5 minutes on top of the sauce in the pan.

COOK'S TIP

Polenta is typical of northern Italian cuisine. It is often fried or toasted and used to mop up the juices of the main course.

Italian Sausage & Bean Casserole

Serves 4

INGREDIENTS

8 Italian sausages	1 green (bell) pepper	2 tbsp sun-dried tomato paste
1 tbsp olive oil	225 g/8 oz fresh tomatoes, skinned	1 x 400 g/14 oz can cannelini beans
1 large onion, chopped	and chopped or 1 x 400 g/	mashed potato or rice, to serve
2 garlic cloves, chopped	14 oz can tomatoes, chopped	

1 Deseed the (bell) pepper and cut it into thin strips.

2 Prick the Italian sausages all over with a fork. Cook them, under a preheated grill (broiler), for 10–12 minutes, turning occasionally, until brown all over. Set aside and keep warm.

3 Heat the oil in a large frying pan (skillet). Add the onion, garlic and (bell) pepper to the frying pan (skillet) and cook for 5 minutes, stirring occasionally, or until softened.

4 Add the tomatoes to the frying pan (skillet) and leave the mixture to simmer for about 5 minutes, stirring occasionally, or until slightly reduced and thickened.

5 Stir the sun-dried tomato paste, cannelini beans and Italian sausages into the mixture in the frying pan (skillet). Cook for 4–5 minutes or until the mixture is piping hot. Add 4–5 tablespoons of water, if the mixture becomes too dry during cooking.

6 Transfer the Italian sausage and bean casserole to serving plates and serve with mashed potato or cooked rice.

COOK'S TIP

Italian sausages are coarse in texture and have quite a strong flavour. They can be found in specialist sausage shops, Italian delicatessens and some larger supermarkets. They are replaceable in this recipe only by game sausages.

Grilled (Broiled) Chicken with Pesto Toasts

Serves 4

INGREDIENTS

8 part-boned chicken thighs
olive oil, for brushing
400 ml/14 fl oz/1²/₃ cups passata
 (sieved tomatoes)

120 ml/4 fl oz/¹/₂ cup green or red
 pesto sauce
12 slices French bread
90 g/3 oz/1 cup freshly grated
 Parmesan cheese

60 g/2 oz/¹/₂ cup pine nuts or flaked
 (slivered) almonds
salad leaves, to serve

1 Arrange the chicken in a single layer in a wide flameproof dish and brush lightly with oil. Place under a preheated grill (broiler) for about 15 minutes, turning occasionally, until golden brown.

2 Pierce the chicken with a skewer to ensure that there is no trace of pink in the juices.

3 Pour off any excess fat. Warm the passata (sieved tomatoes) and half the pesto sauce in a small pan and pour over the chicken. Grill (broil) for a few more minutes, turning until coated.

4 Meanwhile, spread the remaining pesto on to the slices of bread. Arrange the bread over the chicken and sprinkle with the Parmesan cheese. Scatter the pine nuts over the cheese. Grill (broil) for 2–3 minutes, or until browned and bubbling. Serve with a selection of salad leaves.

COOK'S TIP

Although leaving the skin on the chicken means that it will have a higher fat content, many people like the rich taste and crispy skin especially when it is blackened by the barbecue (grill). The skin also keeps in the cooking juices.

Boned Chicken with Parmesan

Serves 6

INGREDIENTS

1 chicken, weighing about 2.25 kg/5 lb

8 slices mortadella or salami

125 g/4¹/₂ oz/2 cups fresh white or
    brown breadcrumbs

125 g/4¹/₂ oz/1 cup freshly grated
    Parmesan cheese

2 garlic cloves, crushed

6 tbsp chopped fresh basil or parsley

1 egg, beaten

pepper

fresh spring vegetables, to serve

---

1 Bone the chicken, keeping the skin intact. Dislocate each leg by breaking it at the thigh joint. Cut down each side of the backbone, taking care not to pierce the breast skin.

2 Pull the backbone clear of the flesh and discard. Remove the ribs, severing any attached flesh with a sharp knife.

3 Scrape the flesh from each leg and cut away the bone at the joint with a knife or shears.

4 Use the bones for stock. Lay out the boned chicken on a board, skin side down. Arrange the mortadella slices over the chicken, overlapping slightly.

5 Put the breadcrumbs, Parmesan, garlic and basil or parsley in a bowl. Season well with pepper and mix. Stir in the beaten egg to bind the mixture together. Pile the mixture down the middle of the boned chicken, roll the meat around it and tie securely with fine cotton string.

6 Place in a roasting dish and brush lightly with olive oil. Roast in a preheated oven, 200°C/400°F/Gas Mark 6, for 1¹/₂ hours or until the juices run clear when pierced.

7 Serve hot or cold, in slices, with fresh spring vegetables.

VARIATION

Replace the mortadella with rashers of streaky bacon, if preferred.

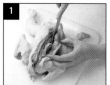

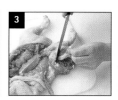

Italian Chicken Spirals

Serves 4

INGREDIENTS

4 skinless, boneless, chicken breasts
25 g/1 oz/1 cup fresh basil leaves
15 g/$^1/_2$ oz/2 tbsp hazelnuts
1 garlic clove, crushed

250 g/9 oz/2 cups wholemeal
(whole wheat) pasta spirals
2 sun-dried tomatoes or fresh
tomatoes
1 tbsp lemon juice

1 tbsp olive oil
1 tbsp capers
60 g/2 oz/$^1/_2$ cup black olives
salt and pepper

1 Beat the chicken breasts with a rolling pin to flatten evenly.

2 Place the basil and hazelnuts in a food processor and process until finely chopped. Mix with the garlic, salt and pepper.

3 Spread the basil mixture over the chicken breasts and roll up from one short end to enclose the filling. Wrap the chicken roll tightly in foil so that they hold their shape, then seal the ends well.

4 Bring a large pan of lightly salted water to the boil and cook the pasta until tender, but still firm to the bite.

5 Place the chicken parcels in a steamer basket or colander set over the pan, cover tightly, and steam for 10 minutes. Meanwhile, dice the tomatoes.

6 Drain the pasta and return to the pan with the lemon juice, olive oil, tomatoes, capers and olives. Heat through.

7 Pierce the chicken with a skewer to make sure that the juices run clear and not pink, then slice the chicken, arrange over the pasta and serve.

VARIATION

Sun-dried tomatoes have a wonderful, rich flavour, but if you can't find them use fresh tomatoes.

Parma-Wrapped Chicken Cushions

Serves 4

INGREDIENTS

125 g/4¹/₂ oz/¹/₂ cup frozen spinach,
    defrosted
125 g/4¹/₂ oz/¹/₂ cup ricotta cheese
pinch grated nutmeg
4 skinless, boneless chicken breasts,
    each weighing 175 g/6 oz

4 Parma ham (prosciutto) slices
25 g/1 oz/2 tbsp butter
1 tbsp olive oil
12 small onions or shallots
125 g/4¹/₂ oz/1¹/₂ cups button
    mushrooms, sliced

1 tbsp plain (all-purpose) flour
150 ml/¹/₄ pint/²/₃ cup dry white or
    red wine
300 ml/¹/₂ pint/1¹/₄ cups chicken stock
salt and pepper

1 Put the spinach into a sieve (strainer) and press out the water with a spoon. Mix with the ricotta and nutmeg and season with salt and pepper to taste.

2 Using a sharp knife, slit each chicken breast through the side and enlarge each cut to form a pocket. Fill with the spinach mixture, reshape the chicken breasts, wrap each breast tightly in a slice of ham and secure with cocktail sticks. Cover and chill in the refrigerator.

3 Heat the butter and oil in a frying pan (skillet) and brown the chicken breasts for 2 minutes on each side. Transfer the chicken to a large, shallow ovenproof dish and keep warm until required.

4 Fry the onions and mushrooms for 2–3 minutes until lightly browned. Stir in the plain (all-purpose) flour then gradually add the wine and stock. Bring to the boil, stirring constantly. Season and spoon the mixture around the chicken.

5 Cook the chicken uncovered in a preheated oven, 200°C/400°F/Gas Mark 6, for 20 minutes. Turn the breasts over and cook for a further 10 minutes. Remove the cocktail sticks and serve with the sauce, together with carrot purée and green beans, if wished.

Chicken Pepperonata

Serves 4

INGREDIENTS

8 skinless chicken thighs
2 tbsp wholemeal. (whole wheat) flour
2 tbsp olive oil
1 small onion, sliced thinly

1 garlic clove, crushed
1 each large red, yellow and green (bell) peppers, sliced thinly
400 g/14 oz can chopped tomatoes
1 tbsp chopped oregano

salt and pepper
fresh oregano, to garnish
crusty wholemeal (whole wheat) bread, to serve

1 Remove the skin from the chicken thighs and toss the thighs in the flour.

2 Heat the oil in a wide pan and fry the chicken quickly until sealed and lightly browned, then remove from the pan. Add the onion to the pan and gently fry until soft. Add the garlic, (bell) peppers, tomatoes and oregano, then bring to the boil, stirring.

3 Arrange the chicken over the vegetables, season well with salt and pepper, then cover the pan tightly and simmer for 20–25 minutes or until the chicken is completely cooked and tender.

4 Season to taste, garnish with oregano and serve with crusty wholemeal (whole wheat) bread.

COOK'S TIP

If you do not have fresh oregano, use canned tomatoes with herbs already added.

COOK'S TIP

For extra flavour, halve the (bell) peppers and grill (broil) under a preheated grill (broiler) until the skins are charred. Leave to cool then remove the skins and seeds. Slice the (bell) peppers thinly and use in the recipe.

Fish & Seafood

Fish markets in Italy are fascinating, with a huge
variety of fish on display, but as most of the catch
comes from the Mediterranean, it is not always
easy to find an equivalent elsewhere.

Pasta is a natural partner for fish and seafood.
Both are cooked quickly to preserve their flavour
and texture, they are packed full of nutritional
goodness and the varieties available are almost
infinite. The superb recipes in this chapter
demonstrate the full range of these qualities. Try
a quick, easy and satisfying recipe, or one of the
more unusual and sophisticated dishes. There are
meals to suit all tastes – freshwater and sea fish,
shellfish and other seafood – and to suit all pockets.
All are easy to make; the only problem is
choosing which one to cook next.

Cannelloni Filetti di Sogliola

Serves 6

INGREDIENTS

12 small fillets of sole
(about 115 g/4 oz each)
150 ml/¼ pint/⅝ cup red wine
90 g/3 oz/6 tbsp butter
115 g/4 oz/3⅛ cups sliced
button mushrooms
4 shallots, finely chopped

115 g/4 oz tomatoes, chopped
2 tbsp tomato purée (paste)
60 g/2 oz/½ cup plain (all
purpose) flour, sifted
150 ml/¼ pint/⅝ cup of
warm milk
2 tbsp double (heavy) cream

6 dried cannelloni tubes
175 g/6 oz cooked, peeled
prawns (shrimp), preferably
freshwater
salt and pepper
1 fresh dill sprig, to garnish

1 Brush the fillets with a little wine. Season and roll up, skin side inwards. Secure with a skewer or cocktail stick (toothpick).

2 Arrange the fish rolls in a single layer in a large frying pan (skillet), add the remaining red wine and poach for 4 minutes. Remove from the pan and reserve the cooking liquid.

3 Melt the butter in another pan. Fry the mushrooms and shallots

for 2 minutes, then add the tomatoes and tomato purée (paste). Season the flour and stir it into the pan. Stir in the reserved cooking liquid and half the milk. Cook over a low heat, stirring, for 4 minutes. Remove from the heat and stir in the cream.

4 Bring a pan of salted water to the boil. Add the cannelloni and cook for 8 minutes, until tender but still firm to the bite. Drain and set aside to cool.

5 Remove the skewers or cocktail sticks from the fish rolls. Put 2 sole fillets into each cannelloni tube with 3–4 prawns (shrimp) and a little red wine sauce. Arrange the cannelloni in an ovenproof dish, pour over the sauce and bake in a preheated oven at 200°C/400°F/Gas 6 for 20 minutes.

6 Serve the cannelloni with the red wine sauce, garnished with a sprig of dill.

Sea Bass with Olive Sauce on a Bed of Macaroni

Serves 4

INGREDIENTS

450 g/1 lb dried macaroni
1 tbsp olive oil
8 x 115 g/4 oz sea bass
    medallions

TO GARNISH:
lemon slices
shredded leek
shredded carrot

SAUCE:
25 g/1 oz/2 tbsp butter
4 shallots, chopped
2 tbsp capers
175 g/6 oz/1$^1/_2$ cups stoned
    (pitted) green olives, chopped
4 tbsp balsamic vinegar

300 ml/$^1/_2$ pint/1$^1/_4$ cups fish stock
300 ml/$^1/_2$ pint/1$^1/_4$ cups double
    (heavy) cream
juice of 1 lemon
salt and pepper

1 For the sauce, melt the butter in a frying pan (skillet) and cook the shallots for 4 minutes. Add the capers and olives and cook for 3 minutes.

2 Stir in the balsamic vinegar and fish stock, bring to the boil and reduce by half. Stir in the cream and reduce again by half. Season to taste and stir in the lemon juice. Remove the pan from the heat, set aside and keep warm.

3 Bring a large pan of lightly salted water to the boil. Add the pasta and olive oil and cook for about 12 minutes, until tender but still firm to the bite.

4 Lightly grill (broil) the sea bass medallions for 3–4 minutes on each side, until cooked through, but still moist and delicate.

5 Drain the pasta and transfer to individual serving dishes. Top the pasta with the fish medallions and pour over the olive sauce. Garnish with lemon slices, shredded leek and shredded carrot and serve.

Spaghetti alla Bucaniera

Serves 4

INGREDIENTS

90 g/3 oz/³/₄ cup plain
(all purpose) flour

450 g/1 lb brill or sole fillets,
skinned and chopped

450 g/1 lb hake fillets, skinned
and chopped

90 g/3 oz/6 tbsp butter

4 shallots, finely chopped

2 garlic cloves, crushed

1 carrot, diced

1 leek, finely chopped

300 ml/¹/₂ pint/1¹/₄ cups dry
(hard) cider

300 ml/¹/₂ pint/1¹/₄ cups medium
sweet cider

1 tbsp tarragon vinegar

2 tsp anchovy essence (extract)

450 g/1 lb dried spaghetti

1 tbsp olive oil

salt and pepper

chopped fresh parsley, to garnish

crusty brown bread, to serve

1 Season the flour with salt and pepper. Sprinkle 25 g/1 oz/¹/₄ cup of the seasoned flour on to a shallow plate. Press the fish pieces into the seasoned flour to coat thoroughly.

2 Melt the butter in a flameproof casserole. Add the fish fillets, shallots, garlic, carrot and leek and cook over a low heat, stirring frequently, for about 10 minutes.

3 Sprinkle over the remaining seasoned flour and cook, stirring constantly, for 2 minutes. Gradually stir in the cider, tarragon vinegar and anchovy essence (extract). Bring to the boil and simmer over a low heat for 35 minutes. Alternatively, bake in a preheated oven at 180°C/350°F/Gas 4 for 30 minutes.

4 About 15 minutes before the end of the

cooking time, bring a pan of lightly salted water to the boil. Add the spaghetti and olive oil and cook for 12 minutes, or until tender but still firm to the bite. Drain the pasta and transfer to a serving dish.

5 Arrange the fish on top of the spaghetti and pour over the sauce. Garnish with chopped parsley and serve immediately with warm, crusty brown bread.

Steamed Pasta Pudding

Serves 4

INGREDIENTS

115 g/4 oz/1 cup dried short-cut
    macaroni or other short
    pasta
1 tbsp olive oil
15 g/¹/₂ oz/1 tbsp butter, plus
    extra for greasing
450 g/1 lb white fish fillets, such
    as cod or haddock

2-3 fresh parsley sprigs
6 black peppercorns
125 ml/4 fl oz/¹/₂ cup double
    (heavy) cream
2 eggs, separated
2 tbsp chopped fresh dill or
    parsley
pinch of freshly grated nutmeg

60 g/2 oz/²/₃ cup freshly grated
    Parmesan cheese
salt and pepper
fresh dill or parsley sprigs, to
    garnish
tomato sauce, to serve

1 Bring a pan of salted water to the boil. Add the pasta and olive oil and cook until tender. Drain, return to the pan, add the butter, cover and keep warm.

2 Place the fish, parsley, peppercorns and enough water to cover in a frying pan (skillet). Bring to the boil, cover and simmer for 10 minutes. Remove the fish and reserve the cooking liquid.

3 Skin the fish and cut into bite-size pieces. Combine the cream, egg yolks, chopped dill or parsley, nutmeg and cheese and mix with the pasta in a bowl. Carefully spoon in the fish. Add enough of the reserved cooking liquid to make a moist, but firm mixture. Whisk the egg whites until stiff, then fold them into the mixture.

4 Grease a heatproof bowl and spoon the

fish mixture to within 4 cm/1½ inches of the rim. Cover with greased greaseproof (baking) paper and foil and tie securely with string.

5 Stand the bowl on a trivet in a saucepan. Add boiling water to reach halfway up the sides. Cover and steam for 1½ hours. Invert the pudding on to a serving plate. Garnish and serve with the tomato sauce.

Red Mullet Fillets with Orecchiette, Amaretto & Orange Sauce

Serves 4

INGREDIENTS

90 g/3 oz/3³/₄ cup plain
  (all purpose) flour
8 red mullet fillets
25 g/1 oz/2 tbsp butter
150 ml/¹/₄ pint/⁵/₈ cup fish stock
1 tbsp crushed almonds
1 tsp pink peppercorns
1 orange, peeled and cut

into segments
1 tbsp orange liqueur
grated rind of 1 orange
450 g/1 lb dried orecchiette
1 tbsp olive oil
150 ml/¹/₄ pint/⁵/₈ cup double
  (heavy) cream
4 tbsp amaretto

salt and pepper

TO GARNISH:
2 tbsp snipped fresh chives
1 tbsp toasted almonds

1 Season the flour and sprinkle into a shallow bowl. Press the fish fillets into the flour to coat. Melt the butter in a frying pan (skillet) and fry the fish over a low heat for 3 minutes, until browned.

2 Add the fish stock to the pan and cook for 4 minutes. Carefully remove the fish, cover with foil and keep warm.

3 Add the almonds, pink peppercorns, half the orange, the orange liqueur and orange rind to the pan. Simmer until the liquid has reduced by half.

4 Meanwhile, bring a large saucepan of lightly salted water to the boil. Add the orecchiette and olive oil and cook for 15 minutes, until tender but still firm to the bite.

5 Season the sauce and stir in the cream and amaretto. Cook for 2 minutes. Coat the fish with the sauce in the pan.

6 Drain the pasta and transfer to a serving dish. Top with the fish fillets and their sauce. Garnish with the remaining orange segments, the chives and toasted almonds. Serve.

Vermicelli with Fillets of Red Mullet

Serves 4

INGREDIENTS

1 kg/2¼ lb red mullet fillets
300 ml/½ pint/1¼ cups dry white wine
4 shallots, finely chopped
1 garlic clove, crushed
3 tbsp mixed fresh herbs
finely grated rind and juice of 1 lemon

pinch of freshly grated nutmeg
3 anchovy fillets, roughly chopped
2 tbsp double (heavy) cream
1 tsp cornflour (cornstarch)
450 g/1 lb dried vermicelli
1 tbsp olive oil
salt and pepper

TO GARNISH:
1 fresh mint sprig
lemon slices
lemon rind

1 Put the red mullet fillets in a large casserole. Pour over the wine and add the shallots, garlic, herbs, lemon rind and juice, nutmeg and anchovies. Season with salt and pepper to taste. Cover and bake in a preheated oven at 180°C/350°F/Gas 4 for 35 minutes.

2 Carefully transfer the mullet to a warm dish. Set aside and keep warm.

3 Pour the cooking liquid into a pan and bring to the boil. Simmer for 25 minutes, until reduced by half. Mix the cream and cornflour (cornstarch) and stir into the sauce to thicken.

4 Bring a pan of salted water to the boil. Add the vermicelli and olive oil and cook until tender, but still firm to the bite. Drain the pasta and transfer to a warm serving dish.

5 Arrange the red mullet fillets on top of the vermicelli and pour over the sauce. Garnish with a fresh mint sprig, slices of lemon and strips of lemon rind. Serve immediately.

COOK'S TIP

The best red mullet is sometimes called golden mullet, although it is bright red in colour.

Spaghetti al Tonno

Serves 4

INGREDIENTS

200 g/7 oz can tuna, drained
60 g/2 oz can anchovies, drained
250 ml/9 fl oz/1⅛ cups
olive oil
60 g/2 oz/1 cup roughly chopped

flat leaf parsley, plus extra to
garnish
150 ml/¼ pint/⅝ cup crème
fraîche
450 g/1 lb dried spaghetti

25 g/1 oz/2 tbsp butter
salt and pepper
black olives, to garnish
crusty bread, to serve

1 Remove any bones
from the tuna. Put the
tuna into a food processor
or blender, together with
the anchovies, 225 ml/
8 fl oz/1 cup of the olive oil
and the flat leaf parsley.
Process until smooth.

2 Spoon the crème
fraîche into the food
processor or blender and
process again for a few
seconds to blend
thoroughly. Season to taste.

3 Bring a large pan of
lightly salted water to
the boil. Add the spaghetti

and the remaining olive oil
and cook until tender, but
still firm to the bite.

4 Drain the spaghetti,
return to the pan and
place over a medium heat.
Add the butter and toss
well to coat. Spoon in the
sauce and quickly toss into
the spaghetti, using 2 forks.

5 Remove the pan from
the heat and divide the
spaghetti between 4 warm
individual serving plates.
Garnish with olives and
parsley and serve with
warm, crusty bread.

VARIATION

*If liked, you could add
1–2 garlic cloves to the
sauce, substitute 25 g/
1 oz/½ cup chopped fresh
basil for half the parsley and
garnish with capers instead
of black olives.*

Casserole of Fusilli & Smoked Haddock with Egg Sauce

Serves 4

INGREDIENTS

25 g/1 oz/2 tbsp butter, plus extra for greasing	pinch of freshly grated nutmeg	1 tbsp lemon juice
450 g/1 lb smoked haddock fillets, cut into 4 slices	3 tbsp double (heavy) cream	salt and pepper
600 ml/1 pint/2½ cups milk	1 tbsp chopped fresh parsley, plus extra to garnish	boiled new potatoes and beetroot (beet), to serve
25 g/1 oz/¼ cup plain (all purpose) flour	2 eggs, hard boiled (hard cooked) and mashed	
	450 g/1 lb/4 cups dried fusilli	

1 Grease a casserole with butter. Put the haddock in the casserole and pour over the milk. Bake in a preheated oven at 200°C/400°G/Gas 6 for 15 minutes. Carefully pour the cooking liquid into a jug (pitcher) without breaking up the fish.

2 Melt the butter in a saucepan and stir in the flour. Gradually whisk in the reserved cooking liquid. Season with salt, pepper and nutmeg. Stir in the cream, parsley and mashed eggs and cook for 2 minutes.

3 Meanwhile, bring a large saucepan of salted water to the boil. Add the fusilli and lemon juice and cook until tender, but still firm to the bite.

4 Drain the pasta and tip it over the fish. Top with the sauce and return to the oven for 10 minutes.

5 Garnish and serve the casserole with boiled new potatoes and beetroot (beet).

VARIATION

You can use any type of dried pasta for this casserole. Try penne, conchiglie or rigatoni.

Ravioli of Lemon Sole & Haddock

Serves 4

INGREDIENTS

450 g/1 lb lemon sole fillets,
    skinned
450 g/1 lb haddock fillets,
    skinned
3 eggs beaten
450 g/1 lb cooked potato
    gnocchi

175 g/6 oz/3 cups fresh
    breadcrumbs
50 ml/2 fl oz/¼ cup double
    (heavy) cream
450 g/1 lb Basic Pasta Dough

300 ml/½ pint/1¼ cups Italian
    Red Wine Sauce
60 g/2 oz/⅔ cup freshly grated
    Parmesan cheese
salt and pepper

1 Flake the fish fillets in a large mixing bowl.

2 Mix the eggs, cooked potato gnocchi, breadcrumbs and cream in a bowl until combined. Add the fish and season the mixture to taste.

3 Roll out the pasta dough on to a lightly floured surface and cut out 7.5 cm/3 inch rounds.

4 Place a spoonful of the fish stuffing on each round. Dampen the edges slightly and fold the pasta rounds over, pressing together to seal.

5 Bring a large saucepan of lightly salted water to the boil. Add the ravioli and cook for 15 minutes.

6 Drain the ravioli, using a slotted spoon, and transfer to a large serving dish. Pour over the Italian Red Wine Sauce, sprinkle over the Parmesan cheese and serve immediately.

COOK'S TIP

For square ravioli, divide the dough into two. Wrap half in cling film and thinly roll out the other half. Cover with a clean, damp tea towel while rolling the remaining dough. Spoon the filling at regular intervals and brush the gaps with water or beaten egg. Cover with the second sheet of dough and press firmly between the filling to seal and expel any air. Cut out the shapes with a knife.

Poached Salmon Steaks with Penne

Serves 4

INGREDIENTS
---

4 x 275 g/10 oz fresh salmon steaks
60 g/2 oz/4 tbsp butter
175 ml/6 fl oz/³/₄ cup dry white
    wine
sea salt
8 peppercorns
fresh dill sprig
fresh tarragon sprig
1 lemon, sliced

450 g/1 lb dried penne
2 tbsp olive oil
lemon slices and fresh
    watercress, to garnish

LEMON & WATERCRESS SAUCE:
25 g/1 oz/2 tbsp butter
25 g/1 oz/¹/₄ cup plain (all
    purpose) flour

150 ml/¹/₄ pint/⁵/₈ cup warm milk
juice and finely grated rind of
    2 lemons
60 g/2 oz watercress, chopped
salt and pepper

1 Put the salmon in a large, non-stick pan. Add the butter, wine, a pinch of sea salt, the peppercorns, dill, tarragon and lemon. Cover, bring to the boil, and simmer for 10 minutes.

2 Using a slotted spoon, carefully remove the salmon. Strain and reserve the cooking liquid. Remove and discard the salmon skin and centre

bones. Place on a warm dish, cover and keep warm.

3 Bring a pan of salted water to the boil. Add the penne and 1 tbsp of oil and cook for 12 minutes. Drain and sprinkle over the remaining oil. Place on a serving dish, top with the salmon and keep warm.

4 To make the sauce, melt the butter and stir in the flour for 2 minutes.

Stir in the milk and about 7 tbsp of the reserved cooking liquid. Add the lemon juice and rind and cook, stirring, for a further 10 minutes.

5 Stir in the watercress and seasoning.

6 Pour the sauce over the salmon and penne, garnish with slices of lemon and fresh watercress and serve immediately.

Spaghetti with Smoked Salmon

Serves 4

INGREDIENTS

450 g/1 lb dried buckwheat
  spaghetti
2 tbsp olive oil
90 g/3 oz/¹/₂ cup crumbled
  feta cheese
salt

fresh coriander (cilantro) or
  parsley leaves, to garnish
SAUCE:
300 ml/¹/₂ pint/1¹/₄ cups double
  (heavy) cream
150 ml/¹/₄ pint/⁵/₈ cup whisky or
  brandy

125 g/4¹/₂ oz smoked salmon
pinch of cayenne pepper
black pepper
2 tbsp chopped fresh coriander
  (cilantro) or parsley

1 Bring a large pan of lightly salted water to the boil. Add the spaghetti and 1 tbsp of the olive oil and cook until tender, but still firm to the bite. Drain and return to the pan with the remaining olive oil. Cover, set aside and keep warm.

2 Pour the cream into a small saucepan and bring to simmering point, but do not let it boil. Pour the whisky or brandy into another small saucepan and bring to simmering point, but do not allow it to boil. Remove both pans from the heat and mix together the cream and whisky or brandy.

3 Cut the smoked salmon into thin strips and add to the cream mixture. Season with cayenne and black pepper. Just before serving, stir in the fresh coriander (cilantro) or parsley.

4 Transfer the spaghetti to a warm serving dish, pour over the sauce and toss thoroughly with 2 large forks. Scatter over the crumbled feta cheese, garnish with the coriander (cilantro) or parsley leaves and serve immediately.

COOK'S TIP

Serve this rich and luxurious dish with a green salad tossed in a lemony dressing.

Trout with Pasta colle Acciughe & Smoked Bacon

Serves 4

INGREDIENTS

4 x 275 g/9¹/₂ oz trout, gutted
and cleaned
12 anchovies in oil, drained
and chopped
2 apples, peeled, cored and sliced
4 fresh mint sprigs

juice of 1 lemon
12 slices rindless, smoked,
fatty bacon
butter, for greasing
450 g/1 lb dried tagliatelle
1 tbsp olive oil
salt and pepper

TO GARNISH:
2 apples, cored and sliced
4 fresh mint sprigs

1 Open up the cavities of each trout and wash with warm salt water.

2 Season each cavity with salt and black pepper. Divide the anchovies, sliced apples and mint sprigs between each of the cavities. Sprinkle the lemon juice into each cavity.

3 Carefully cover the whole of each trout, except the head and tail, with three slices of smoked bacon in a spiral.

4 Arrange the trout on a deep, greased baking (cookie) sheet with the loose ends of bacon tucked underneath. Season with black pepper and bake in a preheated oven at 200°C/400°F/Gas 6 for about 20 minutes, turning the trout over after 10 minutes.

5 Bring a large pan of salted water to the boil. Add the tagliatelle and oil and cook for about 12 minutes, until tender but still firm to the bite. Drain and transfer to a warm serving dish.

6 Remove the trout from the oven and arrange on the tagliatelle. Garnish with sliced apples and fresh mint sprigs and serve immediately.

Farfalle with a Medley of Seafood

Serves 4

INGREDIENTS

12 raw tiger prawns (shrimp)
12 raw shrimp
125 g/4¹/₂ oz freshwater prawns (shrimp)
450 g/1 lb fillet of sea bream
60 g/2 oz/4 tbsp butter
12 scallops, shelled
juice and finely grated rind of 1 lemon

pinch of saffron powder or threads
1 litre/1³/₄ pints/4 cups vegetable stock
150 ml/¹/₄ pint/⁵/₈ cup rose petal vinegar
450 g/1 lb dried farfalle
1 tbsp olive oil

150 ml/¹/₄ pint/⁵/₈ cup white wine
1 tbsp pink peppercorns
115 g/4 oz baby carrots
150 ml/¹/₄ pint/⁵/₈ cup double (heavy) cream or fromage frais
salt and pepper
fresh parsley, to garnish

1 Peel and devein the prawns (shrimp) and shrimp. Thinly slice the sea bream. Melt the butter in a pan, add the sea bream, scallops, prawns (shrimp) and shrimp and cook for 1–2 minutes.

2 Season with black pepper. Add the lemon juice and rind. Carefully add the saffron to the cooking juices (not to the seafood).

3 Remove the seafood from the pan, set aside and keep warm.

4 Return the pan to the heat and add the vegetable stock. Bring to the boil and reduce by one third. Add the rose petal vinegar and cook for 4 minutes, until reduced.

5 Bring a pan of salted water to the boil. Add the farfalle and olive oil and

cook until tender, but still firm to the bite. Drain and transfer to a serving plate, topped with the seafood.

6 Add the wine, peppercorns, and carrots to the pan and reduce the sauce for 6 minutes. Add the cream or fromage frais and simmer for 2 minutes. Pour the sauce over the seafood and pasta, garnish and serve.

Seafood Lasagne

Serves 4

INGREDIENTS

450 g/1 lb finnan haddock,
    filleted, skin removed and
    flesh flaked
115 g/4 oz prawns (shrimp)
115 g/4 oz sole fillet, skin
    removed and flesh sliced
juice of 1 lemon

60 g/2 oz/4 tbsp butter
3 leeks, very thinly sliced
60 g/2 oz/½ cup plain
    (all purpose) flour
about 600 ml/1 pint/2½
    cups milk
2 tbsp clear honey

200g/7 oz /1¾ cups grated
    mozzarella cheese
450g/1 lb pre-cooked lasagne
60 g/2 oz/⅔ cup freshly grated
    Parmesan cheese
black pepper

1 Put the haddock fillet, prawns (shrimp) and sole fillet into a large bowl and season with black pepper and lemon juice. Set aside while you start to make the sauce.

2 Melt the butter in a large saucepan. Add the leeks and cook, stirring occasionally, for 8 minutes. Add the flour and cook, stirring constantly, for 1 minute. Gradually stir in enough milk to make a thick, creamy sauce.

3 Blend in the honey and mozzarella cheese and cook for a further 3 minutes. Remove from the heat and mix in the fish and prawns (shrimp).

4 Make alternate layers of fish sauce and lasagne in an ovenproof dish, finishing with a layer of fish sauce. Sprinkle over the grated Parmesan cheese and bake in a preheated oven at 180°C/350°F/Gas 4 for 30 minutes. Serve immediately.

VARIATION

For a cider sauce, substitute 1 finely chopped shallot for the leeks, 300 ml/ ½ pint/1¼ cups cider and 300 ml/½ pint/1¼ cups double (heavy) cream for the milk and 1 tsp mustard for the honey. For a Tuscan sauce, substitute 1 finely chopped fennel bulb for the leeks and omit the honey.

Spaghetti with Seafood Sauce

Serves 4

INGREDIENTS

225 g/8 oz dried spaghetti,
    broken into 15 cm/6 inch
    lengths
2 tbsp olive oil
300 ml/¹/₂ pint/1¹/₄ cups
    chicken stock
1 tsp lemon juice
1 small cauliflower, cut into
    florets (flowerets)
2 carrots, thinly sliced

115 g/4 oz mangetouts (snow
    peas)
60 g/2 oz/4 tbsp butter
1 onion, sliced
225 g/8 oz courgettes
    (zucchini), sliced
1 garlic clove, chopped
350 g/12 oz frozen, cooked,
    peeled prawns (shrimp),
    defrosted

2 tbsp chopped fresh parsley
25 g/1 oz/¹/₃ cup freshly grated
    Parmesan cheese
¹/₂ tsp paprika
salt and pepper
4 unpeeled, cooked prawns
    (shrimp), to garnish

1 Bring a pan of lightly salted water to the boil. Add the spaghetti and 1 tbsp of the olive oil and cook until tender, but still firm to the bite. Drain, toss with the remaining olive oil, cover and keep warm.

2 Bring the chicken stock and lemon juice to the boil. Add the cauliflower and carrots and cook for 3–4 minutes.

Remove from the pan and set aside. Cook the mangetouts (snow peas) for 1–2 minutes then set aside with the other vegetables.

3 Melt half the butter in a frying pan (skillet) and fry the onion and courgettes (zucchini) for 3 minutes. Add the garlic and prawns (shrimp) and cook for a further 2–3 minutes. Stir in the

reserved vegetables and heat through. Season to taste and stir in the remaining butter.

4 Transfer the spaghetti to a warm serving dish. Mix in the sauce and the chopped parsley until coated. Sprinkle over the Parmesan cheese and paprika, garnish with the unpeeled prawns (shrimp) and serve immediately.

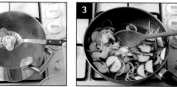

Macaroni & Prawn (Shrimp) Bake

Serves 4

INGREDIENTS

350 g/12 oz/3 cups dried short-cut macaroni	175 g/6 oz mushrooms, thinly sliced	60 g/2 oz/⅔ cup freshly grated Parmesan cheese
1 tbsp olive oil, plus extra for brushing	175 g/6 oz peeled, cooked prawns (shrimp)	2 large tomatoes, sliced
90 g/3 oz/6 tbsp butter, plus extra for greasing	pinch of cayenne pepper	1 tsp dried oregano
2 small fennel bulbs, thinly sliced and fronds reserved	300 ml/½ pint/1¼ cups Béchamel Sauce (see Cook's Tip, below)	salt and pepper

1 Bring a pan of salted water to the boil. Add the pasta and oil and cook until tender, but still firm to the bite. Drain, return to the pan and toss in 25 g/1 oz/2 tbsp of the butter. Cover and keep warm.

2 Fry the fennel in the remaining butter for 3–4 minutes. Stir in the mushrooms and fry for 2 minutes. Stir in the prawns (shrimp), then remove the pan from the heat.

3 Stir the pasta, cayenne pepper and prawn (shrimp) mixture into the Béchamel sauce. Pour into a greased ovenproof dish. Sprinkle over the Parmesan cheese and arrange the tomato slices around the edge. Brush the tomatoes with olive oil and sprinkle over the oregano.

4 Bake in a preheated oven at 180°C/350°F/ Gas 4 for 25 minutes, until golden brown. Serve.

COOK'S TIP

For Béchamel sauce, melt 25 g/1 oz/2 tbsp butter. Stir in 25 g/1 oz/¼ cup flour and cook for 2 minutes. Gradually, stir in 300 ml/ ½ pint/1¼ cups warm milk. Add 2 tbsp finely chopped onion, 5 white peppercorns and 2 parsley sprigs. Season with salt, dried thyme and grated nutmeg. Simmer, stirring, for 15 minutes. Strain.

Pasta Parcels

Serves 4

INGREDIENTS

450 g/1 lb dried fettuccine	750 g/1 lb 10 oz large raw	125 ml/4 fl oz/¹/₂ cup dry white
150 ml/¹/₄ pint/⁶/₈ cup Pesto	prawns (shrimp), peeled and	wine
Sauce	deveined	salt and pepper
4 tsp extra virgin olive oil	2 garlic cloves, crushed	lemon wedges, to serve

1 Cut out 4 × 30 cm/ 12 inch squares of greaseproof (baking) paper.

2 Bring a large saucepan of lightly salted water to the boil. Add the fettuccine and cook for 2–3 minutes, until just softened. Drain and set aside.

3 Mix together the fettuccine and half of the Pesto Sauce. Spread out the paper squares and put 1 tsp olive oil in the middle of each. Divide the fettuccine between the squares, then divide the

prawns (shrimp) and place on top of the fettuccine.

4 Mix together the remaining Pesto Sauce and the garlic and spoon it over the prawns (shrimp). Season each parcel with salt and black pepper and sprinkle with the white wine.

5 Dampen the edges of the greaseproof (baking) paper and wrap the parcels loosely, twisting the edges to seal.

6 Place the parcels on a baking (cookie) sheet

and bake in a preheated oven at 200°C/400°F/ Gas 6 for 10–15 minutes. Transfer the parcels to 4 individual serving plates and serve immediately.

COOK'S TIP

Traditionally, these parcels are designed to look like money bags. The resemblance is more effective with greaseproof (baking) paper than with foil.

Farfallini Buttered Lobster

Serves 4

INGREDIENTS

2 x 700 g/1 lb 9 oz lobsters, split
    into halves
juice and grated rind of
    1 lemon
115 g/4 oz/¹/₂ cup butter
4 tbsp fresh white breadcrumbs
2 tbsp brandy

5 tbsp double (heavy) cream
    or crème fraîche
450 g/1 lb dried farfallini
1 tbsp olive oil
60 g/2 oz/²/₃ cup freshly grated
    Parmesan cheese
salt and pepper

TO GARNISH:
1 kiwi fruit, sliced
4 unpeeled, cooked king prawns
    (shrimp)
fresh dill sprigs

1 Carefully discard the stomach sac, vein and gills from each lobster. Remove all the meat from the tail and chop. Crack the claws and legs, remove the meat and chop. Transfer the meat to a bowl and add the lemon juice and rind.

2 Clean the shells thoroughly and place in a warm oven at 170°C/325°/Gas 3 to dry out.

3 Melt 25 g/1 oz/2 tbsp of the butter in a frying pan (skillet). Add the breadcrumbs and fry for about 3 minutes, until crisp and golden brown.

4 Melt the remaining butter in a saucepan and gently cook the lobster meat. Add the brandy and cook for a further 3 minutes, then add the cream or crème fraîche and season to taste.

5 Bring a large pan of lightly salted water to the boil. Add the farfallini and olive oil and cook for about 12 minutes, until tender but still firm to the bite. Drain and spoon the pasta into the clean lobster shells. Top with the buttered lobster and sprinkle with the grated Parmesan cheese and the breadcrumbs. Grill (broil) for 2–3 minutes, until golden brown.

6 Transfer the lobster shells to a warm serving dish, garnish and serve immediately.

Pasta Shells with Mussels

Serves 4–6

INGREDIENTS

1.25 kg/2³/₄ lb mussels
225 ml/8 fl oz/1 cup dry white wine
2 large onions, chopped
115 g/4 oz/¹/₂ cup unsalted butter

6 large garlic cloves, finely chopped
5 tbsp chopped fresh parsley
300 ml/¹/₂ pint/1¹/₄ cups double (heavy) cream

400 g/14 oz dried pasta shells
1 tbsp olive oil
salt and pepper
crusty bread, to serve

1 Scrub and debeard the mussels under cold running water. Discard any that do not close immediately when tapped. Put the mussels in a pan with the wine and half of the onions. Cover and cook over a medium heat, shaking the pan frequently, until the shells open.

2 Remove from the heat. Drain the mussels and reserve the cooking liquid. Discard any mussels that have not opened. Strain the cooking liquid and reserve.

3 Fry the remaining onion in the butter for 2–3 minutes. Stir in the garlic and cook for 1 minute. Gradually stir in the reserved cooking liquid, parsley and cream. Season and leave to simmer.

4 Cook the pasta with the oil in a pan of salted water until just tender, but still firm to the bite. Drain, return to the pan, cover and keep warm.

5 Reserve a few mussels for the garnish and

remove the remainder from their shells. Stir the shelled mussels into the cream sauce and warm briefly. Transfer the pasta to a serving dish. Pour over the sauce and toss well to coat. Garnish with the reserved mussels and serve with warm, crusty bread.

COOK'S TIP

Pasta shells are ideal because the sauce collects in the cavities and impregnates the pasta with flavour.

Saffron Mussel Tagliatelle

Serves 4

INGREDIENTS

1 kg/2¼ lb mussels
150 ml/¼ pint/⅝ cup white wine
1 medium onion, finely chopped
25 g/1 oz/2 tbsp butter
2 garlic cloves, crushed
2 tsp cornflour (cornstarch)

300 ml/½ pint/1¼ cups double (heavy) cream
pinch of saffron threads or saffron powder
1 egg yolk
juice of ½ lemon

450 g/1 lb dried tagliatelle
1 tbsp olive oil
salt and pepper
3 tbsp chopped fresh parsley, to garnish

1 Scrub and debeard the mussels under cold running water. Discard any that do not close when sharply tapped. Put the mussels in a pan with the wine and onion. Cover and cook over a high heat until the shells open.

2 Drain and reserve the cooking liquid. Discard any mussels that are still closed. Reserve a few mussels for the garnish and remove the remainder from their shells.

3 Strain the cooking liquid into a saucepan. Bring to the boil and reduce by about a half. Remove from the heat.

4 Melt the butter in a saucepan and fry the garlic for 2 minutes, until golden brown. Stir in the cornflour (cornstarch) and cook, stirring, for 1 minute. Gradually stir in the cooking liquid and the cream. Crush the saffron threads and add to the pan. Season to taste and simmer

over a low heat for 2–3 minutes, until thickened.

5 Stir in the egg yolk, lemon juice and shelled mussels. Do not allow the mixture to boil.

6 Bring a pan of salted water to the boil. Add the pasta and oil and cook until tender. Drain and transfer to a serving dish. Add the mussel sauce and toss. Garnish with the parsley and reserved mussels and serve.

Baked Scallops with Pasta in Shells

Serves 4

INGREDIENTS

12 scallops

3 tbsp olive oil

350 g/12 oz/3 cups small, dried wholemeal (wholewheat) pasta shells

150 ml/¼ pint/⅝ cup fish stock

1 onion, chopped

juice and finely grated rind of 2 lemons

150 ml/¼ pint/⅝ cup double (heavy) cream

225 g/8 oz/2 cups grated Cheddar cheese

salt and pepper

crusty brown bread, to serve

1 Remove the scallops from their shells. Scrape off the skirt and the black intestinal thread. Reserve the white part (the flesh) and the orange part (the coral or roe). Carefully ease the flesh and coral from the shell with a short, but very strong knife.

2 Wash the shells thoroughly and dry them well. Put the shells on a baking (cookie) sheet, sprinkle lightly with about two thirds of the olive oil and set aside.

3 Meanwhile, bring a large saucepan of lightly salted water to the boil. Add the pasta shells and remaining olive oil and cook for about 12 minutes, until tender, but still firm to the bite. Drain and spoon about 25 g/1 oz of pasta into each scallop shell.

4 Put the scallops, fish stock and onion in an ovenproof dish and season to taste with pepper. Cover with foil and bake in a preheated oven at 180°C/350°F/Gas 4 for 8 minutes.

5 Remove the dish from the oven. Remove the foil and, using a slotted spoon, transfer the scallops to the shells. Add 1 tbsp of the cooking liquid to each shell, drizzle with lemon juice and a little cream, and top with grated cheese.

6 Increase the oven temperature to 230°C/450°F/Gas 8 and return the scallops to the oven for 4 minutes. Serve the scallops in their shells with crusty brown bread and butter.

Vermicelli with Clams

Serves 4

INGREDIENTS

400 g/14 oz dried vermicelli,
    spaghetti or other long pasta
2 tbsp olive oil
25 g/1 oz/2 tbsp butter
2 onions, chopped
2 garlic cloves, chopped

2 x 200 g/7 oz jars clams in brine
125 ml/4 fl oz/¹/₂ cup white wine
4 tbsp chopped fresh parsley
¹/₂ tsp dried oregano
pinch of freshly grated nutmeg
salt and pepper

TO GARNISH:
fresh basil sprigs

1 Bring a large pan of lightly salted water to the boil. Add the pasta and half the olive oil and cook until tender, but still firm to the bite. Drain, return to the pan and add the butter. Cover the pan, shake well and keep warm.

2 Heat the remaining oil in a saucepan over a medium heat. Add the onions and fry until they are translucent. Stir in the garlic and cook for 1 minute.

3 Strain the liquid from 1 jar of clams and add the liquid to the pan, together with the wine. Stir, bring to simmering point and simmer for 3 minutes. Drain the second jar of clams and discard the liquid.

4 Add the clams, parsley and oregano to the saucepan and season with pepper and nutmeg. Lower the heat and cook until the sauce is completely heated through.

5 Transfer the pasta to a serving dish and pour over the sauce. Garnish with the basil and serve.

COOK'S TIP

There are many different types of clams found along almost every coast in the world. Those traditionally used in this dish are the tiny ones – only 2.5–5 cm/ 1–2 inches across – known in Italy as vongole.

Squid & Macaroni Stew

Serves 4–6

INGREDIENTS

225 g/8 oz/2 cups dried short-cut
   macaroni or other small
   pasta shapes
7 tbsp olive oil
2 onions, sliced

350 g/12 oz prepared squid, cut
   into 4 cm/1½ inch strips
225 ml/8 fl oz/1 cup fish stock
150 ml/¼ pint/⅝ cup red wine
2 tbsp tomato purée (paste)

350 g/12 oz tomatoes, skinned
   and thinly sliced
1 tsp dried oregano
2 bay leaves
2 tbsp chopped fresh parsley
salt and pepper
crusty bread, to serve

1 Bring a large pan of
salted water to the boil.
Add the pasta and 1 tbsp of
oil and cook for 3 minutes.
Drain and keep warm.

2 Heat the remaining oil
in a pan and fry the
onions until translucent.
Add the squid and stock
and simmer for 5 minutes.
Pour in the wine and add
the tomato purée (paste),
tomatoes, oregano and bay
leaves. Bring the sauce to
the boil, season to taste and
cook for 5 minutes.

3 Stir the pasta into the
pan, cover and simmer
for 10 minutes, or until the
squid and macaroni are
tender and the sauce has
thickened. If the sauce
remains too liquid, uncover
the pan and continue
cooking for a few minutes.

4 Discard the bay leaves.
Reserve a little parsley
and stir the remainder into
the pan. Transfer to a warm
serving dish and sprinkle
over the remaining parsley.
Serve with crusty bread.

COOK'S TIP

*To prepare squid, peel off the
outer skin, then cut off the
head and tentacles. Extract
the transparent flat oval bone
from the body and discard.
Remove the sac of black ink,
then turn the body sac inside
out. Wash in cold water. Cut
off the tentacles and discard
the rest; wash thoroughly.*

Pasta Vongole

Serves 4

INGREDIENTS

675 g/1½ lb fresh clams or	mussels, defrosted if frozen	2 tbsp chopped tarragon
1 x 290 g/10 oz can clams,	2 tbsp olive oil	salt and pepper
drained	2 cloves garlic, finely chopped	675 g/1½ lb fresh pasta or 350
400 g/14 oz mixed seafood, such	150 ml/5 fl oz/⅔ cup white wine	g/12 oz dried pasta
as prawns (shrimps), squid and	150 ml/5 fl oz/⅔ cup fish stock	

1 If you are using fresh clams, scrub them clean and discard any that are already open.

2 Heat the oil in a large frying pan (skillet). Add the garlic and the clams to the pan and cook for 2 minutes, shaking the pan to ensure that all of the clams are coated in the oil.

3 Add the remaining seafood mixture to the pan and cook for a further 2 minutes.

4 Pour the wine and stock over the mixed

seafood and garlic and bring to the boil. Cover the pan, reduce the heat and leave to simmer for 8–10 minutes or until the shells open. Discard any clams or mussels that do not open.

5 Meanwhile, cook the pasta in a saucepan of boiling water according to the instructions on the packet or until it is cooked through, but still has 'bite'. Drain.

6 Stir the tarragon into the sauce and season to taste.

7 Transfer the pasta to a serving plate and pour over the sauce.

VARIATION

Red clam sauce can be made by adding 8 tablespoons of passata (tomato purée) to the sauce along with the stock in step 4. Follow the same cooking method.

Smoked Cod Polenta

Serves 4

INGREDIENTS

350 g/12 oz instant polenta
1.5 litres/2¾ pints/6½ cups water
200 g/7 oz chopped frozen
   spinach, defrosted

50 g/1¾ oz/3 tbsp butter
50 g/1¾ oz pecorino cheese, grated
200 ml/7 fl oz/¾ cup milk

450 g/1 lb smoked cod fillet,
   skinned and boned
4 eggs, beaten
salt and pepper

1 Cook the polenta, using 1.5 litres/2¼ pints/6½ cups of water to 350 g/12 oz polenta, stirring occasionally. Alternatively, follow the instructions on the packet.

2 Stir the spinach, butter and half of the pecorino cheese into the polenta. Season to taste with salt and pepper.

3 Divide the polenta among 4 individual ovenproof dishes, spreading the polenta evenly across the bottom and up the sides of the dishes.

4 In a large frying pan (skillet), bring the milk to the boil. Add the fish and cook for 8–10 minutes, turning once, or until tender. Remove the fish with a perforated spoon.

5 Remove the pan from the heat. Pour the eggs into the milk in the pan and mix together.

6 Using a fork, flake the fish into smaller pieces and place it in the centre of the dishes.

7 Pour the milk and egg mixture over the fish.

8 Sprinkle with the remaining cheese and bake in a preheated oven at 190°C/375°F/ Gas Mark 5 for 25–30 minutes or until set and golden. Serve hot.

VARIATION

Try using 350 g/12 oz cooked chicken breast with 2 tablespoons of chopped tarragon, instead of the fish, if you prefer.

Celery & Salt Cod Casserole

Serves 4

INGREDIENTS

250 g/9 oz salt cod, soaked
    overnight
1 tbsp oil
4 shallots, finely chopped
2 garlic cloves, chopped

3 celery sticks, chopped
1 x 400 g/14 oz can tomatoes,
    chopped
150 ml/5 fl oz/²⁄₃ cup fish stock
50 g/1³⁄₄ oz pine nuts

2 tbsp roughly chopped tarragon
2 tbsp capers
crusty bread or mashed potato,
    to serve

1 Drain the salt cod, rinse it under plenty of running water and drain again thoroughly. Remove and discard any skin and bones. Pat the fish dry with paper towels and cut it into chunks.

2 Heat the oil in a large frying pan (skillet). Add the shallots and garlic and cook for 2–3 minutes. Add the celery and cook for a further 2 minutes, then add the tomatoes and stock.

3 Bring the mixture to the boil, reduce the heat and leave to simmer for 5 minutes.

4 Add the fish and cook for 10 minutes or until tender.

5 Meanwhile, place the pine nuts on a baking tray (cookie sheet). Place under a preheated grill (broiler) and toast for 2–3 minutes or until golden.

6 Stir the tarragon, capers and pine nuts into the fish casserole and heat gently to warm through.

7 Transfer to serving plates and serve with fresh crusty bread or mashed potato.

COOK'S TIP

Salt cod is a useful ingredient to keep in the storecupboard and once soaked, can be used in the same way as any other fish. It does, however, have a stronger flavour than normal, and it is, of course, slightly salty. It can be found in fishmongers, larger supermarkets and delicatessens.

Salt Cod Fritters

Makes 28 cakes

INGREDIENTS

100 g/3½ oz self-raising flour	1 small red onion, finely chopped	TO SERVE:
1 egg, beaten	1 small fennel bulb, finely chopped	crisp salad, chilli relish, cooked
150 ml/5 fl oz/⅔ cup milk	1 red chilli, finely chopped	rice and fresh vegetables
250 g/9 oz salt cod, soaked overnight	2 tbsp oil	

1 Sift the flour into a large bowl. Make a well in the centre of the flour and add the egg.

2 Using a wooden spoon, gradually draw in the flour, slowly adding the milk, and mix to form a smooth batter. Leave to stand for 10 minutes.

3 Drain the salt cod and rinse it under cold running water. Drain again thoroughly.

4 Remove and discard the skin and any bones from the fish, then mash the flesh with a fork.

5 Place the fish in a large bowl and combine with the onion, fennel and chilli. Add the mixture to the batter and blend together.

6 Heat the oil in a large frying pan (skillet) and, taking about 1 tablespoon of the mixture at a time, spoon it into the hot oil. Cook the fritters, in batches, for 3–4 minutes on each side until golden and slightly puffed. Keep warm while cooking the remaining mixture.

7 Serve with salad and a chilli relish for a light meal or with vegetables and rice.

COOK'S TIP

If you prefer larger fritters, use 2 tablespoons per fritter and cook for slightly longer.

Sardinian Red Mullet

Serves 4

INGREDIENTS

50 g/1¾ oz sultanas
150 ml/5 fl oz/⅝ cup red wine
2 tbsp olive oil
2 medium onions, sliced

1 courgette (zucchini) cut into
5 cm/2 inch sticks
2 oranges
2 tsp coriander seeds, lightly crushed

4 red mullet, boned and filleted
1 x 50 g/1¾ oz can anchovy fillets,
drained
2 tbsp chopped, fresh oregano

1 Place the sultanas in a bowl. Pour over the red wine and leave to soak for 10 minutes.

2 Heat the oil in a large frying pan (skillet). Add the onions and sauté for 2 minutes.

3 Add the courgettes (zucchini) to the pan and fry for a further 3 minutes or until tender.

4 Using a zester, pare long, thin strips from one of the oranges. Using a sharp knife, remove the skin from both of the oranges, then segment the oranges by slicing between the lines of pith.

5 Add the orange zest to the frying pan (skillet). Add the red wine, sultanas, red mullet and anchovies to the pan and leave to simmer for 10–15 minutes or until the fish is cooked through.

6 Stir in the oregano, set aside and leave to cool. Place the mixture in a large bowl and leave to chill, covered, in the refrigerator for at least 2 hours to allow the flavours to mingle. Transfer to serving plates and serve.

COOK'S TIP

Red mullet is usually available all year round – frozen, if not fresh – from your fishmonger or supermarket. If you cannot get hold of it try using telapia. This dish can also be served warm, if you prefer.

Herrings with Hot Pesto Sauce

Serves 4

INGREDIENTS

4 whole herrings or small
   mackerel, cleaned and gutted
2 tbsp olive oil

225 g/8 oz tomatoes, peeled,
   deseeded and chopped
8 canned anchovy fillets, chopped

about 30 fresh basil leaves
50 g/1¾ oz pine nuts
2 garlic cloves, crushed

1 Cook the herrings under a preheated grill (broiler) for about 8–10 minutes on each side, or until the skin is slightly charred on both sides.

2 Meanwhile, heat 1 tablespoon of the olive oil in a large saucepan.

3 Add the tomatoes and anchovies to the saucepan and cook over a medium heat for 5 minutes.

4 Meanwhile, place the basil, pine nuts, garlic and remaining oil into a food processor and blend to form a smooth paste.

Alternatively, pound the ingredients by hand in a mortar and pestle.

5 Add the pesto mixture to the saucepan containing the tomato and anchovy mixture, and stir to heat through.

6 Spoon some of the pesto sauce on to warm individual serving plates. Place the fish on top and pour the rest of the pesto sauce over the fish. Serve immediately.

COOK'S TIP

Try barbecuing (grilling) the fish for an extra char-grilled flavour, if you prefer.

Grilled (Broiled) Stuffed Sole

Serves 4

INGREDIENTS

1 tbsp olive oil	2 tbsp lemon thyme	salt and pepper
25 g/1 oz/2 tbsp butter	50 g/1³/₄ oz breadcrumbs	lemon wedges, to garnish
1 small onion, finely chopped	1 tbsp lemon juice	fresh green salad leaves, to serve
1 garlic clove, chopped	4 small whole sole, gutted and	
3 sun-dried tomatoes, chopped	cleaned	

1 Heat the oil and butter in a frying pan (skillet) until it just begins to froth.

2 Add the onion and garlic to the frying pan (skillet) and cook, stirring, for 5 minutes until just softened.

3 To make the stuffing, mix the tomatoes, thyme, breadcrumbs and lemon juice in a bowl, and season to taste.

4 Add the stuffing mixture to the pan, and stir to mix.

5 Using a sharp knife, pare the skin from the bone inside the gut hole of the fish to make a pocket. Spoon the tomato and herb stuffing into the pocket.

6 Cook the fish, under a preheated grill (broiler), for 6 minutes on each side or until golden brown.

7 Transfer the stuffed fish to serving plates and garnish with lemon wedges. Serve immediately with fresh green salad leaves.

COOK'S TIP

Lemon thyme (Thymus x citriodorus) has a delicate lemon scent and flavour. Ordinary thyme can be used instead, but mix it with 1 teaspoon of lemon rind to add extra flavour.

Sole Fillets in Marsala & Cream

Serves 4

INGREDIENTS

STOCK:
600 ml/1 pint/2$\frac{1}{2}$ cups water
bones and skin from the sole fillets
1 onion, peeled and halved
1 carrot, peeled and halved
3 fresh bay leaves

SAUCE;
1 tbsp olive oil
15 g/$\frac{1}{2}$ oz/1 tbsp butter
4 shallots, finely chopped
100 g/3$\frac{1}{2}$ oz baby button
    mushrooms, wiped and halved

1 tbsp peppercorns, lightly crushed
8 sole fillets
100 ml/3$\frac{1}{2}$ fl oz/$\frac{1}{3}$ cup Marsala
150 ml/5 fl oz/$\frac{2}{3}$ pint double
    (heavy) cream

1 To make the stock, place the water, fish bones and skin, onion, carrot and bay leaves in a saucepan and bring to the boil.

2 Reduce the heat and leave the mixture to simmer for 1 hour or until the stock has reduced to about 150 ml/5 fl oz/$\frac{2}{3}$ cup. Drain the stock through a fine sieve, discarding the bones and vegetables, and set aside.

3 To make the sauce, heat the oil and butter in a frying pan (skillet).

Add the shallots and cook, stirring, for 2–3 minutes or until just softened.

4 Add the mushrooms to the frying pan (skillet) and cook, stirring, for a further 2–3 minutes or until they are just beginning to brown.

5 Add the peppercorns and sole fillets to the frying pan (skillet). Fry the sole fillets for 3–4 minutes on each side or until golden brown.

6 Pour the wine and stock over the fish and leave to simmer for 3 minutes. Remove the fish with a fish slice or a perforated spoon, set aside and keep warm.

7 Increase the heat and boil the mixture in the pan for about 5 minutes or until the sauce has reduced and thickened.

8 Pour in the cream, return the fish to the pan and heat through. Serve with the cooked vegetables of your choice.

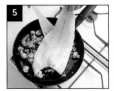

Fresh Baked Sardines

Serves 4

INGREDIENTS

2 tbsp olive oil

2 large onions, sliced into rings

3 garlic cloves, chopped

2 large courgettes (zucchini), cut into sticks

3 tbsp fresh thyme, stalks removed

8 sardine fillets or about 1 kg/2 lb 4 oz whole sardines, filleted

75 g/2¾ oz Parmesan cheese, grated

4 eggs, beaten

150 ml/5 fl oz/⅔ pint milk

salt and pepper

1 Heat 1 tablespoon of the oil in a frying pan (skillet). Add the onions and garlic and sauté for 2–3 minutes.

2 Add the courgettes (zucchini) to the frying pan (skillet) and cook for about 5 minutes or until golden.

3 Stir 2 tablespoons of the thyme into the mixture.

4 Place half of the onions and courgettes (zucchini) in the base of a large ovenproof dish. Top with the sardine fillets and half of the Parmesan cheese.

5 Place the remaining onions and courgettes (zucchini) on top and sprinkle with the remaining thyme.

6 Mix the eggs and milk together in a bowl and season to taste with salt and pepper. Pour the mixture over the vegetables and sardines in the dish. Sprinkle the remaining Parmesan cheese over the top.

7 Bake in a preheated oven at 180°C/350°F/ Gas Mark 4 for 20–25 minutes or until golden and set. Serve hot, straight from the oven.

VARIATION

If you cannot find sardines that are large enough to fillet, use small mackerel instead.

Marinated Fish

Serves 4

INGREDIENTS

4 whole mackerel, cleaned and gutted	2 tbsp extra virgin olive oil finely grated rind and juice of	2 garlic cloves, crushed salt and pepper
4 tbsp chopped marjoram	1 lime	

1 Under gently running water, scrape the mackerel with the blunt side of a knife to remove any scales.

2 Using a sharp knife, make a slit in the stomach of the fish and cut horizontally along until the knife will go no further very easily. Gut the fish and rinse under water. You may prefer to remove the heads before cooking, but it is not necessary.

3 Using a sharp knife, cut 4–5 diagonal slashes on each side of the fish. Place the fish in a shallow, non-metallic dish.

4 To make the marinade, mix together the marjoram, olive oil, lime rind and juice, garlic and salt and pepper in a bowl.

5 Pour the mixture over the fish. Leave to marinate in the refrigerator for 30 minutes.

6 Cook the mackerel, under a preheated grill (broiler), for 5–6 minutes on each side, brushing occasionally with the reserved marinade, until golden.

7 Transfer the fish to serving plates. Pour over any remaining marinade before serving.

COOK'S TIP

If the lime is too hard to squeeze, microwave on high power for 30 seconds to release the juice. This dish is also excellent cooked on the barbecue (grill).

Orange Mackerel

Serves 4

INGREDIENTS

2 tbsp oil	1 tbsp oats	8 mackerel fillets
4 spring onions (scallions), chopped	50 g/1¹/₄ oz mixed green and black	salt and pepper
2 oranges	olives, pitted and chopped	crisp salad, to serve
50 g/1¹/₄ oz ground almonds		

1 Heat the oil in a frying pan (skillet). Add the spring onions (scallions) and cook for 2 minutes.

2 Finely grate the rind of the oranges, then, using a sharp knife, cut away the remaining skin and white pith.

3 Using a sharp knife, segment the oranges by cutting down either side of the lines of pith to loosen each segment. Do this over a plate so that you can reserve any juices. Cut each orange segment in half.

4 Lightly toast the almonds, under a preheated grill (broiler), for 2–3 minutes or until golden; watch them carefully as they brown very quickly.

5 Mix the spring onions (scallions), oranges, ground almonds, oats and olives together in a bowl and season to taste with salt and pepper.

6 Spoon the orange mixture along the centre of each fillet. Roll up each fillet, securing it in place with a cocktail stick (toothpick) or skewer.

7 Bake in a preheated oven at 190°C/375°F/ Gas Mark 5 for 25 minutes until the fish is tender.

8 Transfer to serving plates and serve warm with a salad.

Italian Cod

Serves 4

INGREDIENTS

25 g/1 oz/2 tbsp butter

50 g/1³/₄ oz wholemeal breadcrumbs

25 g/1 oz chopped walnuts

grated rind and juice of 2 lemons

2 sprigs rosemary, stalks removed

2 tbsp chopped parsley

4 cod fillets, each about
 150 g/5¹/₂ oz

1 garlic clove, crushed

3 tbsp walnut oil

1 small red chilli, diced

salad leaves, to serve

1 Melt the butter in a large frying pan (skillet).

2 Remove the frying pan (skillet) from the heat and add the breadcrumbs, walnuts, the rind and juice of 1 lemon, half of the rosemary and half of the parsley.

3 Press the breadcrumb mixture over the top of the cod fillets. Place the cod fillets in a shallow, foil-lined roasting tin (pan).

4 Bake in a preheated oven at 200°C/400°F/Gas Mark 6 for 25–30 minutes.

5 Mix the garlic, the remaining lemon rind and juice, rosemary, parsley and chilli in a bowl. Beat in the walnut oil and mix to combine. Drizzle the dressing over the cod steaks as soon as they are cooked.

6 Transfer to serving plates and serve immediately.

VARIATION

If preferred, the walnuts may be omitted from the crust. In addition, extra virgin olive oil can be used instead of walnut oil, if you prefer.

COOK'S TIP

The 'hotness' of chillies varies so use them with caution. As a general guide, the smaller the chilli the hotter it will be.

Mussel Casserole

Serves 4

INGREDIENTS

1 kg/2 lb 4 oz mussels	1 onion, finely chopped	100 g/3½ oz passata (tomato paste)
150 ml/5 fl oz/ ⅔ cup white wine	3 garlic cloves, chopped	1 tbsp chopped marjoram
1 tbsp oil	1 red chilli, finely chopped	toast or crusty bread, to serve

1 Scrub the mussels to remove any mud or sand.

2 Remove the beards from the mussels by pulling away the hairy bit between the two shells. Rinse the mussels in a bowl of clean water. Discard any mussels that do not close when they are tapped – they are dead and should not be eaten.

3 Place the mussels in a large saucepan. Pour in the wine and cook for 5 minutes, shaking the pan occasionally until the shells open. Remove and discard any mussels that do not open.

4 Remove the mussels from the saucepan with a perforated spoon. Strain the cooking liquid through a fine sieve set over a bowl, reserving the liquid.

5 Heat the oil in a large frying pan (skillet). Add the onion, garlic and chilli and cook for 4–5 minutes or until softened.

6 Add the reserved cooking liquid to the pan and cook for 5 minutes or until reduced.

7 Stir in the passata (tomato paste), marjoram and mussels and cook until hot.

8 Transfer to serving bowls and serve with toast or plenty of crusty bread to mop up the juices.

COOK'S TIP

Finger bowls are individual bowls of warm water with a slice of lemon floating in them. They are used to clean your fingers at the end of a meal.

Stuffed Squid

Serves 4

INGREDIENTS
---

8 squid, cleaned and gutted but
    left whole (ask your
    fishmonger to do this)
6 canned anchovies, chopped
2 garlic cloves, chopped

2 tbsp rosemary, stalks removed
    and leaves chopped
2 sun-dried tomatoes, chopped
150 g/5½ oz breadcrumbs
1 tbsp olive oil

1 onion, finely chopped
200 ml/7 fl oz/¾ cup white wine
200 ml/7 fl oz/¾ cup fish stock
cooked rice, to serve

---

1 Remove the tentacles from the body of the squid and chop the flesh finely.

2 Grind the anchovies, garlic, rosemary and tomatoes to a paste in a mortar and pestle.

3 Add the breadcrumbs and the chopped squid tentacles and mix. If the mixture is too dry to form a thick paste at this point, add 1 teaspoon of water.

4 Spoon the paste into the body sacs of the squid then tie a length of cotton

around the end of each sac to fasten them. Do not overfill the sacs, because they will expand during cooking.

5 Heat the oil in a frying pan (skillet). Add the onion and cook, stirring, for 3–4 minutes or until golden.

6 Add the stuffed squid to the pan and cook for 3–4 minutes or until brown all over.

7 Add the wine and stock and bring to the boil. Reduce the heat, cover and then leave to simmer for 15 minutes.

8 Remove the lid and cook for a further 5 minutes until the squid is tender and the juices reduced. Serve with cooked rice.

COOK'S TIP

If you cannot buy whole squid, use squid pieces and stir the paste into the sauce with the wine and stock.

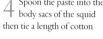

Genoese Seafood Risotto

Serves 4

INGREDIENTS

1.2 litres/2 pints/5 cups hot fish
or chicken stock
350 g/12 oz arborio (risotto) rice,
washed
50 g/1¾ oz/3 tbsp butter

2 garlic cloves, chopped
250 g/9 oz mixed seafood,
preferably raw, such as prawns
(shrimp), squid, mussels, clams
and (small) shrimps

2 tbsp chopped oregano, plus
extra for garnishing
50 g/1¾ oz pecorino or
Parmesan cheese, grated

1 In a large saucepan,
bring the stock to the
boil. Add the rice and cook
for about 12 minutes,
stirring, until the rice is
tender or according to the
instructions on the packet.
Drain thoroughly,
reserving any excess liquid.

2 Heat the butter in a
large frying pan (skillet)
and add the garlic, stirring.

3 Add the raw mixed
seafood to the pan
(skillet) and cook for 5
minutes. If the seafood is
already cooked, fry for
2–3 minutes.

4 Stir the oregano into
the seafood mixture
in the frying pan (skillet).

5 Add the cooked rice to
the pan and cook for
2–3 minutes, stirring, or
until hot. Add the reserved
stock if the mixture gets
too sticky.

6 Add the pecorino or
Parmesan cheese and
mix well.

7 Transfer the risotto to
warm serving dishes
and serve immediately.

COOK'S TIP

*The Genoese are excellent
cooks, and they make
particularly delicious fish
dishes flavoured with the
local olive oil.*

Vegetables, salads, Bakes

The recipes in this chapter offer something special for every occasion: filling vegetarian suppers, unusual vegetable side dishes, main course and side salads. You could even take many of the salads on a picnic and, of course, they are perfect as accompaniments for summer barbecues.

Many of the recipes are classic dishes, others are imaginative and sometimes surprising new combinations of vegetables and pasta. Try making a sophisticated family meal using an unusual vegetable such as fennel. Whatever you choose, in this section you will find a range of superb side dishes to get the tastebuds tingling.

Tagliatelle with Pumpkin

Serves 4

INGREDIENTS

500 g/1 lb 2 oz pumpkin or
    butternut squash, peeled and
    seeded
3 tbsp olive oil
1 onion, finely chopped
2 garlic cloves, crushed

4–6 tbsp chopped fresh parsley
pinch of freshly grated nutmeg
about 250 ml/9 fl oz/1$\frac{1}{4}$ cups
    chicken or vegetable stock
115 g/4 oz Parma ham
    (prosciutto)

250 g/9 oz dried tagliatelle
150 ml/$\frac{1}{4}$ pint/$\frac{5}{8}$ cup double
    (heavy cream)
salt and pepper
freshly grated Parmesan cheese,
    to serve

1 Cut the pumpkin or butternut squash in half and scoop out the seeds. Cut the flesh into 1 cm/$\frac{1}{2}$ inch dice.

2 Heat 2 tbsp of the olive oil in a large saucepan and fry the onion and garlic over a low heat for about 3 minutes, until soft. Add half the parsley and fry for 1 minute.

3 Add the pumpkin or squash pieces and cook for 2–3 minutes. Season to taste with salt, pepper and nutmeg.

4 Add half the stock to the pan, bring to the boil, cover and simmer for 10 minutes, or until the pumpkin or squash is tender, adding more stock if necessary.

5 Add the Parma ham (prosciutto) to the pan and cook, stirring frequently, for 2 minutes.

6 Bring a large pan of lightly salted water to the boil. Add the tagliatelle and the remaining oil and cook for 12 minutes, until tender, but still firm to the bite. Drain and transfer to a warm serving dish.

7 Stir the cream into the pumpkin and ham mixture and heat through. Spoon over the pasta, sprinkle over the remaining parsley and serve immediately.

Aubergine (Eggplant) Cake

Serves 4

INGREDIENTS

1 aubergine (eggplant), thinly sliced
5 tbsp olive oil
250 g/8 oz/2 cups dried fusilli
600 ml/1 pint/2$\frac{1}{2}$ cups Béchamel sauce
90 g/3 oz/$\frac{3}{4}$ cup grated Cheddar cheese
butter, for greasing

25 g/1 oz/$\frac{1}{3}$ cup freshly grated Parmesan cheese
salt and pepper

Lamb sauce:
2 tbsp olive oil
1 large onion, sliced
2 celery sticks (stalks), thinly sliced

450 g/1 lb minced (ground) lamb
3 tbsp tomato purée (paste)
150 g/5$\frac{1}{2}$ oz bottled sun-dried tomatoes, drained and chopped
1 tsp dried oregano
1 tbsp red wine vinegar
150 ml/$\frac{1}{4}$ pint/$\frac{5}{8}$ cup chicken stock

1 Sprinkle the aubergine (eggplant) slices with salt and set aside.

2 Fry the onion and celery in the oil for 3–4 minutes. Add the lamb and fry until browned. Stir in the remaining sauce ingredients and bring to the boil for 20 minutes.

3 Rinse the aubergine (eggplant) slices, drain and pat dry. Heat 4 tbsp of the oil in a frying pan (skillet). Fry the aubergine (eggplant) slices on each side for 4 minutes. Remove from the pan and drain.

4 Cook the fusilli and the remaining oil in a pan of salted boiling water until almost tender. Drain.

5 Gently heat the Béchamel Sauce. Stir in the Cheddar and then stir half of the cheese sauce into the fusilli.

6 Make layers of fusilli, lamb sauce and aubergine (eggplant) in a greased dish. Top with the remaining cheese sauce. Sprinkle with Parmesan and bake in a preheated oven at 190°C/375°F/Gas 5 for 25 minutes. Serve hot or cold.

Fettuccine all'Alfredo

Serves 4

INGREDIENTS

25 g/1 oz/2 tbsp butter
200 ml/7 fl oz/⅞ cup double
   (heavy) cream
460 g/1 lb fresh fettuccine
1 tbsp olive oil

90 g/3 oz/1 cup freshly grated
   Parmesan cheese, plus extra
   to serve
pinch of freshly grated nutmeg
salt and pepper

fresh parsley sprigs, to garnish

1 Put the butter and
150 ml/¼ pint/⅝ cup
of the cream in a large
saucepan and bring the
mixture to the boil over a
medium heat. Reduce the
heat and then simmer
gently for about
1½ minutes, or until
slightly thickened.

2 Meanwhile, bring a
large pan of lightly
salted water to the boil.
Add the fettuccine and
olive oil and cook for 2–3
minutes, until tender but
still firm to the bite. Drain
the fettuccine, then pour
over the cream sauce.

3 Using 2 forks, toss the
fettuccine in the sauce
over a low heat until
thoroughly coated.

4 Add the remaining
cream, the Parmesan
cheese and nutmeg to the
fettuccine mixture and
season to taste. Toss
thoroughly to coat while
gently heating through.

5 Transfer the fettuccine
mixture to a warm
serving plate and garnish
with the fresh parsley
sprigs. Serve immediately,
handing extra grated
Parmesan cheese separately.

VARIATION

*This classic Roman dish is
often served with the
addition of strips of ham
and fresh peas. Add 225 g/
8 oz/2 cups shelled cooked
peas and 175 g/6 oz ham
strips with the Parmesan
cheese in step 4.*

Macaroni Bake

Serves 4

INGREDIENTS

460 g/1 lb/4 cups dried short-cut macaroni	460 g/1 lb potatoes, thinly sliced	(heavy) cream
1 tbsp olive oil	460 g/1 lb onions, sliced	salt and pepper
60 g/2 oz/4 tbsp beef dripping	225 g/8 oz/2 cups grated mozzarella cheese	crusty brown bread and butter, to serve
	150 ml/5 fl oz/⅔ cup double	

1 Bring a large saucepan of lightly salted water to the boil. Add the macaroni and olive oil and cook for about 12 minutes, until tender but still firm to the bite. Drain the macaroni thoroughly and set aside.

2 Melt the dripping in a large flameproof casserole, then remove from the heat.

3 Make alternate layers of potatoes, onions, macaroni and grated cheese in the dish, seasoning well

with salt and pepper between each layer and finishing with a layer of cheese on top. Finally, pour the cream over the top layer of cheese.

4 Bake in a preheated oven at 200°C/400°F/ Gas 6 for 25 minutes. Remove the dish from the oven and carefully brown the top of the bake under a hot grill (broiler).

5 Serve the bake straight from the dish with crusty brown bread and butter as a main course.

Alternatively, serve as a vegetable accompaniment with your favourite main course.

VARIATION

For a stronger flavour, use mozzarella affumicata, *a smoked version of this cheese, or* Gruyère (Swiss) *cheese instead of the mozzarella.*

Creamy Pasta & Broccoli

Serves 4

INGREDIENTS

60 g/2 oz/4 tbsp butter
1 large onion, finely chopped
450 g/1 lb dried ribbon pasta
460 g/1 lb broccoli, broken into
    florets (flowerets)

150 ml/¼ pint/⅔ cup boiling
    vegetable stock
1 tbsp plain (all purpose) flour
150 ml/¼ pint/⅔ cup single
    (light) cream

60 g/2 oz/½ cup grated
    mozzarella cheese
freshly grated nutmeg
salt and white pepper
fresh apple slices, to garnish

1 Melt half of the butter in a large saucepan over a medium heat. Add the onion and fry for 4 minutes.

2 Add the pasta and broccoli to the pan and cook, stirring constantly, for 2 minutes. Add the vegetable stock, bring back to the boil and simmer for a further 12 minutes. Season well with salt and white pepper.

3 Meanwhile, melt the remaining butter in a saucepan over a medium heat. Stir in the flour and cook for 2 minutes. Gradually stir in the cream and bring to simmering point, but do not boil. Add the grated cheese and season with salt and a little freshly grated nutmeg.

4 Drain the pasta and broccoli mixture and pour over the cheese sauce. Cook, stirring occasionally, for about 2 minutes. Transfer the pasta and broccoli mixture to a warm, large, deep serving dish and serve garnished with slices of fresh apple.

VARIATION

This dish would also be delicious and look just as colourful made with Cape broccoli, which is actually a purple variety of cauliflower and not broccoli at all.

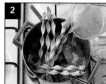

Paglia e Fieno

Serves 4

INGREDIENTS

60 g/2 oz/4 tbsp butter
900 g/1 lb fresh peas, shelled
200 ml/7 fl oz/⅞ cup double (heavy) cream

460 g/1 lb mixed fresh green and white spaghetti or tagliatelle
1 tbsp olive oil
pinch of freshly grated nutmeg

60 g/2/ oz/⅔ cup freshly grated Parmesan cheese, plus extra to serve
salt and pepper

1 Melt the butter in a large saucepan. Add the peas and cook, over a low heat, for 2–3 minutes.

2 Using a measuring jug (pitcher), pour 150 ml/ 5 fl oz/⅝ cup of the cream into the pan, bring to the boil and simmer for 1–1½ minutes, until slightly thickened. Remove the pan from the heat.

3 Meanwhile, bring a large pan of lightly salted water to the boil.

Add the spaghetti or tagliatelle and olive oil and cook for 2–3 minutes, until just tender but still firm to the bite. Remove the pan from the heat, drain the pasta thoroughly and return to the pan.

4 Add the peas and cream sauce to the pasta. Return the pan to the heat and add the remaining cream and the Parmesan cheese and season to taste with salt, black pepper and grated nutmeg.

5 Using 2 forks, gently toss the pasta to coat with the peas and cream sauce, while heating through.

6 Transfer the pasta to a serving dish and serve immediately, with extra Parmesan cheese.

Green Tagliatelle with Garlic

Serves 4

INGREDIENTS

2 tbsp walnut oil
1 bunch spring onions (scallions), sliced
2 garlic cloves, thinly sliced
250 g/8 oz/3¼ cups sliced mushrooms
450 g/1 lb fresh green and white tagliatelle

1 tbsp olive oil
225 g/8 oz frozen spinach, thawed and drained
115 g/4 oz/½ cup full-fat soft cheese with garlic and herbs
4 tbsp single (light) cream

60 g/2 oz/½ cup chopped, unsalted pistachio nuts
2 tbsp shredded fresh basil
salt and pepper
fresh basil sprigs, to garnish
Italian bread, to serve

1 Heat the walnut oil in a large frying pan (skillet). Add the spring onions (scallions) and garlic and fry for 1 minute, until just softened.

2 Add the mushrooms to the pan, stir well, cover and cook over a low heat for about 5 minutes, until softened.

3 Meanwhile, bring a large saucepan of lightly salted water to the boil. Add the tagliatelle and olive oil and cook for 3–5 minutes, until tender but still firm to the bite. Drain and return to the saucepan.

4 Add the spinach to the frying pan (skillet) and heat through for 1–2 minutes. Add the cheese to the pan and allow to melt slightly. Stir in the cream and continue to cook, without allowing the mixture to come to the boil, until warmed through.

5 Pour the sauce over the tagliatelle, season with salt and black pepper to taste and mix well. Heat through gently, stirring constantly, for 2–3 minutes.

6 Transfer the pasta to a serving dish and sprinkle with the pistachio nuts and shredded basil. Garnish with the basil sprigs and serve with the Italian bread of your choice.

Spaghetti Olio e Aglio

Serves 4

INGREDIENTS

125 ml/4 fl oz/$\frac{1}{2}$ cup olive oil
3 garlic cloves, crushed
460 g/1 lb fresh spaghetti

3 tbsp roughly chopped fresh
parsley

salt and pepper

1 Reserve 1 tbsp of the olive oil and heat the remainder in a medium saucepan. Add the garlic and a pinch of salt and cook over a low heat, stirring constantly, until golden brown, then remove the pan from the heat. Do not allow the garlic to burn as it will taint its flavour. (If it does burn, you will have to start all over again!)

2 Meanwhile, bring a large saucepan of lightly salted water to the boil. Add the spaghetti and remaining olive oil and cook for 2–3 minutes, until tender, but still firm to the bite. Drain the spaghetti thoroughly and return to the pan.

3 Add the oil and garlic mixture to the spaghetti and toss to coat thoroughly. Season with pepper, add the chopped fresh parsley and toss to coat again.

4 Transfer the spaghetti to a warm serving dish and serve immediately.

COOK'S TIP

It is worth buying the best-quality olive oil for dishes such as this one which makes a feature of its flavour. Extra virgin oil is produced from the first pressing and has the lowest acidity. It is more expensive than other types of olive oil, but has the finest flavour. Virgin olive oil is slightly more acid, but is also well flavoured. Oil simply labelled pure has usually been heat-treated and refined by mechanical means and, consequently, lacks character and flavour.

Patriotic Pasta

Serves 4

INGREDIENTS

460 g/1 lb/4 cups dried farfalle	460 g/1 lb cherry tomatoes	salt and pepper
4 tbsp olive oil	90 g/3 oz rocket (arugula)	Pecorino cheese, to garnish

1 Bring a large saucepan of lightly salted water to the boil. Add the farfalle and 1 tbsp of the olive oil and cook until tender, but still firm to the bite. Drain the farfalle thoroughly and return to the pan.

2 Cut the cherry tomatoes in half and trim the rocket (arugula).

3 Heat the remaining olive oil in a large saucepan. Add the tomatoes and cook for 1 minute. Add the farfalle and the rocket (arugula) and stir gently to mix. Heat through and season to taste with salt and black pepper.

4 Meanwhile, using a vegetable peeler, shave thin slices of Pecorino cheese.

5 Transfer the farfalle and vegetables to a warm serving dish. Garnish with the Pecorino cheese shavings and serve immediately.

COOK'S TIP

Pecorino cheese is a hard sheep's milk cheese which resembles Parmesan and is often used for grating over a variety of dishes. It has a sharp flavour and is only used in small quantities.

COOK'S TIP

Rocket (arugula) is a small plant with irregular-shaped leaves rather like those of turnip tops (greens). The flavour is distinctively peppery and slightly reminiscent of radish. It has always been popular in Italy, both in salads and for serving with pasta and has recently enjoyed a revival in Britain and the United States, where it has now become very fashionable.

Mediterranean Spaghetti

Serves 4

INGREDIENTS

2 tbsp olive oil
1 large, red onion, chopped
2 garlic cloves, crushed
1 tbsp lemon juice
4 baby aubergines (eggplants), quartered

600 ml/1 pint/2½ cups passata (sieved tomatoes)
2 tsp caster (superfine) sugar
2 tbsp tomato purée (paste)
400 g/14 oz can artichoke hearts, drained and halved

115 g/4 oz/1 cup stoned (pitted) black olives
350 g/12 oz dried spaghetti
25 g/1 oz/2 tbsp butter
salt and pepper
fresh basil sprigs, to garnish
olive bread, to serve

1 Heat 1 tbsp of the olive oil in a large frying pan (skillet). Add the onion, garlic, lemon juice and aubergines (eggplants) and cook over a low heat for 4–5 minutes, until the onion and aubergines (eggplants) are lightly golden brown.

2 Pour in the passata (sieved tomatoes), season to taste with salt and black pepper and stir in the caster (superfine) sugar and tomato purée (paste). Bring to the boil, then simmer, stirring occasionally, for 20 minutes.

3 Gently stir in the artichoke hearts and black olives and cook for 5 minutes.

4 Meanwhile, bring a large saucepan of lightly salted water to the boil. Add the spaghetti and the remaining oil and cook for 7–8 minutes, until tender but still firm to the bite.

5 Drain the spaghetti thoroughly and toss with the butter. Transfer the spaghetti to a large serving dish.

6 Pour the vegetable sauce over the spaghetti, garnish with the sprigs of fresh basil and serve immediately with olive bread.

Spinach & Wild Mushroom Lasagne

Serves 4

INGREDIENTS

115 g/4 oz/8 tbsp butter, plus extra for greasing	225 g/8 oz/2 cups grated Cheddar cheese	8 sheets pre-cooked lasagne
2 garlic cloves, finely chopped	$^1/_4$ tsp freshly grated nutmeg	salt and pepper
115 g/4 oz shallots	1 tsp chopped fresh basil	watercress salad, to serve
225 g/8 oz wild mushrooms, such as chanterelles	60 g/2 oz plain (all purpose) flour	
450 g/1 lb spinach, cooked, drained and finely chopped	600 ml/1 pint/2$^1/_2$ cups hot milk	
	60 g/2 oz/$^2/_3$ cup grated Cheshire cheese	

1 Lightly grease an ovenproof dish.

2 Melt 60 g/2 oz/4 tbsp of the butter in a saucepan. Add the garlic, shallots and wild mushrooms and fry over a low heat for 3 minutes. Stir in the spinach, Cheddar cheese, nutmeg and basil. Season well and set aside.

3 Melt the remaining butter in another saucepan over a low heat.

Stir in the flour and cook for 1 minute. Gradually stir in the hot milk, whisking constantly until smooth. Stir in 25 g/1 oz/$^1/_4$ cup of the Cheshire cheese and season to taste.

4 Spread half of the mushroom and spinach mixture over the base of the prepared dish. Cover with a layer of lasagne and then with half of the cheese sauce. Repeat and then sprinkle over the

remaining cheese. Bake in a preheated oven at 200°C/ 400°F/Gas 6 for 30 minutes, until golden brown. Serve hot.

VARIATION

Substitute 4 (bell) peppers for the spinach. Roast in a preheated oven at 200°C/ 400°F/Gas 6 for 20 minutes. Rub off the skins under cold water, deseed and chop before using.

Ravioli with Vegetable Stuffing

Serves 4

INGREDIENTS

450 g/1 lb Basic Pasta Dough
1 tbsp olive oil
90 g/3 oz/6 tbsp butter
150 ml/5 fl oz/⅔ cup single
(light) cream
75 g/3 oz/1 cup freshly grated
Parmesan cheese

STUFFING:
2 large aubergines (eggplants)
3 large courgettes (zucchini)
6 large tomatoes
1 large green (bell) pepper
1 large red (bell) pepper
3 garlic cloves
1 large onion

120 ml/4 fl oz/½ cup olive oil
60 g/2 oz tomato purée (paste)
½ tsp chopped fresh basil
salt and pepper
fresh basil sprig, to garnish

1 To make the stuffing, cut the aubergines (eggplants) and courgettes (zucchini) into 2.5 cm/1 inch chunks. Sprinkle the aubergine (eggplant) with salt and set aside for 20 minutes. Rinse and drain.

2 Blanch the tomatoes in boiling water for 2 minutes. Drain, skin and chop the flesh. Core and seed the (bell) peppers and cut into 2.5 cm/1 inch dice. Chop the garlic and onion.

3 Heat the oil in a saucepan and fry the garlic and onion for 3 minutes. Stir in the remaining stuffing ingredients and season with salt and pepper. Cover and simmer for 20 minutes, stirring frequently.

4 Roll out the pasta dough and cut out 7.5 cm/3 inch rounds. Put a spoonful of the vegetable stuffing on each round. Dampen the edges slightly

and fold the pasta rounds over, pressing to seal.

5 Bring a pan of salted water to the boil. Add the ravioli and the oil and cook for 3–4 minutes. Drain and transfer to a dish, dotting each layer with butter. Pour over the cream and sprinkle over the Parmesan cheese. Bake in a preheated oven at 200°C/400°F/Gas 6 for 20 minutes. Garnish and serve

Courgette (Zucchini) & Aubergine (Eggplant) Lasagne

Serves 6

INGREDIENTS

1 kg/2¼ lb aubergines (eggplants)

8 tbsp olive oil

25 g/1 oz/2 tbsp garlic and herb butter

450 g/1 lb courgettes (zucchini), sliced

225 g/8 oz/2 cups grated mozzarella cheese

600 ml/1 pint/2½ cups passata (sieved tomatoes)

6 sheets pre-cooked green lasagne

600 ml/1 pint/2½ cups Béchamel Sauce

60 g/2 oz/⅔ cup freshly grated Parmesan cheese

1 tsp dried oregano

salt and black pepper

1 Thinly slice the aubergines (eggplants), sprinkle with salt and set aside for 20 minutes. Rinse and pat dry.

2 Heat 4 tbsp of the oil in a large frying pan (skillet). Fry half the aubergine (eggplant) slices over a low heat for 6–7 minutes, until golden. Drain then repeat with the remaining oil and aubergine (eggplant) slices.

3 Melt the garlic and herb butter in the frying pan (skillet) and fry the courgettes (zucchini) for 5–6 minutes, until golden brown. Drain.

4 Place half the aubergine (eggplant) and courgette (zucchini) slices in a large ovenproof dish. Season with pepper and sprinkle over half the mozzarella cheese. Spoon over half the passata (sieved

tomatoes) and top with 3 sheets of lasagne. Repeat the process, ending with a layer of lasagne.

5 Spoon over the Béchamel sauce and sprinkle over the Parmesan cheese and oregano. Put the dish on a baking (cookie) sheet and bake in a preheated oven at 220°C/425°F/Gas 7 for 30–35 minutes, until golden brown. Serve.

Pasta & Bean Casserole

Serves 6

INGREDIENTS

225 g/8 oz/1¼ cups dried haricot (navy) beans, soaked overnight and drained
225 g/8 oz dried penne
6 tbsp olive oil
850 ml/1½ pints /3½ cups vegetable stock
2 large onions, sliced

2 garlic cloves, chopped
2 bay leaves
1 tsp dried oregano
1 tsp dried thyme
5 tbsp red wine
2 tbsp tomato purée (paste)
2 celery sticks (stalks), sliced
1 fennel bulb, sliced

115 g/4 oz/1½ cups sliced mushrooms
250 g/8 oz tomatoes, sliced
1 tsp dark muscovado sugar
4 tbsp dry white breadcrumbs
salt and pepper
salad leaves (greens) and crusty bread, to serve

1 Put the haricot (navy) beans in a large saucepan and add cold water to cover. Bring to the boil and boil vigorously for 20 minutes. Drain, set aside and keep warm.

2 Bring a large saucepan of lightly salted water to the boil. Add the penne and 1 tbsp of the olive oil and cook for about 3 minutes. Drain the pasta, set aside and keep warm.

3 Put the beans in a large, flameproof casserole. Add the vegetable stock and stir in the remaining olive oil, the onions, garlic, bay leaves, oregano, thyme, wine and tomato purée (paste). Bring to the boil, then cover and cook in a preheated oven at 180°C/350°F/Gas 4 for 2 hours.

4 Add the penne, celery, fennel, mushrooms and tomatoes to the casserole and season to taste with salt and pepper. Stir in the muscovado sugar and sprinkle over the breadcrumbs. Cover the dish and cook in the oven for 1 further hour.

5 Serve hot with salad leaves (greens) and crusty bread.

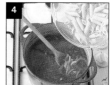

Creamed Spaghetti & Mushrooms

Serves 4

INGREDIENTS

60 g/2 oz/4 tbsp butter

2 tbsp olive oil

6 shallots, sliced

450 g/1 lb/6 cups sliced
button mushrooms

1 tsp plain (all purpose) flour

150 ml/¼ pint/⅔ cup double
(heavy) cream

2 tbsp port

115 g/4 oz sun-dried
tomatoes, chopped

freshly grated nutmeg

450g /1 lb dried spaghetti

1 tbsp freshly chopped parsley

salt and pepper

6 triangles of fried white bread,
to serve

1 Heat the butter and 1 tbsp of the oil in a large pan. Add the shallots and cook over a medium heat for 3 minutes. Add the mushrooms and cook over a low heat for 2 minutes. Season with salt and black pepper, sprinkle over the flour and cook, stirring constantly, for 1 minute.

2 Gradually stir in the cream and port, add the sun-dried tomatoes and a pinch of grated nutmeg and cook over a low heat for 8 minutes.

3 Bring a large saucepan of lightly salted water to the boil. Add the spaghetti and remaining olive oil and cook for 12–14 minutes, until tender but still firm to the bite.

4 Drain the spaghetti and return to the pan. Pour over the mushroom sauce and cook for 3 minutes. Transfer the spaghetti and mushroom sauce to a large serving plate and sprinkle over the chopped parsley. Serve with crispy triangles of fried bread.

VARIATION

Non-vegetarians could add 115 g/4 oz Parma ham (prosciutto), cut into thin strips and heated gently in 25 g/1 oz/2 tbsp butter, to the pasta along with the mushroom sauce.

Vegetable Pasta Stir-Fry

Serves 4

INGREDIENTS

400 g/14 oz dried wholemeal
(wholewheat) pasta shells or
other short pasta shapes
1 tbsp olive oil
2 carrots, thinly sliced
115 g/4 oz baby corn cobs
3 tbsp corn oil
2.5 cm/1 inch piece fresh root
ginger, thinly sliced
1 large onion, thinly sliced

1 garlic clove, thinly sliced
3 celery sticks (stalks), thinly
sliced
1 small red (bell) pepper, cored,
seeded and cut into
matchstick strips
1 small green (bell) pepper, cored,
seeded and cut into
matchstick strips
1 tsp cornflour (cornstarch)

2 tbsp water
3 tbsp soy sauce
3 tbsp dry sherry
1 tsp clear honey
a dash of hot pepper sauce
(optional)
salt
red (bell) pepper, finely sliced, to
garnish

1 Bring a large pan of
salted water to the boil.
Add the pasta and olive oil
and cook until tender, but
still firm to the bite. Drain
and keep warm.

2 Bring a saucepan of
lightly salted water to
the boil. Add the carrots
and corn cobs and cook
for 2 minutes. Drain,
refresh in cold water and
drain again.

3 Heat the corn oil in a
preheated wok or large
frying pan (skillet). Add the
ginger and stir-fry over a
medium heat for 1 minute.
Remove the ginger with a
slotted spoon and discard.

4 Add the onion, garlic,
celery and (bell)
peppers to the pan and stir-
fry for 2 minutes. Add the
carrots and baby corn cobs
and stir-fry for a further

2 minutes. Stir in the
drained pasta.

5 Mix the cornflour
(cornstarch) and water
to make a smooth paste.
Stir in the soy sauce,
sherry and honey. Pour the
cornflour mixture into the
pasta and cook, stirring
occasionally, for 2 minutes.
Stir in the pepper sauce, if
liked. Transfer to a serving
dish, garnish and serve.

Macaroni & Corn Pancakes

Serves 4

INGREDIENTS

2 corn cobs
60 g/2 oz/4 tbsp butter
115 g/4 oz red (bell) peppers,
    cored, seeded and finely
    diced
285 g/10 oz/2^1/$_2$ cups dried short-
    cut macaroni

150 ml/^{1}/$_4$ pint/ ^{5}/$_8$ cup double
    (heavy) cream
25 g/1 oz/^{1}/$_4$ cup plain (all
    purpose) flour
4 egg yolks
4 tbsp olive oil
salt and pepper

TO SERVE:
oyster mushrooms
fried leeks

1 Bring a pan of water to the boil, add the corn cobs and cook for about 8 minutes. Drain and refresh under cold running water for 3 minutes. Carefully cut away the kernels and set aside to dry.

2 Melt 25 g/1 oz/2 tbsp of the butter in a frying pan (skillet). Add the (bell) peppers and cook over a low heat for 4 minutes. Drain and pat dry with kitchen paper (towels).

3 Bring a large saucepan of lightly salted water to the boil. Add the macaroni and cook for about 12 minutes, until tender but still firm to the bite. Drain the macaroni and leave to cool in cold water until required.

4 Beat together the cream, flour, a pinch of salt and the egg yolks in a bowl until smooth. Add the corn and (bell) peppers to the cream and egg mixture. Drain the macaroni and

then toss into the corn and cream mixture. Season well with black pepper to taste.

5 Heat the remaining butter with the oil in a large frying pan (skillet). Drop spoonfuls of the mixture into the pan and press down until the mixture forms a flat pancake. Fry until golden on both sides, and all the mixture is used up. Serve with oyster mushrooms and fried leeks.

Vermicelli Flan

Serves 4

INGREDIENTS

75 g/3 oz/6 tbsp butter, plus extra, for greasing	1 green (bell) pepper, cored, seeded and sliced into thin rings	freshly grated nutmeg
225 g/8 oz dried vermicelli or spaghetti	150 ml/¼ pint/⅝ cup milk	1 tbsp freshly grated Parmesan cheese
1 tbsp olive oil	3 eggs, lightly beaten	salt and pepper
1 onion, chopped	2 tbsp double (heavy) cream	tomato and basil salad, to serve
140 g/5 oz button mushrooms	1 tsp dried oregano	

1 Generously grease a 20 cm/8 inch loose-based flan tin (pan).

2 Bring a large pan of lightly salted water to the boil. Add the vermicelli and olive oil and cook until tender, but still firm to the bite. Drain, return to the pan and toss in 25 g/1 oz/ 2 tbsp of the butter to coat.

3 Press the pasta on to the base and around the sides of the flan tin (pan) to make a flan case.

4 Melt the remaining butter in a frying pan (skillet) and fry the onion until it is translucent.

5 Add the mushrooms and (bell) pepper rings to the frying pan (skillet) and cook, stirring, for 2–3 minutes. Spoon the onion, mushroom and (bell) pepper mixture into the flan case and press it evenly into the base.

6 Beat together the milk, eggs and cream, stir in

the oregano and season to taste with nutmeg and black pepper. Carefully pour the mixture over the vegetables and sprinkle over the cheese.

7 Bake the flan in a preheated oven at 180°C/350°F/Gas 4 for 40–45 minutes, until the filling has set.

8 Slide the flan out of the tin (pan) and serve warm with a tomato and basil salad.

Fettuccine with Olive, Garlic & Walnut Sauce

Serves 4–6

INGREDIENTS

2 thick slices wholemeal
(wholewheat) bread, crusts
removed
300 ml/$^1/_2$ pint/1$^1/_4$ cups milk
275 g/9$^1/_2$ oz/2$^1/_2$ cups shelled
walnuts

2 garlic cloves, crushed
115 g/4 oz/1 cup stoned (pitted)
black olives
60 g/2 oz/$^2/_3$ cup freshly grated
Parmesan cheese
8 tbsp extra virgin olive oil

150 ml/$^1/_4$ pint/$^5/_8$ cup double
(heavy) cream
460 g/1 lb fresh fettuccine
salt and pepper
2–3 tbsp chopped fresh parsley

1 Put the bread in a
shallow dish, pour
over the milk and set aside
to soak until the liquid has
been absorbed.

2 Spread the walnuts out
on a baking (cookie)
sheet and toast in a
preheated oven at
190°C/375°F/Gas 5 for
about 5 minutes, until
golden. Set aside to cool.

3 Put the soaked bread,
walnuts, garlic, olives,

Parmesan cheese and
6 tbsp of the olive oil in a
food processor and work
to make a purée. Season
to taste with salt and
black pepper and add
the cream.

4 Bring a large pan of
lightly salted water to
the boil. Add the fettuccine
and 1 tbsp of the remaining
oil and cook for
2–3 minutes, until tender
but still firm to the bite.
Drain the fettuccine

thoroughly and toss with
the remaining olive oil.

5 Divide the fettuccine
between individual
serving plates and spoon
the olive, garlic and walnut
sauce on top. Sprinkle over
the fresh parsley and serve.

Linguine with Braised Fennel

Serves 4

INGREDIENTS

6 fennel bulbs
150 ml/¼ pint/⅝ cup
    vegetable stock
25 g/1 oz/2 tbsp butter

6 slices rindless, smoked bacon,
    diced
6 shallots, quartered
25 g/1 oz/¼ cup plain (all
    purpose) flour

7 tbsp double (heavy) cream
1 tbsp Madeira
450 g/1 lb dried linguine
1 tbsp olive oil
salt and pepper

1 Trim the fennel bulbs, then gently peel off and reserve the first layer of the bulbs. Cut the bulbs into quarters and put them in a large saucepan, together with the vegetable stock and the reserved outer layers. Bring to the boil, lower the heat and simmer for 5 minutes.

2 Using a slotted spoon, transfer the fennel to a large dish. Discard the outer layers of the fennel bulb. Bring the vegetable stock to the boil and allow to reduce by half. Set aside.

3 Melt the butter in a frying pan (skillet). Add the bacon and shallots and fry for 4 minutes. Add the flour, reduced stock, cream and Madeira and cook, stirring constantly, for 3 minutes, until the sauce is smooth. Season to taste and pour over the fennel.

4 Bring a large saucepan of lightly salted water to the boil. Add the linguine and olive oil and cook for 10 minutes, until tender but still firm to the bite. Drain and transfer to a deep ovenproof dish.

5 Add the fennel and sauce and braise in a preheated oven at 180°C/ 350°F/Gas 4 for 20 minutes. Serve immediately.

COOK'S TIP

Fennel will keep in the salad drawer of the refrigerator for 2–3 days, but it is best eaten as fresh as possible. Cut surfaces turn brown quickly, so do not prepare it too much in advance of cooking.

Baked Aubergine (Eggplant)
with Pasta

Serves 4

INGREDIENTS

225 g/8 oz dried penne or
   other short pasta shapes
4 tbsp olive oil, plus extra for
   brushing
2 aubergines (eggplants)
1 large onion, chopped

2 garlic cloves, crushed
400 g/14 oz can chopped
   tomatoes
2 tsp dried oregano
60 g/2 oz mozzarella cheese,
   thinly sliced

25 g/1 oz/⅓ cup freshly grated
   Parmesan cheese
2 tbsp dry breadcrumbs
salt and pepper
salad leaves (greens), to serve

1 Bring a pan of salted water to the boil. Add the pasta and 1 tbsp of the olive oil and cook until tender. Drain, return to the pan, cover and keep warm.

2 Cut the aubergines (eggplants) in half lengthways and score around the inside, being careful not to pierce the shells. Scoop out the flesh then brush the insides of the shells with oil. Chop the flesh and set aside.

3 Fry the onion in the remaining oil until translucent. Add the garlic and fry for 1 minute. Stir in the chopped aubergine (eggplant) and fry for 5 minutes. Add the tomatoes, oregano and seasoning. Bring to the boil and simmer for 10 minutes. Remove from the heat and stir in the pasta.

4 Brush a baking (cookie) sheet with oil and arrange the aubergine

(eggplant) shells in a single layer. Divide half the tomato and pasta mixture between them. Sprinkle over the mozzarella, then pile the remaining tomato and pasta mixture on top. Mix the Parmesan cheese and breadcrumbs and sprinkle over the top.

5 Bake in a preheated oven at 200°C/400°C/ Gas 6 for 25 minutes, until golden brown. Serve with salad leaves (greens).

Pasta with Green Vegetable Sauce

Serves 4

INGREDIENTS

225 g/8 oz/2 cups dried gemelli
    or other pasta shapes
1 tbsp olive oil
1 head green broccoli, cut into
    florets (flowerets)
2 courgettes (zucchini), sliced
225 g/8 oz asparagus spears

115 g/4 oz mange tout
    (snow peas)
115 g/4 oz frozen peas
25 g/1 oz/2 tbsp butter
3 tbsp vegetable stock
4 tbsp double (heavy) cream
freshly grated nutmeg

2 tbsp chopped fresh parsley
2 tbsp freshly grated
    Parmesan cheese
salt and pepper

1 Bring a large saucepan of lightly salted water to the boil. Add the pasta and olive oil and cook until tender, but still firm to the bite. Drain, return to the pan, cover and keep warm.

2 Steam the broccoli, courgettes (zucchini), asparagus spears and mangetout (snow peas) over a pan of boiling salted water until they begin to soften. Remove from the heat and refresh in cold water. Drain and set aside.

3 Bring a small pan of lightly salted water to the boil. Add the frozen peas and cook for 3 minutes. Drain the peas, refresh in cold water and then drain again. Set aside with the other vegetables.

4 Put the butter and vegetable stock in a pan over a medium heat. Add all of the vegetables, reserving a few of the asparagus spears, and toss until they have thoroughly heated through.

5 Stir in the double (heavy) cream and heat through, without bringing to the boil. Season to taste with salt, pepper and nutmeg.

6 Transfer the pasta to a warmed serving dish and stir in the chopped parsley. Spoon over the vegetable sauce and sprinkle over the Parmesan cheese. Arrange the reserved asparagus spears in a pattern on top and serve immediately.

Tagliatelle with Garlic Butter

Serves 4

INGREDIENTS

450 g/1 lb strong white flour, plus extra for dredging 2 tsp salt	4 eggs, beaten 3 tbsp olive oil 75 g/2³/₄ oz/5 tbsp butter, melted	3 garlic cloves, finely chopped 2 tbsp chopped, fresh parsley pepper

1 Sift the flour into a large bowl and stir in the salt.

2 Make a well in the middle of the dry ingredients and add the eggs and 2 tablespoons of oil. Using a wooden spoon, stir in the eggs, gradually drawing in the flour. After a few minutes the dough will be too stiff to use a spoon and you will need to use your fingers.

3 Once all of the flour has been incorporated, turn the dough out on to a floured surface and knead for about 5 minutes, until smooth and elastic. If you find the dough is too wet, add a little more flour and continue kneading. Cover with cling film (plastic wrap) and leave to rest for at least 15 minutes.

4 The basic dough is now ready; roll out the pasta thinly and create the pasta shapes required. This can be done by hand or using a pasta machine. Results from a machine are usually neater and thinner, but not necessarily better.

5 To make the tagliatelle by hand, fold the thinly rolled pasta sheets into 3 and cut out long, thin stips, about 1 cm/¹/₂ inch wide.

6 To cook, bring a large pan of water to the boil, add 1 tablespoon of oil and the pasta. It will take 2–3 minutes to cook, and the texture should have a slight bite to it. Drain thoroughly.

7 Mix together the butter, garlic and parsley. Stir into the pasta and serve immediately with plenty of black pepper.

COOK'S TIP

Generally allow about 150 g/5¹/₂ oz fresh pasta or about 100 g/3¹/₂ dried pasta per person.

Spicy Tomato Tagliatelle

Serves 4

INGREDIENTS

50 g/1¾ oz/3 tbsp butter
1 onion, finely chopped
1 garlic clove, crushed
2 small red chillies, deseeded
 and diced

450 g/1 lb fresh tomatoes,
 skinned, deseeded and diced
200 ml/7 fl oz/⅞ cup vegetable stock
2 tbsp tomato purée
1 tsp sugar

salt and pepper
675 g/1½ lb fresh green and white
 tagliatelle, or 350 g/12 oz dried

1 Melt the butter in a large saucepan. Add the onion and garlic and cook for 3–4 minutes or until softened.

2 Add the chillies to the pan and continue cooking for about 2 minutes.

3 Add the tomatoes and stock, reduce the heat and leave to simmer for 10 minutes, stirring.

4 Pour the sauce into a food processor and blend for 1 minute until smooth. Alternatively, push the sauce through a sieve.

5 Return the sauce to the pan and add the tomato purée, sugar, and salt and pepper to taste. Gently reheat over a low heat, until piping hot.

6 Cook the tagliatelle in a pan of boiling water according to the instructions on the packet or until it is cooked, but still has 'bite'. Drain the tagliatelle, transfer to serving plates and serve with the tomato sauce.

VARIATION

Try topping your pasta dish with 50 g/1¼ oz pancetta or unsmoked bacon, diced and dry-fried for 5 minutes until crispy.

Basil & Tomato Pasta

Serves 4

INGREDIENTS

1 tbsp olive oil	450 g/1 lb tomatoes, halved	salt and pepper
2 sprigs rosemary	1 tbsp sun-dried tomato paste	675 g/1½ lb fresh farfalle or
2 cloves garlic, unpeeled	12 fresh basil leaves, plus extra	350 g/12 oz dried farfalle
	to garnish	

1 Place the oil, rosemary, garlic and tomatoes, skin side up, in a shallow roasting tin (pan).

2 Drizzle with a little oil and cook under a preheated grill (broiler) for 20 minutes or until the tomato skins are slightly charred.

3 Peel the skin from the tomatoes. Roughly chop the tomato flesh and place in a pan.

4 Squeeze the pulp from the garlic cloves and mix with the tomato flesh and sun-dried tomato paste.

5 Roughly tear the fresh basil leaves into smaller pieces and then stir them into the sauce. Season with a little salt and pepper to taste.

6 Cook the farfalle in a saucepan of boiling water according to the instructions on the packet or until it is cooked through, but still has 'bite'. Drain.

7 Gently heat the tomato and basil sauce.

8 Transfer the farfalle to serving plates and serve with the basil and tomato sauce.

COOK'S TIP

This sauce tastes just as good when served cold in a pasta salad.

Basil & Pine Nut Pesto

Serves 4

INGREDIENTS

about 40 fresh basil leaves, washed and dried	50 g/1¾ oz Parmesan cheese, finely grated	675 g/1½ lb fresh pasta or 350 g/12 oz dried pasta
3 garlic cloves, crushed	2–3 tbsp extra virgin olive oil	
25 g/1 oz pine nuts	salt and pepper	

1 Rinse the basil leaves and pat them dry with paper towels.

2 Put the basil leaves, garlic, pine nuts and grated Parmesan into a food processor and blend for about 30 seconds or until smooth. Alternatively, pound the ingredients by hand, using a mortar and pestle.

3 If you are using a food processor, keep the motor running and slowly add the olive oil. Alternatively, add the oil drop by drop while stirring briskly. Season with salt and pepper.

4 Meanwhile, cook the pasta in a saucepan of boiling water according to the instructions on the packet or until it is cooked through, but still has 'bite'. Drain.

5 Transfer the pasta to a serving plate and serve with the pesto. Toss to mix well and serve hot.

COOK'S TIP

You can store pesto in the refrigerator for about 4 weeks. Cover the surface of the pesto with olive oil before sealing the container or bottle, to prevent the basil from oxidising and turning black.

VARIATION

Try making a walnut version of this pesto. Substitute 25 g/1 oz walnuts for the pine nuts and add 1 tablespoon walnut oil in step 2.

Pasta & Sicilian Sauce

Serves 4

INGREDIENTS

450 g/1lb tomatoes, halved
25 g/1 oz pine nuts
50 g/1¾ oz sultanas

1 x 50 g/1¾ oz can anchovies,
    drained and halved lengthways
2 tbsp concentrated tomato purée

675 g/1½ lb fresh or 350 g/12 oz
    dried penne

1 Cook the tomatoes under a preheated grill (broiler) for about 10 minutes. Leave to cool slightly, then once cool enough to handle, peel off the skin and dice the flesh.

2 Place the pine nuts on a baking tray (cookie sheet) and lightly toast under the grill (broiler) for 2–3 minutes or until golden.

3 Soak the sultanas in a bowl of warm water for about 20 minutes. Drain the sultanas thoroughly.

4 Place the tomatoes, pine nuts and sultanas in a small pan and gently heat.

5 Add the anchovies and tomato purée, heating the sauce for a further 2–3 minutes or until hot.

6 Cook the pasta in a saucepan of boiling water according to the instructions on the packet or until it is cooked through, but still has 'bite'. Drain thoroughly.

7 Transfer the pasta to a serving plate and serve with the hot Sicilian sauce.

VARIATION

Add 100 g/3½ oz bacon, grilled for 5 minutes until crispy, then chopped, instead of the anchovies, if you prefer.

COOK'S TIP

If you are making fresh pasta, remember that pasta dough prefers warm conditions and responds well to handling. Do not leave to chill and do not use a marble surface for kneading.

Tortelloni

Makes 36 pieces

INGREDIENTS

about 300 g/10 1/2 oz fresh pasta rolled out to thin sheets	3 garlic clove, crushed	25 g/1 oz pecorino cheese, finely grated, plus extra to garnish
75 g/2 3/4 oz/5 tbsp butter	50 g/1 3/4 oz mushrooms, wiped and finely chopped	1 tbsp oil
50 g/1 3/4 oz shallots, finely chopped	1/2 stick celery, finely chopped	salt and pepper

1 Using a serrated pasta cutter, cut 5 cm/2 inch squares from the sheets of fresh pasta. To make 36 tortelloni you will need 72 squares. Once the pasta is cut, cover the squares with cling film (plastic wrap) to stop them drying out.

2 Heat 25 g/1 oz/3 tbsp of the butter in a frying pan (skillet). Add the shallots, 1 crushed garlic clove, the mushrooms and celery and cook for 4–5 minutes.

3 Remove the pan from the heat, stir in the cheese and season with salt and pepper.

4 Spoon 1/2 teaspoon of the mixture on to the middle of 36 pasta squares. Brush the edges of the squares with water and top with the remaining 36 squares. Press the edges together to seal. Leave to rest for 5 minutes.

5 Bring a large pan of water to the boil, add the oil and cook the tortelloni, in batches, for 2–3 minutes. The tortelloni will rise to the surface when cooked and the pasta should be tender with a slight 'bite'. Remove from the pan with a perforated spoon and drain thoroughly.

6 Meanwhile, melt the remaining butter in a pan. Add the remaining garlic and plenty of pepper and cook for 1–2 minutes.

7 Transfer the tortelloni to serving plates and pour over the garlic butter. Garnish with grated pecorino cheese and serve immediately.

Milanese Sun-Dried Tomato Risotto

Serves 4

INGREDIENTS

1 tbsp olive oil	about 15 strands saffron	100 g/3^1/$_2$ oz frozen peas, defrosted
25 g/1 oz/2 tbsp butter	150 ml/5 fl oz/^{2}/$_3$ cup white wine	50 g/1^3/$_4$ oz Parma ham
1 large onion, finely chopped	850 ml/1^1/$_2$ pints/3^3/$_4$ cup hot	(prosciutto), shredded
350 g/12 oz arborio (risotto) rice,	vegetable or chicken stock	75 g/2^3/$_4$ oz Parmesan cheese, grated
washed	8 sun-dried tomatoes, cut into strips	

1 Heat the oil and butter in a large frying pan (skillet). Add the onion and cook for 4–5 minutes or until softened.

2 Add the rice and saffron to the frying pan (skillet), stirring well to coat the rice in the oil, and cook for 1 minute.

3 Add the wine and stock slowly to the rice mixture in the pan, a ladleful at a time, stirring and making sure that all the liquid is absorbed before adding the next ladleful of liquid.

4 About half-way through adding the stock, stir in the tomatoes.

5 When all of the wine and stock is incorporated, the rice should be cooked. Test by tasting a grain – if it is still crunchy, add a little more water and continue cooking. It should take at least 15 minutes to cook.

6 Stir in the peas, Parma ham (prosciutto) and cheese. Cook for 2–3 minutes, stirring, until hot. Serve with extra Parmesan.

COOK'S TIP

Italian rice is a round, short-grained variety with a nutty flavour, which is essential for a good risotto. Arborio is the very best kind to use. The finished dish should have moist but separate grains. This is achieved by adding the hot stock a little at a time, only adding more when the last addition is fully absorbed. Don't leave the risotto to cook by itself: it needs constant watching to see when more liquid is required.

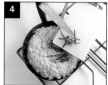

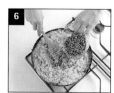

Wild Mushroom Risotto

Serves 4

INGREDIENTS

2 tbsp olive oil
1 large onion, finely chopped
1 garlic clove, crushed
200 g /7 oz mixed wild and
  cultivated mushrooms, such as
  ceps, oyster, porcini and button,
  wiped and sliced if large

250 g/9 oz arborio (risotto) rice,
  washed
pinch saffron threads
700 ml/1¼ pt/scant 3 cups hot
  vegetable stock
100 g/3½ oz Parmesan cheese,
  grated, plus extra for serving

2 tbsp chopped thyme
salt and pepper

1 Heat the oil in a large
frying pan (skillet).
Add the onions and garlic
and sauté for 3–4 minutes
or until softened.

2 Add the mushrooms to
the pan and cook for a
further 3 minutes or until they
are just beginning to brown.

3 Add the rice and saffron
to the pan and stir to
coat the rice in the oil.

4 Mix together the stock
and the wine and add to
the pan, a ladleful at a time.

Stir the rice mixture and
allow the liquid to be fully
absorbed before adding more
liquid, a ladleful at a time.

5 When all of the
wine and stock is
incorporated, the rice
should be cooked. Test by
tasting a grain – if it is still
crunchy, add a little more
water and continue
cooking. It should take at
least 15 minutes to cook.

6 Stir in the cheese and
thyme, and season with
freshly ground black pepper.

7 Transfer the risotto to
serving dishes and
serve sprinkled with extra
Parmesan cheese.

COOK'S TIP

*Wild mushrooms each have
their own distinctive flavours
and make a change from
button mushrooms. However,
they can be quite expensive, so
you can always use a mixture
with chestnut (crimini) or
button mushrooms instead.*

Chicken Risotto alla Milanese

Serves 4

INGREDIENTS

125 g/4¹/₂ oz/¹/₂ cup butter
900 g/2 lb chicken meat, sliced thinly
1 large onion, chopped
500 g/1 lb 2 oz/2¹/₂ cups risotto rice

600 ml/1 pint/2¹/₂ cups chicken stock
150 ml/¹/₂ pint/²/₃ cup white wine
1 tsp crumbled saffron
salt and pepper

60 g/2 oz/¹/₂ cup grated Parmesan
cheese, to serve

1 Heat 60 g/2 oz/4 tbsp of butter in a deep frying pan (skillet), and fry the chicken and onion until golden brown.

2 Add the rice, stir well, and cook for 15 minutes.

3 Heat the stock until boiling and gradually add to the rice. Add the white wine, saffron, salt and pepper to taste and mix well. Simmer gently for 20 minutes, stirring occasionally, and adding more stock if the risotto becomes too dry.

4 Leave to stand for a few minutes and just before serving add a little more stock and simmer for a further 10 minutes. Serve the risotto, sprinkled with the grated Parmesan cheese and the remaining butter.

COOK'S TIP

A risotto should have moist but separate grains. Stock should be added a little at a time and only when the last addition has been completely absorbed.

VARIATION

The possibilities for risotto are endless – try adding the following just at the end of cooking time: cashew nuts and sweetcorn, lightly sautéed courgettes (zucchini) and basil, or artichokes and oyster mushrooms.

Golden Chicken Risotto

Serves 4

INGREDIENTS

2 tbsp sunflower oil

15 g/^{1}/$_2$ oz/1 tbsp butter or margarine

1 medium leek, thinly sliced

1 large yellow (bell) pepper, diced

3 skinless, boneless chicken breasts, diced

350 g/12 oz round grain (arborio) rice

few strands saffron

1.5 litres/2^3/$_4$ pints/6^1/$_4$ cups chicken stock

200 g/7 oz can baby sweetcorn (baby corn)

60 g/2 oz/^{1}/$_2$ cup toasted unsalted peanuts

60 g/2 oz/^{1}/$_2$ cup grated Parmesan cheese

salt and pepper

1 Heat the oil and butter or margarine in a large saucepan. Fry the leek and (bell) pepper for 1 minute then stir in the chicken and cook, stirring until golden brown.

2 Stir in the rice and cook for 2–3 minutes.

3 Stir in the saffron strands, and salt and pepper to taste. Add the stock, a little at a time, cover and cook over a low heat, stirring occasionally, for about 20 minutes, until the rice is tender and most of the liquid is absorbed. Do not let the risotto dry out – add more stock if necessary.

4 Stir in the baby sweetcorn (baby corn), peanuts and Parmesan cheese, then adjust the seasoning to taste. Serve hot.

COOK'S TIP

Risottos can be frozen, before adding the Parmesan cheese, for up to 1 month, but remember to reheat this risotto thoroughly as it contains chicken.

Niçoise with Pasta Shells

Serves 4

INGREDIENTS

350 g/12 oz dried small pasta
    shells
1 tbsp olive oil
115 g/4 oz French (green) beans
50 g/1³/₄ oz can anchovies,
    drained
25 ml/1 fl oz/¹/₈ cup milk

2 small crisp lettuces
460 g/1 lb or 3 large beef
    tomatoes
4 hard-boiled (hard-cooked) eggs
225 g/8 oz can tuna, drained
115 g/4 oz/1 cup stoned (pitted)
    black olives

salt and pepper

VINAIGRETTE DRESSING:
50 ml/2 fl oz extra virgin olive oil
25 ml/1 fl oz white wine vinegar
1 tsp wholegrain mustard
salt and pepper

1 Bring a large saucepan of lightly salted water to the boil. Add the pasta and the olive oil and cook until tender, but still firm to the bite. Drain and refresh in cold water.

2 Bring a small saucepan of lightly salted water to the boil. Add the beans and cook for 10–12 minutes, until tender but still firm to the bite. Drain, refresh in cold water, drain

thoroughly once more and then set aside.

3 Put the anchovies in a shallow bowl, pour over the milk and set aside for 10 minutes. Meanwhile, tear the lettuces into large pieces. Blanch the tomatoes in boiling water for 1–2 minutes, then drain, skin and roughly chop the flesh. Shell the eggs and cut into quarters. Cut the tuna into large chunks.

4 Drain the anchovies and the pasta. Put all of the salad ingredients, the beans and the olives into a large bowl and gently mix together.

5 To make the vinaigrette dressing, beat together all the ingredients and keep in the refrigerator until required. Just before serving, pour the vinaigrette dressing over the salad.

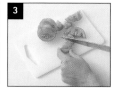

Pasta & Herring Salad

Serves 4

INGREDIENTS

250 g/9 oz dried pasta shells	2 large tart apples	6 pickled gherkins (dill pickles)
5 tbsp olive oil	2 baby frisée lettuces	2 tbsp capers
400 g/14 oz rollmop herrings in brine	2 baby beetroot (beet)	3 tbsp of tarragon vinegar
	4 hard-boiled (hard-cooked) eggs	salt and pepper
6 boiled potatoes	6 pickled onions	

1 Bring a large saucepan of lightly salted water to the boil. Add the pasta and 1 tbsp of the olive oil and cook until tender, but still firm to the bite. Drain the pasta thoroughly and then refresh in cold water.

2 Cut the herrings, potatoes, apples, frisée lettuces and beetroot (beet) into small pieces. Put all of these ingredients into a large salad bowl.

3 Drain the pasta thoroughly and add to the salad bowl. Toss lightly to mix the pasta and herring mixture together.

4 Carefully shell and slice the eggs. Garnish the salad with the slices of egg, pickled onions gherkins (dill pickles) and capers, sprinkle with the remaining olive oil and the tarragon vinegar and serve immediately.

COOK'S TIP

Store this salad, without the dressing, in a container in the refrigerator.

COOK'S TIP

Tarragon vinegar is available from most supermarkets, but you can easily make your own. Add a bunch of fresh tarragon to a bottle of white or red wine vinegar and leave to infuse for 48 hours. It is important to ensure that the tarragon is as fresh as possible and to discard any blemished leaves.

Neapolitan Seafood Salad with Campanelle

Serves 4

INGREDIENTS

450 g/1 lb prepared squid, cut into strips

750 g/1 lb 10 oz cooked mussels

450 g/1 lb cooked cockles in brine

150 ml/¹/₄ pint/⁵/₈ cup white wine

300 ml/¹/₂ pint/1¹/₄ cups olive oil

225 g/8 oz/2 cups dried campanelle or other small pasta shapes

juice of 1 lemon

1 bunch chives, snipped

1 bunch fresh parsley, finely chopped

4 large tomatoes, quartered or sliced

mixed salad leaves (greens)

salt and pepper

sprigs of fresh basil, to garnish

1 Put all of the seafood into a large bowl, pour over the wine and half the olive oil, and set aside for 6 hours.

2 Put the seafood mixture into a saucepan and simmer over a low heat for 10 minutes. Set aside to cool.

3 Bring a large saucepan of lightly salted water to the boil. Add the pasta and 1 tbsp of the remaining olive oil and cook until tender, but still firm to the bite. Drain thoroughly and refresh in cold water.

4 Strain off about half of the cooking liquid from the seafood and discard the rest. Mix in the lemon juice, chives, parsley and the remaining olive oil. Season to taste with salt and pepper. Drain the pasta and add to the seafood.

5 Cut the tomatoes into quarters. Shred the salad leaves (greens) and arrange them at the base of a salad bowl. Spoon in the seafood salad and garnish with the quartered or sliced tomatoes and a sprig of basil.

Pasta Salad with Red & White Cabbage

Serves 4

INGREDIENTS

260 g/9 oz/2 ¼ cups dried short-cut
   macaroni
5 tbsp olive oil
1 large red cabbage, shredded

1 large white cabbage, shredded
2 large apples, diced
260 g/9 oz cooked smoked bacon
   or ham, diced

8 tbsp wine vinegar
1 tbsp sugar
salt and pepper

1 Bring a large saucepan of lightly salted water to the boil. Add the macaroni and 1 tbsp of the olive oil and cook until tender, but still firm to the bite. Drain the pasta, then refresh in cold water. Drain again and set aside.

2 Bring a large saucepan of lightly salted water to the boil. Add the shredded red cabbage and cook for 5 minutes. Drain thoroughly and set aside to cool.

3 Bring a large saucepan of lightly salted water to the boil. Add the white cabbage and cook for 5 minutes. Drain thoroughly and set aside to cool.

4 In a large bowl, mix together the pasta, red cabbage and apple. In a separate bowl, mix together the white cabbage and bacon or ham.

5 In a small bowl, mix together the remaining oil, the vinegar and sugar and season to taste. Pour the dressing over each of the 2 cabbage mixtures and, finally, mix them all together. Serve.

VARIATION

Alternative dressings for this salad can be made with 4 tbsp olive oil, 4 tbsp red wine, 4 tbsp red wine vinegar and 1 tbsp sugar. Or substitute 3 tbsp olive oil and 1 tbsp walnut or hazelnut oil for the olive oil.

Dolcelatte, Nut & Pasta Salad

Serves 4

INGREDIENTS

225 g/8 oz/2 cups dried pasta shells
1 tbsp olive oil
115 g/4 oz/1 cup shelled and
  halved walnuts
225 g/8 oz dolcelatte cheese,
  crumbled

mixed salad leaves (greens), such
  as radicchio, escarole, rocket
  (arugula), lamb's lettuce (corn
  salad) and frisée
salt

DRESSING:
2 tbsp walnut oil
4 tbsp extra virgin olive oil
2 tbsp red wine vinegar
salt and pepper

1 Bring a large saucepan of lightly salted water to the boil. Add the pasta shells and olive oil and cook until just tender, but still firm to the bite. Drain the pasta, refresh under cold running water, drain thoroughly again and set aside.

2 Spread out the shelled walnut halves on to a baking (cookie) sheet and toast under a preheated grill (broiler) for 2–3 minutes. Set aside to cool.

3 To make the dressing, whisk together the walnut oil, olive oil and vinegar in a small bowl, and season to taste with salt and black pepper.

4 Arrange the salad leaves (greens) in a large serving bowl. Pile the cooled pasta in the middle of the salad leaves (greens) and sprinkle over the dolcelatte cheese. Pour the dressing over the pasta salad, scatter over the walnut halves and toss together to mix. Serve immediately.

COOK'S TIP

Dolcelatte is a semi-soft, blue-veined cheese from Italy. Its texture is creamy and smooth and the flavour is delicate, but piquant. You could substitute Roquefort as an alternative. Whichever cheese you choose, it is essential that it is of the best quality and in peak condition.

Goat's Cheese with Penne, Pear & Walnut Salad

Serves 4

INGREDIENTS

260 g/9 oz dried penne	2 ripe pears, cored and diced	4 tomatoes, quartered
5 tbsp olive oil	1 fresh basil sprig	1 small onion, sliced
1 head radicchio, torn into pieces	1 bunch of watercress, trimmed	1 large carrot, grated
1 Webbs lettuce, torn into pieces	2 tbsp lemon juice	250 g/9 oz goat's cheese, diced
7 tbsp chopped walnuts	3 tbsp garlic vinegar	salt and pepper

1 Bring a large saucepan of lightly salted water to the boil. Add the penne and 1 tbsp of the olive oil and cook until tender, but still firm to the bite. Drain the pasta, refresh under cold running water, drain thoroughly again and set aside to cool.

2 Place the radicchio and Webbs lettuce in a large salad bowl and mix together well. Top with the pasta, walnuts, pears, basil and watercress.

3 Mix together the lemon juice, the remaining olive oil and the vinegar in a measuring jug (pitcher). Pour the mixture over the salad ingredients and toss to coat the salad leaves well.

4 Add the tomato quarters, onion slices, grated carrot and diced goat's cheese and toss together, using 2 forks, until well mixed. Leave the salad to chill in the refrigerator for about 1 hour before serving.

Pasta & Garlic Mayonnaise Salad

Serves 4

INGREDIENTS

2 large lettuces	juice of 4 lemons	250 ml/9 fl oz/1^{1}/$_{8}$ cups fresh
260 g/9 oz dried penne	1 head of celery, sliced	garlic mayonnaise (see Cook's
1 tbsp olive oil	115 g/4 oz/^{3}/$_{4}$ cup shelled,	Tip, below right)
8 red eating apples	halved walnuts	salt

1 Wash, drain and pat dry the lettuce leaves with kitchen paper (towels). Transfer them to the refrigerator for 1 hour until crisp.

2 Meanwhile, bring a large saucepan of lightly salted water to the boil. Add the pasta and olive oil and cook until tender, but still firm to the bite. Drain the pasta and refresh under cold running water. Drain thoroughly again and set aside.

3 Core and dice the apples, place them in a small bowl and sprinkle with the lemon juice. Mix together the pasta, celery, apples and walnuts and toss the mixture in the garlic mayonnaise (see Cook's Tip, right). Add more mayonnaise, if liked.

4 Line a salad bowl with the lettuce leaves, spoon the pasta salad into the lined bowl and serve.

COOK'S TIP

Sprinkling the apples with lemon juice will prevent them from turning brown.

COOK'S TIP

To make homemade garlic mayonnaise, beat 2 egg yolks with a pinch of salt and 6 crushed garlic cloves. Start beating in 350 ml/ 12 fl oz/1^{1}/$_{2}$ cups olive oil, 1–2 tsp at a time, using a balloon whisk or electric mixer. When about one quarter of the oil has been incorporated, beat in 1–2 tbsp white wine vinegar. Continue beating in the oil, adding it in a thin, continuous stream. Finally, stir in 1 tsp Dijon mustard and season to taste.

Fusilli, Avocado, Tomato & Mozzarella Salad

Serves 4

INGREDIENTS

2 tbsp pine nuts (kernels)	2 tbsp lemon juice	DRESSING:
175 g/6 oz/1¹/₂ cups dried fusilli	3 tbsp chopped fresh basil	6 tbsp extra virgin olive oil
1 tbsp olive oil	salt and pepper	2 tbsp white wine vinegar
6 tomatoes	fresh basil sprigs, to garnish	1 tsp wholegrain mustard
225 g/8 oz mozzarella cheese		pinch of sugar
1 large avocado pear		

1 Spread the pine nuts (kernels) out on a baking (cookie) sheet and toast under a preheated grill (broiler) for 1–2 minutes. Remove and set aside to cool.

2 Bring a large saucepan of lightly salted water to the boil. Add the fusilli and olive oil and cook until tender, but still firm to the bite. Drain the pasta and refresh in cold water. Drain again and set aside to cool.

3 Thinly slice the tomatoes and the mozzarella cheese.

4 Cut the avocado pear in half, remove the stone (pit) and skin. Cut into thin slices lengthways and sprinkle with lemon juice to prevent discoloration.

5 To make the dressing, beat together all the dressing ingredients and season to taste with salt and black pepper.

6 Arrange the tomatoes, mozzarella cheese and avocado pear alternately in overlapping slices on a large serving platter.

7 Toss the pasta with half of the dressing and the chopped basil and season to taste. Spoon the pasta into the centre of the platter and pour over the remaining dressing. Sprinkle over the pine nuts (kernels), garnish with fresh basil sprigs and serve.

Pasta-Stuffed Tomatoes

Serves 4

INGREDIENTS

5 tbsp extra virgin olive oil, plus
    extra for greasing
8 beef tomatoes or large round
    tomatoes
115 g/4 oz/1 cup dried ditalini or
    other very small pasta shapes

8 black olives, stoned (pitted) and
    finely chopped
2 tbsp finely chopped fresh basil
1 tbsp finely chopped fresh
    parsley

60 g/2 oz/⅔ cup freshly grated
    Parmesan cheese
salt and pepper
fresh basil sprigs, to garnish

1 Brush a baking
(cookie) sheet with
olive oil.

2 Slice the tops off the
tomatoes and reserve
to make 'lids'. If the
tomatoes will not stand up,
cut a thin slice off the
bottom of each tomato.

3 Scoop out the tomato
pulp into a strainer,
but do not pierce the
tomato shells. Invert the
tomato shells, pat dry and
then set aside to drain.

4 Bring a large pan of
lightly salted water to
the boil. Add the pasta and
1 tbsp of the remaining
olive oil and cook until
tender, but still firm to the
bite. Drain and set aside.

5 Put the olives, chopped
basil, parsley and
Parmesan cheese into a
large mixing bowl and stir
in the drained tomato pulp.
Add the pasta to the bowl.
Stir in the remaining olive
oil and season to taste with
salt and pepper.

6 Spoon the pasta
mixture into the
tomato shells and replace
the lids. Arrange the
tomatoes on the baking
(cookie) sheet and bake in
a preheated oven at
190°C/375°F/Gas 5 for
15–20 minutes.

7 Remove the tomatoes
from the oven and
allow to cool until just
warm. Arrange on a
serving dish, garnish with
the fresh basil sprigs
and serve.

Rare Beef Pasta Salad

Serves 4

INGREDIENTS

450 g/1 lb rump or sirloin steak
  in one piece
450 g/1 lb dried fusilli
5 tbsp olive oil

2 tbsp lime juice
2 tbsp Thai fish sauce (see Cook's
  Tip, below right)
2 tsp clear honey
4 spring onions (scallions), sliced

1 cucumber, peeled and cut into
  2.5 cm/1 inch chunks
3 tomatoes, cut into wedges
3 tsp finely chopped fresh mint
salt and pepper

1 Season the steak with salt and black pepper. Grill (broil) or pan-fry the steak for 4 minutes on each side. Allow to rest for 5 minutes, then slice thinly across the grain.

2 Meanwhile, bring a large saucepan of lightly salted water to the boil. Add the fusilli and 1 tbsp of the olive oil and cook until tender, but still firm to the bite. Drain the fusilli, refresh in cold water and drain again. Toss the fusilli in the remaining oil.

3 Combine the lime juice, fish sauce and honey in a small saucepan and cook over a medium heat for 2 minutes.

4 Add the spring onions (scallions), cucumber, tomatoes and mint to the pan, then add the steak and mix well. Season to taste with salt.

5 Transfer the fusilli to a large, warm serving dish and top with the steak and salad mixture. Serve just warm or allow to cool.

COOK'S TIP

Thai fish sauce, also known as nam pla, is made from salted anchovies and has quite a strong flavour, so it should be used with discretion. It is available from some supermarkets and from Oriental food stores.

Beetroot (Beet) Cannolicchi

Serves 4

INGREDIENTS

300 g/11 oz dried ditalini rigati
5 tbsp olive oil
2 garlic cloves, chopped
400 g/14 oz can chopped
   tomatoes

400 g/14 oz cooked beetroot
   (beet), diced
2 tbsp chopped fresh basil leaves
1 tsp mustard seeds
salt and pepper

TO SERVE:
mixed salad leaves (greens),
   tossed in olive oil
4 Italian plum tomatoes, sliced

1 Bring a large pan of salted water to the boil. Add the pasta and 1 tbsp of the oil and cook for about 10 minutes, until tender, but still firm to the bite. Drain and set aside.

2 Heat the remaining oil in a large saucepan and fry the garlic for 3 minutes. Add the chopped tomatoes and cook for 10 minutes.

3 Remove the pan from the heat and carefully add the beetroot (beet), basil, mustard seeds and pasta and season to taste with salt and black pepper.

4 Serve on a bed of mixed salad leaves (greens) tossed in olive oil, and sliced plum tomatoes.

COOK'S TIP

Mustard seeds come from three different plants and may be black, brown or white. Black and brown mustard seeds have a stronger, more pungent flavour than white mustard.

COOK'S TIP

To cook raw beetroot (beet), trim off the leaves about 5 cm/2 inches above the root and ensure that the skin is not broken. Boil in very lightly salted water for 30–40 minutes, until tender. Leave to cool and rub off the skin.

Chilli & (Bell) Pepper Pasta Salad

Serves 4

INGREDIENTS

2 red (bell) peppers, halved and deseeded	4 tomatoes, halved	675 g/1¹/₂ lb fresh pasta or 350 g/
1 small red chilli	50 g/1³/₄ oz ground almonds	12 oz dried pasta
2 garlic cloves	7 tbsp olive oil	fresh oregano leaves, to garnish

1 Place the (bell) peppers, skin-side up, on a baking tray (cookie sheet) with the chilli and garlic. Cook under a preheated grill (broiler) for 15 minutes or until charred. After 10 minutes turn the tomatoes skin-side up.

2 Place the (bell) peppers and chillies in a polythene bag and leave to sweat for 10 minutes.

3 Remove the skin from the (bell) peppers and chillies and slice the flesh into strips, using a sharp knife.

4 Peel the garlic and peel and deseed the tomatoes.

5 Place the almonds on a baking tray (cookie sheet) and place under grill (broiler) for 2–3 minutes until golden.

6 Using a food processor, blend the (bell) pepper, chilli, garlic and tomatoes to make a purée. Keep the motor running and slowly add the olive oil to form a thick sauce. Alternatively, mash the mixture with a fork and beat in the olive oil, drop by drop.

7 Stir the toasted ground almonds into the mixture.

8 Warm the sauce in a saucepan until it is heated through.

9 Cook the pasta in a saucepan of boiling water according to the instructions on the packet or until it is cooked through, but still has 'bite'. Drain the pasta and transfer to a serving dish. Pour over the sauce and toss to mix. Garnish with fresh oregano leaves.

VARIATION

Add 2 tablespoons of red wine vinegar to the sauce and use as a dressing for a cold pasta salad, if you wish.

Pizza Margherita

Serves 4

INGREDIENTS

BASIC PIZZA DOUGH:
7 g/¼ oz dried yeast
1 tsp sugar
250 ml/9 fl oz/1 cup hand-hot water
350 g/12 oz strong flour
1 tsp salt
1 tbsp olive oil

TOPPING:
1 x 400 g/14 oz can tomatoes, chopped
2 garlic cloves, crushed
2 tsp dried basil
1 tbsp olive oil

2 tbsp tomato purée
100 g/3½ oz Mozzarella cheese, chopped
2 tbsp freshly grated Parmesan cheese
salt and pepper

1 Place the yeast and sugar in a measuring jug and mix with 50 ml/2 fl oz/4 tbsp of the water. Leave the yeast mixture in a warm place for 15 minutes or until frothy.

2 Mix the flour with the salt and make a well in the centre. Add the oil, the yeast mixture and the remaining water. Using a wooden spoon, mix to form a dough.

3 Turn the dough out on to a floured surface and knead for 4–5 minutes or until smooth.

4 Return the dough to the bowl, cover with an oiled sheet of cling film (plastic wrap) and leave to rise for 30 minutes or until doubled in size.

5 Knead the dough for 2 minutes. Stretch the dough with your hands, then place it on an oiled baking tray (cookie sheet), pushing out the edges until even and to the shape required. The dough should be no more than 6 mm/¼ inch thick because it will rise during cooking.

6 To make the topping, place the tomatoes, garlic, dried basil, olive oil and salt and pepper to taste in a large frying pan (skillet) and leave to simmer for 20 minutes or until the sauce has thickened. Stir in the tomato purée and leave to cool slightly.

7 Spread the topping evenly over the pizza base. Top with the Mozzarella and Parmesan cheeses and bake in a preheated oven at 200°C/400°F/Gas Mark 6 for 20–25 minutes. Serve hot.

Gorgonzola Pizza

Serves 4

INGREDIENTS

PIZZA DOUGH:
7 g/¼ oz dried yeast
1 tsp sugar
250 ml/9 fl oz/1 cup hand-hot water
175 g/6 oz wholemeal flour
175 g/6 oz strong white flour

1 tsp salt
1 tbsp olive oil

TOPPING:
400 g/14 oz pumpkin or squash,
    peeled and cubed

1 tbsp olive oil
1 pear, cored, peeled and sliced
100 g/3½ oz Gorgonzola cheese
1 sprig fresh rosemary, to garnish

1 Place the yeast and sugar in a measuring jug and mix with 50 ml/2 fl oz/4 tbsp of the water. Leave the yeast mixture in a warm place for 15 minutes or until frothy.

2 Mix both of the flours with the salt and make a well in the centre. Add the oil, the yeast mixture and the remaining water. Using a wooden spoon, mix to form a dough.

3 Turn the dough out on to a floured surface and knead for 4–5 minutes or until smooth.

4 Return the dough to the bowl, cover with an oiled sheet of cling film (plastic wrap) and leave to rise for 30 minutes or until doubled in size.

5 Remove the dough from the bowl. Knead the dough for 2 minutes. Using a rolling pin, roll out the dough to form a long oval shape, then place it on an oiled baking tray (cookie sheet), pushing out the edges until even. The dough should be no more than 6 mm/¼ inch thick because it will rise during cooking.

6 To make the topping, place the pumpkin in a shallow roasting tin (pan). Drizzle with the olive oil and cook under a preheated grill (broiler) for 20 minutes or until soft and lightly golden.

7 Top the dough with the pear and the pumpkin, brushing with the oil from the tin (pan). Sprinkle over the Gorgonzola. Bake in a preheated oven, at 200°C/400°F/Gas Mark 6 for 15 minutes or until the base is golden. Garnish with a sprig of rosemary.

Onion, Ham & Cheese Pizza

Serves 4

INGREDIENTS

1 portion of Basic Pizza Dough	250 g/9 oz onions, sliced into rings	100 g/3½ oz Mozzarella cheese,
	2 garlic cloves, crushed	sliced
TOPPING:	1 red (bell) pepper, diced	2 tbsp rosemary, stalks removed
2 tbsp olive oil	100 g/3½ oz raw ham (prosciutto),	and roughly chopped
	cut into strips	

1 Place the yeast and sugar in a measuring jug and mix with 50 ml/2 fl oz/4 tbsp of the water. Leave the yeast mixture in a warm place for 15 minutes or until frothy.

2 Mix the flour with the salt and make a well in the centre. Add the oil, the yeast mixture and the remaining water. Using a wooden spoon, mix to form a dough.

3 Turn the dough out on to a floured surface and knead for 4–5 minutes or until smooth. Return the dough to the bowl, cover with an oiled sheet of cling film (plastic wrap) and leave to rise for 30 minutes or until doubled in size.

4 Remove the dough from the bowl. Knead the dough for 2 minutes. Using a rolling pin, roll out the dough to form a square shape, then place it on an oiled baking tray (cookie sheet), pushing out the edges until even. The dough should be no more than 6 mm/¼ inch thick because it will rise during cooking.

5 To make the topping, heat the oil in a pan. Add the onions and garlic and cook for 3 minutes. Add the (bell) pepper and fry for a further 2 minutes.

6 Cover the pan and cook the vegetables over a low heat for 10 minutes, stirring occasionally, until the onions are slightly caramelized. Leave to cool slightly.

7 Spread the topping evenly over the pizza base. Place strips of ham (prosciutto), Mozzarella and rosemary over the top. Bake in a preheated oven at 200°C/400°F/Gas Mark 6 for 20–25 minutes. Serve hot.

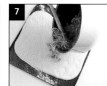

Sun-Dried Tomatoes & Ricotta Pizza

Serves 4

INGREDIENTS

1 portion Basic Pizza Dough	TOPPING: 4 tbsp sun-dried tomato paste 150 g/5¹/₂ oz ricotta cheese	10 sun-dried tomatoes 1 tbsp fresh thyme salt and pepper

1 Place the yeast and sugar in a measuring jug and mix with 50 ml/2 fl oz/4 tbsp of the water. Leave the yeast mixture in a warm place for 15 minutes or until frothy.

2 Mix the flour with the salt and make a well in the centre. Add the oil, the yeast mixture and the remaining water. Using a wooden spoon, mix to form a dough.

3 Turn the dough out on to a floured surface and knead for 4–5 minutes or until smooth.

4 Return the dough to the bowl, cover with an oiled sheet of cling film (plastic wrap) and leave to rise for 30 minutes or until doubled in size.

5 Remove the dough from the bowl. Knead the dough for 2 minutes.

6 Using a rolling pin, roll out the dough to form a circle, then place it on an oiled baking tray (cookie sheet), pushing out the edges until even. The dough should be no more than 6 mm/¹/₄ inch thick because it will rise during cooking.

7 Spread the sun-dried tomato paste over the dough, then add spoonfuls of ricotta.

8 Cut the sun-dried tomatoes into strips and arrange these on top of the pizza.

9 Sprinkle the thyme, and salt and pepper to taste over the top of the pizza. Bake in a preheated oven at 200°C/400°F/Gas Mark 6 for 30 minutes or until the crust is golden. Serve hot.

Mushroom Pizza

Serves 4

INGREDIENTS

1 portion Basic Pizza Dough	2 garlic cloves, crushed	200 g/7 oz mushrooms150 g/5¹/₂
	1 tsp dried basil	oz Mozzarella cheese, grated
TOPPING:	1 tbsp olive oil	salt and pepper
1 x 400 g/14 oz can chopped	2 tbsp tomato purée	basil leaves, to garnish
tomatoes		

1 Place the yeast and sugar in a measuring jug and mix with 50 ml/2 fl oz/4 tbsp of the water. Leave the yeast mixture in a warm place for 15 minutes or until frothy.

2 Mix the flour with the salt and make a well in the centre. Add the oil, the yeast mixture and the remaining water. Using a wooden spoon, mix to form a dough.

3 Turn the dough out on to a floured surface and knead for 4–5 minutes or until smooth. Return the dough to the bowl, cover

with an oiled sheet of cling film (plastic wrap) and leave to rise for 30 minutes or until doubled in size.

4 Remove the dough from the bowl. Knead the dough for 2 minutes. Using a rolling pin, roll out the dough to form an oval or a circular shape, then place it on an oiled baking tray (cookie sheet), pushing out the edges until even. The dough should be no more than 6 mm/¹/₄ inch thick because it will rise during cooking.

5 Using a sharp knife, chop the mushrooms into slices.

6 To make the topping, place the tomatoes, garlic, dried basil, olive oil and salt and pepper in a large pan and simmer for 20 minutes or until the sauce has thickened. Stir in the tomato purée and leave to cool slightly.

7 Spread the sauce over the base of the pizza, top with the sliced mushrooms and scatter over the Mozzarella.

8 Bake in a preheated oven at 200°C/400°F/Gas Mark 6 for 25 minutes. Just before serving, garnish with fresh basil leaves.

Mini-Pizzas

Makes 8

1 portion Basic Pizza Dough	100 g/3¹/₂ oz passata (tomato paste)	50 g/1³/₄ oz black olives, pitted and
	75 g/2³/₄ oz pancetta, diced	chopped
TOPPING:		1 tbsp mixed dried herbs
2 courgettes (zucchini)		2 tbsp olive oil

1 Place the yeast and sugar in a measuring jug and mix with 50 ml/2 fl oz/4 tbsp of the water. Leave the yeast mixture in a warm place for 15 minutes or until frothy.

2 Mix the flour with the salt and make a well in the centre. Add the oil, the yeast mixture and the remaining water. Using a wooden spoon, mix to form a dough.

3 Turn the dough out on to a floured surface and knead for 4–5 minutes or until smooth. Return the dough to the bowl,

cover with an oiled sheet of cling film (plastic wrap) and leave to rise for 30 minutes or until doubled in size.

4 Knead the dough for 2 minutes and divide it into 8 balls. Roll out each portion thinly to form circles or squares, then place them on an oiled baking tray (cookie sheet), pushing out the edges until even. The dough should be no more than 6 mm/ ¹/₄ inch thick because it will rise during cooking.

5 To make the topping, grate the courgettes (zucchini) finely. Cover

with paper towels and leave to stand for 10 minutes to absorb some of the juices.

6 Spread 2–3 teaspoons of the passata (tomato paste) over the pizza bases and top each with the grated courgettes (zucchini), pancetta and olives. Season with freshly ground black pepper, a sprinkling of mixed dried herbs and drizzle with olive oil.

7 Bake in a preheated oven at 200°C/400°F/ Gas Mark 6 for 15 minutes or until crispy. Season and serve hot.

Pizza with Tomato Sauce & Roasted (Bell) Peppers

Serves 4

INGREDIENTS

225 g/8 oz plain (all-purpose) flour
125 g/4¹/₂ oz butter, diced
¹/₂ tsp salt
2 tbsp dried Parmesan cheese
1 egg, beaten
2 tbsp cold water

2 tbsp olive oil
1 large onion, finely chopped
1 garlic clove, chopped
1 x 400 g/14 oz can chopped tomatoes
4 tbsp concentrated tomato purée

1 red (bell) pepper, halved
5 sprigs of thyme, stalks removed
6 black olives, pitted and halved
25 g/1 oz Parmesan cheese, grated

1 Sift the flour and rub in the butter to make breadcrumbs. Stir in the salt and dried Parmesan. Add the egg and 1 tablespoon of the water and mix with a round-bladed knife. Add more water if necessary to make a soft dough. Cover with cling film (plastic wrap) and chill for 30 minutes.

2 Meanwhile, heat the oil in a frying pan (skillet) and cook the onions and garlic for about 5 minutes or until golden. Add the tomatoes and cook for 8–10 minutes. Stir in the tomato purée.

3 Place the (bell) peppers, skin- side up, on a baking tray (cookie sheet) and cook under a preheated gril (broiler) for 15 minutes until charred. Place in a plastic bag and leave to sweat for 10 minutes. Peel off the skin and slice the flesh into thin strips.

4 Roll out the dough to fit a 23 cm/ 9 inch loose base fluted flan tin (pan).

Line with foil and bake in a preheated oven at 200°C/400°F/Gas Mark 6 for 10 minutes or until just set. Remove the foil and bake for a further 5 minutes until lightly golden. Leave to cool slightly.

5 Spoon the tomato sauce over the pastry base and top with the (bell) peppers, thyme, olives and fresh Parmesan. Return to the oven for 15 minutes or until the pastry is crisp. Serve warm or cold.

Folded-Over Pizza

makes 4 large or 8 small calzone

INGREDIENTS

1 portion of Basic Pizza Dough	TOPPING:	100 g/3¹⁄₂ oz Mozzarella,
freshly grated Parmesan cheese,	75 g/2³⁄₄ oz mortadella or other	cut into chunks
to serve	Italian pork sausage, chopped	2 tomatoes, diced
	50 g/1³⁄₄ oz Italian sausage, chopped	4 tbsp fresh oregano
	50 g/1³⁄₄ oz Parmesan cheese, sliced	salt and pepper

1 Place the yeast and sugar in a measuring jug and mix with 50 ml/2 fl oz/4 tbsp of the water. Leave the yeast mixture in a warm place for 15 minutes or until frothy.

2 Mix the flour with the salt and make a well in the centre. Add the oil, the yeast mixture and the remaining water. Using a wooden spoon, mix to form a dough.

3 Turn the dough out on to a floured surface and knead for 4–5 minutes or until smooth. Return the dough to the bowl, cover with an oiled sheet of cling film (plastic wrap) and leave to rise for 30 minutes or until doubled in size.

4 Knead the dough for 2 minutes and divide it into 4 pieces. Roll out each portion thinly to form circles. Place them on an oiled baking tray (cookie sheet). The dough should be no more than 6 mm/¹⁄₄ inch thick because it will rise during cooking.

5 To make the topping, place both Italian sausages, the Parmesan and the Mozzarella on one side of each circle. Top with the tomatoes and oregano. Season to taste with salt and pepper.

6 Brush around the edges of the dough with a little water then fold over the circle to form a pasty shape. Squeeze the edges together to seal so that none of the filling leaks out during cooking.

7 Bake in a preheated oven at 200°C/400°F/ Gas Mark 6 for 10–15 minutes or until golden. If you are making the smaller pizzas, reduce the cooking time to 8–10 minutes. Serve with freshly grated Parmesan cheese.

Pizza with Creamy Ham & Cheese Sauce

Serves 4

INGREDIENTS

250 g/9 oz flaky pastry, well chilled
40 g/1½ oz/3 tbsp butter
1 red onion, chopped
1 garlic clove, chopped
40 g/1½ oz strong flour

300 ml/½ pint/1¼ cups milk
50 g/1¾ oz Parmesan cheese, finely
    grated, plus extra for sprinkling
2 eggs, hard-boiled (hard-cooked),
    cut into quarters

100 g/3½ oz Italian pork sausage,
    such as feline salame,
    cut into strips
salt and pepper
sprigs of fresh thyme, to garnish

1 Fold the sheet of flaky pastry in half and coarsely grate it into 4 individual flan tins, 10 cm/4 inch across. Using a floured fork, press the pastry flakes down lightly so that they are even, there are no holes and the pastry comes up the sides of the tin.

2 Line with foil and bake blind in a preheated oven at 220°C/425°F/Gas Mark 7 for 10 minutes. Reduce the heat to 200°C/400°F/Gas Mark 6, remove the foil and cook

for a further 15 minutes or until golden and set.

3 Heat the butter in a pan. Add the onion and garlic and cook for 5–6 minutes or until softened.

4 Add the flour, stirring well to coat the onions. Gradually stir in the milk to make a thick sauce. Season well with salt and pepper and then stir in the Parmesan cheese. Do not reheat once the cheese has been added or the sauce will become stringy.

5 Spread the sauce over the pastry cases. Decorate with the egg and strips of sausage.

6 Sprinkle with a little extra Parmesan cheese, return to the oven and bake for 5 minutes, just to heat through.

7 Serve immediately, garnished with sprigs of fresh thyme.

Olive Oil Bread with Cheese

Makes 1 loaf

INGREDIENTS

15 g/½ oz dried yeast
1 tsp sugar
250 ml/9 fl oz hand-hot water

350 g/12 oz strong flour
1 tsp salt
3 tbsp olive oil

200 g/7 oz pecorino cheese, cubed
½ tbsp fennel seeds, lightly crushed

1 Mix the yeast with the sugar and 100 ml/3½ fl oz/8 tbsp of the water. Leave to ferment in a warm place for about 15 minutes.

2 Mix the flour with the salt. Add 1 tbsp of the oil, the yeast mixture and the remaining water to form a smooth dough. Knead the dough for 4 minutes.

3 Divide the dough into 2 equal portions. Roll out each portion to a form a round 6 mm/¼ inch thick. Place 1 round on a baking tray (cookie sheet). Scatter the cheese and half of the fennel

seeds evenly over the round.

4 Place the second round on top and squeeze the edges together to seal so that the filling does not leak during cooking.

5 Using a sharp knife, make a few slashes in the top of the dough and brush with the remaining olive oil.

6 Sprinkle with the remaining fennel seeds and leave to rise for 20–30 minutes.

7 Bake in a preheated oven at 200°C/400°F/Gas Mark 6 for 30 minutes

or until golden. Serve immediately.

COOK'S TIP

Pecorino is a hard, quite salty cheese, which is sold in most large supermarkets and Italian delicatessens. If you cannot obtain pecorino, use strong Cheddar or Parmesan cheese instead.

Roman Focaccia

Makes 16 squares

INGREDIENTS

7 g/¼ oz dried yeast
1 tsp sugar
300 ml/½ pint/1¼ cups
    hand-hot water

450 g/1 lb strong white flour
2 tsp salt
3 tbsp rosemary, chopped
2 tbsp olive oil

450 g/1 lb mixed red and white
    onions, sliced into rings
4 garlic cloves, sliced

1 Place the yeast and the sugar in a small bowl and mix with 100 ml/3½ fl oz/8 tablespoons of the water. Leave to ferment in a warm place for 15 minutes.

2 Mix the flour with the salt in a large bowl. Add the yeast mixture, half of the rosemary and the remaining water and mix to form a smooth dough. Knead the dough for 4 minutes.

3 Cover the dough with oiled cling film (plastic wrap) and leave to rise for 30 minutes or until doubled in size.

4 Meanwhile, heat the oil in a large pan. Add the onions and garlic and fry for 5 minutes or until softened. Cover the pan and continue to cook for a further 7–8 minutes or until the onions are lightly caramelized.

5 Remove the dough from the bowl and knead it again for 1–2 minutes.

6 Roll the dough out to form a square shape. The dough should be no more than 6 mm/¼ inch thick because it will rise during cooking. Place the

dough on to a large baking tray (cookie sheet), pushing out the edges until even.

7 Spread the onions over the dough, and sprinkle with the remaining rosemary.

8 Bake in a preheated oven 200°C/400°F/Gas Mark 6 for 25–30 minutes or until golden. Cut into 16 squares and serve immediately.

Sun-Dried Tomato Loaf

Makes 1 loaf

INGREDIENTS

7 g/¼ oz dried yeast	1 tsp salt	2 tbsp sun-dried tomato paste or
1 tsp sugar	2 tsp dried basil	tomato purée
300 ml/1¼ cups hand-hot water	450 g/1 lb strong white flour	12 sun-dried tomatoes, cut into strips

1 Place the yeast and sugar in a bowl and mix with 100 ml/3½ fl oz/ 8 tablespoons of the water. Leave to ferment in a warm place for 15 minutes.

2 Place the flour in a bowl and stir in the salt. Make a well in the dry ingredients and add the basil, the yeast mixture, tomato paste and half of the remaining water. Using a wooden spoon, draw the flour into the liquid and mix to form a dough, adding the rest of the water gradually.

3 Turn out the dough on to a floured surface

and knead for 5 minutes or until smooth. Cover with oiled cling film (plastic wrap) and leave in a warm place to rise for about 30 minutes or until doubled in size.

4 Lightly grease a 900 g/ 2 lb loaf tin (pan).

5 Remove the dough from the bowl and knead in the sun-dried tomatoes. Knead again for 2–3 minutes.

6 Place the dough in the tin (pan) and leave to rise for 30–40 minutes. Once it has doubled in size again, bake in a preheated oven at 190°C/375°F/Gas

Mark 5 for 30–35 minutes or until golden and the base sounds hollow when tapped.

COOK'S TIP

You could make mini sun-dried tomato loaves for children. Divide the dough into 8 equal portions, leave to rise and bake in mini-loaf tins (pans) for 20 minutes. Alternatively, make 12 small rounds, leave to rise and bake as rolls for 12–15 minutes.

Roasted (Bell) Pepper Bread

Serves 4

INGREDIENTS

1 red (bell) pepper, halved and deseeded	2 sprigs rosemary	300 ml/½ pint/1¼ cups hand-hot water
1 yellow (bell) pepper, halved and deseeded	1 tbsp olive oil	450 g/1 lb strong white flour
	7 g/¼ oz dried yeast	1 tsp salt
	1 tsp sugar	

1 Grease a 23 cm/ 9 inch deep round cake tin (pan).

2 Place the (bell) peppers and rosemary in a shallow roasting tin (pan). Pour over the oil and roast in a preheated oven, at 200°C/400°F/Gas Mark 6, for 20 minutes or until slightly charred. Remove the skin from the (bell) peppers and cut the flesh into slices.

3 Place the yeast and sugar in a small bowl and mix with 100 ml/3½ fl oz/8 tablespoons of hand-hot water. Leave to ferment in a warm place for about 15 minutes.

4 Mix the flour and salt together in a large bowl. Stir in the yeast mixture and the remaining water and mix to form a smooth dough.

5 Knead the dough for about 5 minutes until smooth. Cover with oiled cling film (plastic wrap) and leave to rise for about 30 minutes or until doubled in size.

6 Cut the dough into 3 equal portions. Roll the portions into rounds slightly larger than the cake tin (pan).

7 Place 1 round in the base of the tin (pan) so that it reaches up the sides of the

tin (pan) by about 2 cm/¾ inch. Top with half of the (bell) pepper mixture.

8 Place the second round of dough on top, followed by the remaining (bell) pepper mixture. Place the last round of dough on top, pushing the edges of the dough down the sides of the tin (pan).

9 Cover the dough with oiled cling film (plastic wrap) and leave to rise for 30–40 minutes. Place in the preheated oven and bake for 45 minutes until golden or the base sounds hollow when lightly tapped. Serve warm.

Green Easter Pie

Serves 4

INGREDIENTS

2 tbsp olive oil	125 ml/4 fl oz/scant $^1/_2$ cup white wine	4 eggs, beaten
1 onion, chopped	50 g/1$^3/_4$oz Parmesan cheese, grated	3 tbsp fresh marjoram, chopped
2 garlic cloves, chopped	100 g/3$^1/_2$ oz frozen peas, defrosted	50 g/1$^3/_4$ oz breadcrumbs
200 g/7 oz arborio (risotto) rice	80 g/3 oz rocket (arugula)	salt and pepper
700 ml/1$^1/_4$ pint/scant 3 cups hot chicken or vegetable stock	2 tomatoes, diced	

1 Light grease and then line the base of a 23 cm/9 inch deep cake tin (pan).

2 Using a sharp knife, roughly chop the rocket (arugula).

3 Heat the oil in a large frying pan (skillet). Add the onion and garlic and cook for 4–5 minutes or until softened.

4 Add the rice to the mixture in the frying pan (skillet), mix well to combine, then begin adding the stock a ladleful at a time. Wait until all of the stock has been absorbed before adding another ladleful of liquid.

5 Continue to cook the mixture, adding the wine, until the rice is tender. This will take at least 15 minutes.

6 Stir in the Parmesan cheese, peas, rocket (arugula), tomatoes, eggs and 2 tablespoons of the marjoram. Season to taste with salt and pepper.

7 Spoon the risotto into the tin (pan) and level the surface by pressing down with the back of a wooden spoon.

8 Top with the breadcrumbs and the remaining marjoram.

9 Bake in a preheated oven, at 180°C/350°F/ Gas Mark 4, for 30 minutes or until set. Cut into slices and serve immediately.

Spinach & Ricotta Pie

Serves 4

INGREDIENTS

225 g/8 oz spinach	2 large eggs, beaten	250 g/9 oz puff pastry, defrosted if
25 g/1 oz pine nuts	50 g/1³/₄ oz ground almonds	frozen
100 g/3¹/₂ oz ricotta cheese	40 g/1¹/₂ oz Parmesan cheese, grated	1 small egg, beaten

1 Rinse the spinach, place in a large saucepan and cook for 4-5 minutes until wilted. Drain thoroughly. When the spinach is cool enough to handle, squeeze out the excess liquid.

2 Place the pine nuts on a baking tray (cookie sheet) and lightly toast under a preheated grill (broiler) for 2–3 minutes or until golden.

3 Place the ricotta, spinach and eggs in a bowl and mix together. Add the pine nuts, beat well, then stir in the ground almonds and Parmesan cheese.

4 Roll out the puff pastry and make 2 x 20 cm/ 8 inch squares. Trim the edges, reserving the pastry trimmings.

5 Place 1 pastry square on a baking tray (cookie sheet). Spoon over the spinach mixture, keeping within 12 mm/¹/₂ inch of the edge of the pastry. Brush the edges with beaten egg and place the second square over the top.

6 Using a round-bladed knife, press the pastry edges together by tapping along the sealed edge. Use the pastry trimmings to make leaves to decorate the pie.

7 Brush the pie with the beaten egg and bake in a preheated oven, at 220°C/425°F/Gas Mark 8, for 10 minutes. Reduce the oven temperature to 190°C/375°F/Gas Mark 5 and bake for a further 25–30 minutes. Serve hot.

COOK'S TIP

Spinach is very nutritious as it is full of iron – this is particularly important for women and elderly people who may lack this in their diet.

Desserts

If when you think about cooking with pasta,
desserts do not usually spring to the forefront of
your mind, you will be amazed by the
wonderfully self-indulgent sweet treats made
from pasta in this chapter.

The Italians love their desserts, but when
there is a special gathering or celebration, then a
special effort is made and the delicacies appear.
The Sicilians are said to have the sweetest tooth of
all, and many Italian desserts are thought to have
originated there. You have to go a very long way to
beat a Sicilian ice cream – they truly are
the best in the world!

Fresh fruit also features in many Italian desserts –
oranges are often peeled and served whole,
marinated in a fragrant syrup and liqueur.

Chocolate, too, is popular for a deliciously wicked
end to a meal. Whatever your preference, there is
sure to be an Italian dessert to tempt and
satisfy you – you'll never be disappointed!

Baked Sweet Ravioli

Serves 4

INGREDIENTS

PASTA:
425 g/15 oz/3³/₄ cups plain
    (all purpose) flour
140 g/ 5 oz/10 tbsp butter, plus
    extra for greasing
140 g/ 5 oz/³/₄ cup caster
    (superfine) sugar
4 eggs

25 g/1 oz yeast
125 ml/4 fl oz warm milk

FILLING:
175 g/6 oz/²/₃ cup chestnut purée
60 g/2 oz/¹/₂ cup cocoa powder
60 g/2 oz/¹/₄ cup caster
    (superfine) sugar

60 g/2 oz/¹/₂ cup chopped
    almonds
60 g/2 oz/1 cup crushed amaretti
    biscuits (cookies)
175 g/6 oz/¹/₆ cup
    orange marmalade

1 To make the sweet pasta dough, sift the flour into a mixing bowl, then mix in the butter, sugar and 3 eggs.

2 Mix the yeast and warm milk in a small bowl until well combined, then mix into the dough.

3 Knead the dough for 20 minutes, cover with a clean cloth and set aside in a warm place for 1 hour to rise.

4 Combine the chestnut purée, cocoa powder, sugar, almonds, crushed amaretti biscuits (cookies) and orange marmalade in a separate bowl.

5 Grease a baking (cookie) sheet.

6 Lightly flour the work surface (counter). Roll out the pasta dough into a thin sheet and cut into 5 cm/2 inch rounds with a plain pastry cutter.

7 Put a spoonful of filling on to each round and then fold in half, pressing the edges to seal. Arrange on the prepared baking (cookie) sheet, spacing the ravioli out well.

8 Beat the remaining egg and brush all over the ravioli to glaze. Bake in a preheated oven at 180°C/350°F/Gas 4 for 20 minutes until golden. Serve hot.

German Noodle Pudding

Serves 4

INGREDIENTS

60 g/2 oz/4 tbsp butter, plus
  extra for greasing
175 g/6 oz ribbon egg noodles
115 g/4 oz/$^1/_2$ cup cream cheese
225 g/8 oz/1 cup cottage cheese
90 g/3 oz/$^1/_2$ cup caster
  (superfine) sugar

2 eggs, lightly beaten
125 ml/4 fl oz/$^1/_2$ cup soured
  cream
1 tsp vanilla essence (extract)
a pinch of ground cinnamon
1 tsp grated lemon rind

25 g/1 oz/$^1/_4$ cup flaked
  (slivered) almonds
25 g/1 oz/$^3/_4$ cup dry
  white breadcrumbs
icing (confectioners') sugar,
  for dusting

1 Grease an ovenproof dish with butter.

2 Bring a large pan of water to the boil. Add the noodles and cook until almost tender. Drain and set aside.

3 Beat together the cream cheese, cottage cheese and caster (superfine) sugar in a mixing bowl. Beat in the eggs, a little at a time, until well combined. Stir in the soured cream, vanilla essence (extract), cinnamon and lemon rind, and fold in the noodles to coat. Transfer the mixture to the prepared dish and smooth the surface.

4 Melt the butter in a frying pan (skillet). Add the almonds and fry, stirring constantly, for about 1–1$^1/_2$ minutes, until lightly coloured. Remove the frying pan (skillet) from the heat and stir the breadcrumbs into the almonds.

5 Sprinkle the almond and breadcrumb mixture over the pudding and bake in a preheated oven at 180°C/350°F/Gas 4 for 35-40 minutes, until just set. Dust with a little icing (confectioners') sugar and serve immediately.

VARIATION

Although not authentic, you could add 3 tbsp raisins with the lemon rind in step 3, if liked.

Honey & Walnut Nests

Serves 4

INGREDIENTS

225 g/8 oz angel hair pasta
115 g/4 oz/8 tbsp butter
175 g/6 oz/1½ cups shelled
   pistachio nuts, chopped

115 g/4 oz/½ cup sugar
115 g/4 oz/½ cup clear honey
150 ml/¼ pint/⅔ cup water
2 tsp lemon juice

salt
Greek-style yogurt, to serve

1 Bring a large saucepan of salted water to the boil. Add the angel hair pasta and cook until tender, but still firm to the bite. Drain the pasta and return to the pan. Add the butter and toss to coat. Set aside to cool.

2 Arrange 4 small flan or poaching rings on a baking (cookie) sheet. Divide the angel hair pasta into 8 equal quantities and spoon 4 of them into the rings. Press down lightly. Top the pasta with half of the nuts, then add the remaining pasta.

3 Bake in a preheated oven at 180°C/350°F/ Gas 4 for 45 minutes, until golden brown.

4 Meanwhile, put the sugar, honey and water in a saucepan and bring to the boil over a low heat, stirring constantly until the sugar has dissolved completely. Simmer for 10 minutes, add the lemon juice and simmer for a further 5 minutes.

5 Using a palette knife (spatula), carefully transfer the angel hair nests to a serving dish. Pour over the honey syrup, sprinkle over the remaining nuts and set aside to cool completely before serving. Serve with the Greek-style yogurt.

COOK'S TIP

Angel hair pasta is also known as capelli d'Angelo. Long and very fine, it is usually sold in small bunches that already resemble nests.

Raspberry Fusilli

Serves 4

INGREDIENTS

175 g/6 oz/$1\frac{1}{2}$ cup fusilli	2 tbsp caster (superfine) sugar	4 tbsp flaked almonds
700g/1 lb 9 oz/4 cups raspberries	1 tbsp lemon juice	3 tbsp raspberry liqueur
		salt

1 Bring a large pan of lightly salted water to the boil. Add the fusilli and cook until tender, but still firm to the bite. Drain the pasta and return to the pan. Set aside to cool.

2 Using a spoon, firmly press 225 g/ 8 oz/$1\frac{1}{3}$ cups of the raspberries through a sieve (strainer) set over a large mixing bowl to form a smooth purée.

3 Put the raspberry purée and sugar in a small saucepan and simmer over a low heat, stirring occasionally, for 5 minutes.

Stir in the lemon juice then set the sauce aside.

4 Add the remaining raspberries to the fusilli in the pan and mix together well. Transfer the raspberry and fusilli mixture to a serving dish.

5 Spread the almonds out on a baking (cookie) sheet and toast under the grill (broiler) until golden brown. Remove and set aside to cool slightly.

6 Stir the raspberry liqueur into the reserved raspberry sauce

and mix together well until very smooth. Pour the raspberry sauce over the fusilli, sprinkle over the toasted almonds and serve.

VARIATION

You could use almost any sweet, really ripe berry for making this dessert. Strawberries and blackberries are especially suitable, combined with the correspondingly flavoured liqueur. Alternatively, you could use a different berry mixed with the fusilli, but still pour over raspberry sauce.

Italian Bread Pudding

Serves 4

INGREDIENTS

15 g/¹/₂ oz/1 tbsp butter
2 small eating apples, peeled,
    cored and sliced into rings
75 g/2³/₄ oz granulated sugar

2 tbsp white wine
100 g/3¹/₂ oz bread, sliced with
    crusts removed (slightly stale
    French baguette is ideal)

300 ml/¹/₂ pint/1¹/₄ cups single
    (light) cream
2 eggs, beaten
pared rind of 1 orange, cut into
    matchsticks

1 Lightly grease a 1.2 litre/ 2 pint deep ovenproof dish with the butter.

2 Arrange the apple rings in the base of the dish. Sprinkle half of the sugar over the apples.

3 Pour the wine over the apple slices. Add the slices of bread, pushing them down with your hands to flatten them slightly.

4 Mix the cream with the eggs, the remaining sugar and the orange rind and pour the mixture over the bread. Leave to soak for 30 minutes.

5 Bake the pudding in a preheated oven, at 180°C/350°F/Gas Mark 4, for 25 minutes until golden and set. Serve warm.

VARIATION

For a variation, try adding dried fruit, such as apricots, cherries or dates, to the pudding, if you prefer.

COOK'S TIP

Single (light) cream is the type of cream most commonly used for cooking. However, this type of cream should not be boiled as it will curdle. Also, always add hot liquids to the cream rather than the cream to the liquids, in order to avoid curdling. Single (light) cream has an 18 per cent fat content.

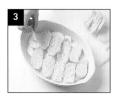

Tuscan Pudding

Serves 4

INGREDIENTS
---

15 g/¹/₂ oz/1 tbsp butter
75 g/2³/₄ oz mixed dried fruit
250 g/9 oz ricotta cheese

3 egg yolks
50 g/1³/₄ oz caster (superfine)
  sugar
1 tsp cinnamon

finely grated rind of 1 orange, plus
  extra to decorate
crème fraîche (soured cream),
  to serve

---

1 Lightly grease 4 mini pudding basins or ramekin dishes with the butter.

2 Put the dried fruit in a bowl and cover with warm water. Leave to soak for 10 minutes.

3 Beat the ricotta cheese with the egg yolks in a bowl. Stir in the caster (superfine) sugar, cinnamon and orange rind and mix to combine.

4 Drain the dried fruit in a sieve set over a bowl. Mix the drained fruit with the ricotta cheese mixture.

5 Spoon the mixture into the basins or ramekin dishes.

6 Bake in a preheated oven, at 180°C/350°F/ Gas Mark 4, for 15 minutes. The tops should be firm to the touch but not brown.

7 Decorate the puddings with grated orange rind. Serve warm or chilled with a dollop of crème fraîche (soured cream).

COOK'S TIP

Crème fraîche (soured cream) has a slightly sour, nutty taste and is very thick. It is suitable for cooking, but has the same fat content as double (heavy) cream. It can be made by stirring cultured buttermilk into double (heavy) cream and refrigerating overnight.

VARIATION

Use the dried fruit of your choice for this delicious recipe.

Cream Custards

Serves 4

INGREDIENTS

450 ml/16 fl oz/2 cups single (light) cream	sugar	3 large eggs, beaten
100 g/3¾ oz caster (superfine)	1 orange	1 tbsp honey
	2 tsp grated nutmeg	1 tsp cinnamon

1 Place the cream and sugar in a large non-stick saucepan and heat gently, stirring, until the sugar caramelizes.

2 Finely grate half of the orange rind and add it to the pan along with the nutmeg.

3 Add the eggs to the mixture in the pan and cook over a low heat for 10–15 minutes, stirring constantly. The custard will eventually thicken.

4 Strain the custard through a fine sieve, into 4 shallow serving dishes. Leave to chill in the refrigerator for 2 hours.

5 Meanwhile, pare the remaining orange rind and cut it into matchsticks.

6 Place the honey and cinnamon in a pan with 2 tablespoons of water and heat gently. Add the orange rind to the pan and cook for 2–3 minutes, stirring, until the mixture has caramelized.

7 Pour the mixture into a bowl and separate out the orange sticks. Leave to cool until set.

8 Once the custards have set, decorate them with the caramelized orange rind and serve.

COOK'S TIP

The cream custards will keep for 1–2 days in the refrigerator. Decorate with the caramelized orange rind just before serving.

Sicilian Orange & Almond Cake

Serves 8

| INGREDIENTS |

4 eggs, separated

125 g/4½ oz caster (superfine) sugar, plus 2 tsp for the cream

finely grated rind and juice of 2 oranges

finely grated rind and juice of 1 lemon

125 g/4½ oz ground almonds

25 g/1 oz self-raising flour

200 ml/7 fl oz/¾ cup whipping

(light) cream

1 tsp cinnamon

25 g/1 oz flaked (slivered) almonds, toasted

icing (confectioners') sugar, to dust

1 Grease and line the base of a 18 cm/7 inch round deep cake tin (pan).

2 Blend the egg yolks with the sugar until the mixture is thick and creamy. Whisk half of the orange rind and all of the lemon rind into the egg yolks.

3 Mix the juice from both oranges and the lemon with the ground almonds and stir into the egg yolks. The mixture will become quite runny at this point. Fold in the flour.

4 Whisk the egg whites until stiff and gently fold into the egg yolk mixture.

5 Pour the mixture into the tin (pan) and bake in a preheated oven, at 180°C/350°F/Gas Mark 4, for 35–40 minutes, until golden and springy to the touch. Leave to cool in the tin (pan) for 10 minutes and then turn out. It is likely to sink slightly at this stage.

6 Whip the cream to form soft peaks. Stir in the remaining orange rind,

cinnamon and sugar.

7 Once the cake is cold, cover with the toasted almonds, dust with icing (confectioners') sugar and serve with the cream.

VARIATION

You could serve this cake with a syrup. Boil the juice and finely grated rind of 2 oranges, 75 g/2¼ oz caster (superfine) sugar and 2 tbsp of water for 5–6 minutes until slightly thickened. Stir in 1 tbsp of orange liqueur just before serving.

Orange & Grapefruit Salad

Serves 4

INGREDIENTS

2 grapefruit, ruby or plain

4 oranges

pared rind and juice of 1 lime

4 tbsp runny honey

2 tbsp warm water

1 sprig of mint, roughly chopped

50 g/1¾ oz chopped walnuts

1 Using a sharp knife, slice the top and bottom from the grapefruits, then slice away the rest of the skin and pith.

2 Cut between each segment of the grapefruit to remove the fleshy part only.

3 Using a sharp knife, slice the top and bottom from the oranges, then slice away the rest of the skin and pith.

4 Cut between each segment of the oranges to remove the fleshy part. Add to the grapefruit.

5 Place the lime rind, 2 tablespoons of lime juice, the honey and the warm water in a small bowl. Whisk with a fork to mix the dressing.

6 Pour the dressing over the segmented fruit, add the chopped mint and mix well. Leave to chill in the refrigerator for 2 hours for the flavours to mingle.

7 Place the chopped walnuts on a baking tray (cookie sheet). Lightly toast the walnuts under a preheated medium grill (broiler) for 2–3 minutes until browned.

8 Sprinkle the toasted walnuts over the fruit and serve.

VARIATION

Instead of the walnuts, you could sprinkle toasted almonds, cashew nuts, hazelnuts or pecans over the fruit, if you prefer.

Zabaglione

Serves 4

INGREDIENTS

5 egg yolks	150 ml/ 5 fl oz/²/₃ cup Marsala or	amaretti biscuits, to serve
100 g/3¹/₂ oz caster (superfine) sugar	sweet sherry	(optional)

1 Place the egg yolks in a large mixing bowl.

2 Add the caster (superfine) sugar to the egg yolks and whisk until the mixture is thick and very pale and has doubled in volume.

3 Place the bowl containing the egg yolk and sugar mixture over a saucepan of gently simmering water.

4 Add the Marsala or sherry to the egg yolk and sugar mixture and continue whisking until the foam mixture becomes warm. This process may take as long as 10 minutes.

5 Pour the mixture, which should be frothy and light, into 4 wine glasses.

6 Serve the zabaglione warm with fresh fruit or amaretti biscuits, if you wish.

VARIATION

Any other type of liqueur may be used instead of the Marsala or sweet sherry, if you prefer. Serve soft fruits, such as strawberries or raspberries, with the zabaglione – it's a delicious combination!

VARIATION

Iced or Semifreddo Zabaglione can be made by following the method here, then continuing to whisk the foam while standing the bowl in cold water. Beat 150 ml/¹/₄ pint/²/₃ cup whipping (light) cream until it just holds its shape. Fold into the foam and freeze for about 2 hours, until just frozen.

Sweet Mascarpone Mousse

Serves 4

450 g/1 lb mascarpone cheese
100 g/3½ oz caster (superfine) sugar
4 egg yolks

400 g/14 oz frozen summer fruits,
  such as raspberries and
  redcurrants

redcurrants, to garnish
amaretti biscuits, to serve

1 Place the mascarpone cheese in a large mixing bowl. Using a wooden spoon, beat the mascarpone cheese until smooth.

2 Stir the egg yolks and sugar into the mascarpone cheese, mixing well. Leave the mixture to chill in the refrigerator for about 1 hour.

3 Spoon a layer of the mascarpone mixture into the bottom of 4 individual serving dishes. Spoon a layer of the summer fruits on top. Repeat the layers in the same order, reserving some of the mascarpone mixture for the top.

4 Leave the mousses to chill in the refrigerator for about 20 minutes. The fruits should still be slightly frozen.

5 Serve the mascarpone mousses with amaretti biscuits.

VARIATION

Try adding 3 tablespoons of your favourite liqueur to the mascarpone cheese mixture in step 1, if you prefer.

COOK'S TIP

Mascarpone (sometimes spelled mascherpone*) is a soft, creamy cheese from Italy. It is becoming increasingly more available, and you should have no difficulty finding cartons in your local supermarket, or Italian delicatessen.*

Lemon Mascarpone Cheesecake

Serves 8

INGREDIENTS

50 g/1³/₄ oz/1¹/₂ tbsp unsalted butter
150 g/5¹/₂ oz ginger biscuits
(cookies), crushed

25 g/1 oz stem ginger (candied),
chopped
500 g/1 lb 2 oz mascarpone cheese

finely grated rind and juice of 2 lemons
100 g/3¹/₂ oz caster (superfine) sugar
2 large eggs, separated
fruit coulis (see Cook's Tip), to serve

1 Grease and line the base of a 25 cm/10 inch spring-form cake tin (pan) or loose-bottomed tin (pan).

2 Melt the butter in a pan and stir in the crushed biscuits (cookies) and chopped ginger. Use the mixture to line the tin (pan), pressing the mixture about 6 mm/¹/₄ inch up the sides.

3 Beat together the cheese, lemon rind and juice, sugar and egg yolks until smooth.

4 Whisk the egg whites until they are stiff and fold into the cheese and lemon mixture.

5 Pour the mixture into the tin (pan) and bake in a preheated oven, at 180°C/ 350°F/Gas Mark 4, for 35–45 minutes until just set. Don't worry if it cracks or sinks – this is quite normal.

6 Leave the cheesecake in the tin (pan) to cool. Serve with fruit coulis (see Cook's Tip).

COOK'S TIP

Fruit coulis can be made by cooking 400 g/14 oz fruit, such as blueberries, for 5 minutes with 2 tablespoons of water. Sieve the mixture, then stir in 1 tablespoon (or more to taste) of sifted icing (confectioners') sugar. Leave to cool before serving.

VARIATION

Ricotta cheese can be used instead of the mascarpone to make an equally delicious cheesecake. However, it should be sieved before use to remove any lumps.

Tiramisu

Serves 6

INGREDIENTS

300 g/10½ oz dark chocolate
400 g/14 oz mascarpone cheese
150 ml/5 fl oz/⅔ cup double
(heavy) cream, whipped until
it just holds its shape

400 ml/14 fl oz black coffee with
50 g/1¾ oz caster (superfine)
sugar, cooled
6 tbsp dark rum or brandy

36 sponge fingers (lady-fingers),
about 400 g/14 oz
cocoa powder, to dust

1 Melt the chocolate in a bowl set over a saucepan of simmering water, stirring occasionally. Leave the chocolate to cool slightly, then stir it into the mascarpone and cream.

2 Mix the coffee and rum together in a bowl. Dip the sponge fingers (lady-fingers) into the mixture briefly so that they absorb the liquid but do not become soggy.

3 Place 3 sponge fingers (lady-fingers) on 3 serving plates.

4 Spoon a layer of the mascarpone and chocolate mixture over the sponge fingers (lady-fingers).

5 Place 3 more sponge fingers (lady-fingers) on top of the mascarpone layer. Spread another layer of mascarpone and chocolate mixture and place 3 more sponge fingers (lady-fingers) on top.

6 Leave the tiramisu to chill in the refrigerator for at least 1 hour. Dust with a little cocoa powder just before serving.

COOK'S TIP

Tiramisu can also be served semi-frozen, like icecream. Freeze the tiramisu for 2 hours and serve immediately as it defrosts very quickly.

VARIATION

Try adding 50 g/1¾ oz toasted, chopped hazelnuts to the chocolate cream mixture in step 1, if you prefer.

Rich Chocolate Loaf

Makes 16 Slices

INGREDIENTS

150 g/5½ oz dark chocolate
75 g/2¾ oz/6 tbsp butter, unsalted
1 x 210 g/7¼ oz tin condensed milk

2 tsp cinnamon
75 g/2¾ oz almonds
75 g/2¾ oz amaretti biscuits, broken

50 g/1¾ oz dried no-need-to-soak
apricots, roughly chopped

1 Line a 675 g/1½ lb loaf tin (pan) with a sheet of kitchen foil.

2 Using a sharp knife, roughly chop the almonds.

3 Place the chocolate, butter, milk and cinnamon in a heavy-based saucepan. Heat gently over a low heat for 3–4 minutes, stirring with a wooden spoon, until the chocolate has melted. Beat the mixture well.

4 Stir the almonds, biscuits and apricots into the chocolate mixture in the pan, stirring with a wooden spoon, until well mixed.

5 Pour the mixture into the prepared tin (pan) and leave to chill in the refrigerator for about 1 hour or until set.

6 Cut the rich chocolate loaf into slices to serve.

COOK'S TIP

To melt chocolate, first break it into manageable pieces. The smaller the pieces, the quicker it will melt.

COOK'S TIP

When baking or cooking with fat, butter has the finest flavour. If possible, it is best to use unsalted butter as an ingredient in puddings and desserts, unless stated otherwise in the recipe. 'Low-fat' spreads are not suitable for cooking.

Pear & Ginger Cake

Serves 4–6

INGREDIENTS

200 g/7 oz/14 tbsp unsalted
   butter, softened
175 g/6 oz caster (superfine) sugar

175 g/6 oz self-raising flour, sifted
3 tsp ginger
3 eggs, beaten

450 g/1 lb dessert (eating) pears,
   peeled, cored and thinly sliced
1 tbsp soft brown sugar

1 Lightly grease and line
the base of a deep 20.5
cm/8 inch cake tin (pan).

2 Using a whisk,
combine 175 g/6 oz of
the butter with the sugar,
flour, ginger and eggs and
mix to form a smooth
consistency.

3 Spoon the cake
mixture into the
prepared tin (pan),
levelling the surface.

4 Arrange the pear slices
over the cake mixture.
Sprinkle with the brown
sugar and dot with the
remaining butter.

5 Bake in a preheated
oven, at 180°C/350°F/
Gas Mark 4, for 35–40
minutes or until the cake is
golden and feels springy to
the touch.

6 Serve the pear and
ginger cake warm,
with ice cream or cream,
if you wish.

COOK'S TIP

*To test whether the cake is
cooked through, insert a fine
metal skewer into the centre
of the cake. If the skewer
comes out clean the cake is
cooked through.*

COOK'S TIP

*Soft, brown sugar is often
known as Barbados sugar. It
is a darker form of light
brown soft sugar.*

Peaches in White Wine

Serves 4

INGREDIENTS

4 large ripe peaches
2 tbsp icing (confectioners')
  sugar, sifted
	pared rind and juice of 1 orange	200 ml/7 fl oz/³⁄₄ cup medium or
		  sweet white wine, chilled

1 Using a sharp knife, halve the peaches, remove the stones and discard them. Peel the peaches, if you prefer. Slice the peaches into thin wedges.

2 Place the peach wedges in a glass serving bowl and sprinkle over the sugar.

3 Using a sharp knife, pare the rind from the orange. Cut the orange rind into matchsticks, place them in a bowl of cold water and set aside.

4 Squeeze the juice from the orange and pour over the peaches together with the wine.

5 Leave the peaches to marinate and chill in the refrigerator for at least 1 hour.

6 Remove the orange rind from the cold water and pat dry with paper towels.

7 Garnish the peaches with the strips of orange rind and serve immediately.

COOK'S TIP

There is absolutely no need to use expensive wine in this recipe, so it can be quire economical to make

COOK'S TIP

The best way to pare the rind thinly from citrus fruits is to use a potato peeler.

Vanilla Ice Cream

Serves 4–6

INGREDIENTS

600 ml/1 pint/2½ cups double (heavy) cream

1 vanilla pod

pared rind of 1 lemon

4 eggs, beaten

2 egg, yolks

175 g/6 oz caster (superfine) sugar

1 Place the cream in a heavy-based saucepan and heat gently, whisking. Add the vanilla pod, lemon rind, eggs and egg yolks and heat until the mixture reaches just below boiling point.

2 Reduce the heat and cook for 8–10 minutes, whisking the mixture continuously, until thickened.

3 Stir the sugar into the cream mixture, set aside and leave to cool.

4 Strain the cream mixture through a sieve.

5 Slit open the vanilla pod, scoop out the tiny black seeds and stir them into the cream.

6 Pour the mixture into a shallow freezing container with a lid and freeze overnight until set. Serve when required.

COOK'S TIP

Ice cream is one of the traditional dishes of Italy. Everyone eats it and there are numerous gelato stalls selling a wide variety of flavours, usually in a cone. It is also serve in scoops, and even sliced!

COOK'S TIP

To make tutti frutti ice cream, soak 100 g/3½ oz mixed dried fruit, such as sultanas, cherries, apricots, candied peel and pineapple, in 2 tablespoons of Marsala or sweet sherry for 20 minutes. Follow the method for vanilla ice cream, omitting the vanilla pod, and stir in the Marsala or sherry-soaked fruit in step 5, just before freezing.

Granita

Serves 4

INGREDIENTS

LEMON GRANITA:

3 lemons

200 ml/7 fl oz/³/₄ cup lemon juice

100 g/3¹/₂ oz caster (superfine) sugar

500 ml/18 fl oz/2¹/₄ cups cold water

COFFEE GRANITA:

2 tbsp instant coffee

2 tbsp sugar

2 tbsp hot water

600 ml/1 pint/2¹/₂ cups cold water

2 tbsp rum or brandy

---

1 To make lemon granita, finely grate the lemon rind. Place the lemon rind, juice and caster (superfine) sugar in a pan. Bring the mixture to the boil and leave to simmer for 5–6 minutes or until thick and syrupy. Leave to cool.

2 Once cooled, stir in the cold water and pour into a shallow freezer container with a lid. Freeze the granita for 4–5 hours, stirring occasionally to break up the ice. Serve as a palate cleanser between dinner courses.

3 To make coffee granita, place the coffee and sugar in a bowl and pour over the hot water, stirring until dissolved.

4 Stir in the cold water and rum or brandy.

5 Pour the mixture into a shallow freezer container with a lid. Freeze the granita for at least 6 hours, stirring every 1–2 hours in order to create a grainy texture. Serve with cream after dinner, if you wish.

COOK'S TIP

If you would prefer a non-alcoholic version of the coffee granita, simply omit the rum or brandy and add extra instant coffee instead.

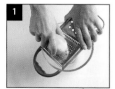

Peaches with Creamy Mascarpone Filling

Serves 4

INGREDIENTS

| 4 peaches | 40 g/1½ oz pecan or walnuts, | 1 tsp sunflower oil |
| 175 g/6 oz mascarpone cheese | chopped | 4 tbsp maple syrup |

1 Cut the peaches in half and remove the stones. If you are preparing this recipe in advance, press the peach halves together again and wrap them in cling film (plastic wrap) until required.

2 Mix the mascarpone and pecan or walnuts together in a small bowl until well combined. Leave to chill in the refrigerator until required.

3 To serve, brush the peaches with a little oil and place on a rack set over medium hot coals.

Barbecue (grill) the peach halves for 5–10 minutes, turning once, until hot.

4 Transfer the peach halves to a dish and top with the mascarpone and nut mixture.

5 Drizzle the maple syrup over the peaches and mascarpone filling and serve at once.

COOK'S TIP

Mascarpone cheese is high in fat; you can use thick natural yogurt instead.

VARIATION

You can use nectarines instead of peaches for this recipe, if you prefer. Remember to choose ripe but fairly firm fruit which won't go soft and mushy when it is barbecued (grilled). Prepare the nectarines in the same way as the peaches and barbecue (grill) for 5–10 minutes.

Index